NIKE EFFECT

JOSHUA HUNT

The NIKE EFFECT

ONE COMPANY'S WAR ON HIGHER EDUCATION, ORGANIZED LABOR, AND CLEAN COMPETITION

MELVILLE HOUSE
BROOKLYN • LONDON

The Nike Effect

Originally published as *The University of Nike* in 2018.

Melville House Publishing
46 John Street
Brooklyn, NY 11201

and

Suite 2000
16/18 Woodford Rd.
London E7 0HA

mhpbooks.com
@melvillehouse

ISBN: 978-1-61219-843-9
ISBN: 978-1-61219-692-3 (eBook)

Designed by Euan Monaghan

Library of Congress Cataloging-in-Publication Data

Names: Hunt, Joshua, author.
Title: The Nike Effect: one company's war on higher education, organized labor, and clean competition / Joshua Hunt.
Description: Brooklyn : Melville House, [2018].
Identifiers: LCCN 2018037658 (print) | LCCN 2018039298 (ebook) | ISBN 9781612196923 (reflowable) | ISBN 9781612198439 (paperback)
Subjects: LCSH: University of Oregon--Finance. | Academic-industrial collaboration--Oregon. | College sports--Corrupt practices--Oregon. | Nike (Firm) | BISAC: SPORTS & RECREATION / Business Aspects. | EDUCATION / Educational Policy & Reform / General.
Classification: LCC LD4353 (ebook) | LCC LD4353 .H86 2018 (print) | DDC 378.795/31--dc23
LC record available at https://lccn.loc.gov/2018037658

Printed in the United States of America

1 3 5 7 9 10 8 6 4 2

Contents

Introduction

In May 2014, I traveled to Eugene, Oregon, to cover a developing story for *The New York Times*: two months earlier, a freshman at the University of Oregon had told local police she'd been gang-raped by three of the school's basketball players. Campus police were aware of the incident just hours after it occurred, and university administrators knew by the following day. But instead of alerting the campus community and suspending the players, they kept the matter quiet and allowed the men to participate in the NCAA basketball tournament.

Throughout March and April, the school's public relations department worked on a media strategy to employ in case the story broke; school administrators quietly brokered a deal that would allow the accused players to transfer to another institution at the end of the academic year, with no incriminating paperwork that might follow them; and campus police were careful to omit from the school's public crime log any mention of the report. When May arrived, it looked as though the school had managed to avoid a major scandal. Then the Eugene Police Department released a graphic twenty-four-page police report the victim had filed, sparking intense media coverage that led to the suspension of the players and, several months later, the resignation of the university's president, Michael Gottfredson.

I was left with a number of nagging questions: Why had the school recruited one of these players despite the fact that his previous college had suspended him for sexually assaulting a fellow student? Why were the players allowed to keep playing basketball with such serious charges hanging over their heads? And why did the school ignore federal laws requiring them to notify the public when crimes of this nature were reported to campus police?

University administrators refused to talk with me, and occasionally locked themselves in their offices until I left the buildings where they worked. The players also refused to talk with me, while their lawyers insisted that the sex had been consensual. The school's office of public records produced mostly useless, heavily redacted records concerning its handling of the incident, and even the school's public relations professionals proved to be tight-lipped: before turning down each of my requests for an interview with some administrator or another, the director of public affairs, Tobin Klinger, would always ask me the same question: "What's your angle?"

And each time I told him I wouldn't have an angle until my notebook was filled with more answers than questions.

I began to hear troubling stories about the University of Oregon's relationship with Nike. Over the course of two decades, the shoe and apparel company's founder, Phil Knight, had become the school's most generous donor. They called him Uncle Phil, not just on campus but around town, and it was easy to see why—when my parents moved the family away from Eugene, in 1995, it was a quiet college town filled with young hippies and former millworkers. Nearly two decades later, it was Niketown, U.S.A.

The University of Oregon, which was once a cash-strapped liberal arts college, had been transformed into a college football powerhouse with an increasingly competitive basketball program. The change was so swift and dramatic, and so obviously tied to Knight's largesse, that Oregon's rivals gave it the derisive nickname the University of Nike—an image it has now embraced. Other schools are embracing that kind of image as well: in 2016, the University of Michigan announced a $169 million contract with Nike, which was the biggest in the history of college sports, until the University of Texas at Austin inked a $250 million Nike deal just months later.

It all began nearly thirty years ago, when Oregonians became the first in the nation to abandon their public universty system by voting for property tax cuts that left state colleges to fend for themselves. A decade later, dozens more states had set out on the same path, which has led us here: in 2017, for the first time, public colleges and universities in most states drew the majority of their revenue from tuition dollars rather than taxpayer support. The American public has, in other words, become a minority shareholder in the nation's public universities. And what happens next is all too clear if you know where to look.

I began with a notebook full of questions, a campus full of rumors, and a sense that the University of Oregon was a canary worth following down a coal mine. My goal was not to write a biography of Phil Knight, whose life and career have been documented more extensively, and more flatteringly, in books authored by his friends, his colleagues, and himself. If my portrait of Knight seems overly critical, it is because I've sought to document a narrow slice of his life that has proven to be consistently controversial—namely, the extent to which his financial support of the University of Oregon has bought him influence over an institution that is meant to serve public, rather than private, interests. Four years after I began investigating Knight's dealings with the university, my notebook had far fewer questions than answers, thanks to well over a hundred interviews, supplemented by many thousands of pages of financial, legal, and archival documents.

At last, I have "my angle."

The NIKE EFFECT

One

TrackTown, U.S.A.

Philip Hampson Knight was seven years old the first time his father took him to a college football game. It was November 3, 1945, and just a few months had passed since the end of the Second World War. Many universities around the country were fielding teams for the first time in two or three years, and fans were eager to see young American men return from the battlefield to the football field. In Portland, Oregon, where the Knight family lived, some 28,000 people—one out of every ten residents of the city—streamed into Multnomah Stadium for the afternoon game, braving overcast skies and periodic showers that had turned the grassy field to mud.

"Oregon vs. Washington," Knight recalled. "I asked, 'Dad, which is the good team?'"

When answering the question, William Knight disregarded the fact that Oregon was losing more games than it was winning that season, and that the Washington Huskies were perched atop the resurgent Pacific Coast Conference. More than athletic excellence or national acclaim, loyalty seemed to be foremost in Knight's mind when he told his son that Oregon was the team he should support.

"He set me straight," Knight said of his father's lesson.

William Knight's loyalty to the University of Oregon began as an accident of geography. Before he grew roots in Wisconsin, where he was born, his parents moved the family west. They raised William in a town called Roseburg, just ninety minutes south of the University of Oregon, where he enrolled after graduating from high school. He spent another three years in Eugene, earning his law degree at the University of Oregon, then briefly returned to Roseburg, where he was elected to serve as a Republican member of the Oregon House of Representatives when he was just twenty-six. It turned out that politics didn't suit Knight, who bristled at the unwieldy nature of representative power. He served just one term before moving to Portland with his wife, Lota Hatfield, in 1938. The couple settled into a comfortable home in an upper-middle-class neighborhood called Eastmoreland, where William quickly found work as legal counsel for the Industrial Relations Association of Oregon, earning himself a reputation as a fierce, union-busting lawyer of considerable clout. Phil was born soon after they arrived in Portland.

William Knight passed both his ambition and his deep love for athletics to his son, who realized by the time he reached middle school that watching from the sidelines was not enough. At Cleveland High School, where he was an honor student, Phil tried his hand at just about any sport that favored a boy with his rail-thin frame: on the basketball court, he proved so unremarkable that few teammates remembered he'd even been on their team. On the tennis court, where his intense shyness was not such a liability, he was capable, if not particularly talented. But it was on the track that he showed great promise, which was perhaps unsurprising given his solitary nature, and the solitary nature of a runner's effort. When Knight graduated from high school in 1955, it was, he said, "pretty much automatic I was going to Oregon."

His decision to enroll at his father's alma mater had less to do with family tradition and geographic convenience than with Knight's determination to be trained and molded by the legendary track and field coach Bill Bowerman, who was building the foundation of his legacy just as Knight was blossoming into a promising middle-distance runner in high school.

"Bowerman was the guy," Knight said.

Bowerman had taken over as Oregon's head track and field

coach in 1948, following the sudden retirement—and near immediate death—of Bill Hayward, who spent forty-four years making the program one of regional dominance and national prominence. In just under a decade, Bowerman had established himself as a worthy heir to his predecessor, who had coached four track world record holders, six American record holders, and nine Olympians.

Knight arrived at the University of Oregon in August 1955, just as the sprawling Eugene campus was anticipating a broader cultural shift in America—the writer Ken Kesey was then a junior at the school, encountering for the first time the "weird, dope-fueled ideas" that would inspire him to write his first novel, *One Flew Over the Cuckoo's Nest*. But Knight had no interest in the emerging counterculture and no plans to use the college experience as a tool of reinvention, as Kesey was doing. He was, if anything, as dedicated as ever to the monkish brand of all-American normalcy that had earned him the white-bread nickname Buck as a child. He even brought the childhood nickname to college with him.

"I hadn't smoked a cigarette, hadn't tried a drug," he wrote in his memoir. "I hadn't broken a rule, let alone a law."

In a time of change and rebellion, Knight was interested in continuity and conformity, majoring in journalism, which had become the family business after his father was made publisher of Portland's *Oregon Journal* newspaper in 1953. Knight occasionally imagined becoming a novelist or a statesman instead of a reporter, but mostly he thought no further ahead than the next running practice or track meet.

Despite more than a half century of track and field excellence at the University of Oregon, the culture and the mythology of the sport had not yet gripped Eugene, a city that is now known as TrackTown, U.S.A. Bowerman's runners were every bit as clean-cut and athletic as Oregon's football players, but for most people they were outsiders, even weirdos, in the world of college athletics. They were forced to buy their running shoes at a hardware store run by John Warren, a retired minor league baseball player who filled their special shoe orders only because he took pity on the boys, whom he'd been tapped to coach as a substitute after Hayward's abrupt retirement. Hugh Luby, who ran Eugene's only sporting goods store, refused to sell running spikes because he felt that the sport was for "sissies."

Bowerman's stable of runners also suffered the indignity of sharing Hayward Field with Oregon's football team, which meant they sometimes didn't have access to the track named for the man who had dedicated his life to building their track and field program. When football practice kept them from training at Hayward Field, Bowerman's boys could sometimes be seen snaking their way around the steep, narrow roads encircling Spencer Butte, a tall volcanic projection that jutted from the craggy earth at the southern edge of the city. Some runners resented sharing the field with the more popular athletes on the football team, but Knight wasn't one of them. He loved college football as much as he ever had. And he was by then too used to being an outsider to hold any grudges about it.

Knight was, in fact, something of an outsider even among the band of misfits populating Bowerman's team of runners. When group photographs were snapped to commemorate a track meet, Knight would often be found near the photograph's creased edges, sometimes close enough to the margins that a picture frame might hide him completely. He was lanky and not especially tall, with a shock of clean-cut blond hair and bug eyes that would give him a nervous, twitchy air if he blinked too fast. His skin was so pale that his fraternity brothers called him "the white mole." And while he appeared less athletic than the other boys in Bowerman's stable, he was, from the very beginning of his college career, an impressive middle-distance runner. On a lesser team, Knight might have been a star. But compared to Bowerman's most important pupil, Jim Grelle, Buck was merely "a good squad man," according to his coach. Still, he managed to earn varsity honors on the track in his sophomore year, and before long he was running the mile in just four minutes and thirteen seconds. But he lacked the genetic gifts that elevated the great runners above the good ones, which just might account for the time he allowed for other pursuits during the summer break.

Each year, when spring term ended, Knight returned home

to Portland and worked part-time in the sports department at the *Oregonian*, a rival newspaper competing against his father's *Oregon Journal*. In 1957, he convinced the newspaper's sports editor to let him cover the annual Civil War game, which pitted the University of Oregon's football team against its bitter cross-state rivals at Oregon State University. It rained hard that day, and Knight spent much of the game kneeling in muddy earth, writing photo captions in real time while an *Oregonian* photographer snapped pictures of the game from the sidelines. Later that day, he could barely read his own notes, which had been soaked through with enough water to make the ink streak down each page of his notebook. But he hardly needed them. In fact, decades later, he still remembered key plays like Jim Shanley's costly fumble near the end of the game.

"That was one of the great games in the rivalry," he said.

The start of Oregon's Civil War football rivalry was uncomfortably close to the end of America's actual Civil War. Less than three decades after the last drops of Confederate and Union blood were spilled, 500 eager spectators gathered around a sawdust field in Corvallis, Oregon, on a crisp, clear Saturday afternoon in November 1894. After Oregon Agricultural College beat the University of Oregon by a score of 16–0, the *Corvallis Gazette* branded the visiting Eugene players "gentlemen" in defeat, noting just one injury—a dislocated shoulder—and an "absence of slugging on either side."

"Slugging" was not the only concern raised about intercollegiate football, which had started on the opposite side of the country in 1869, when Rutgers beat Princeton 6–4 on a makeshift field in New Brunswick, New Jersey. A newspaper editorial penned shortly after the first Oregon Civil War game called on schools to "demand a high grade of classwork from the men on the teams, barring temporarily any man who is neglecting his legitimate occupation, that of study, for the sake of football. It is not at all necessary that training for the games need interfere with the study by any member of the team."

Administrators at Ivy League colleges were especially preoccupied with drafting an "athlete's code of honor." In February 1898, Brown University hosted a conference focused on "the discussion of questions arising out of intercollegiate contests and the objectionable features connected with them," which drew delegates from Columbia, Cornell, Dartmouth, Harvard, Princeton, and the University of Pennsylvania. These delegates agreed on a set of eligibility requirements known as the Providence Rules, and they advanced an idea that remains among the most enduring and controversial aspects of college sports: "It is obvious," they wrote in their report, "that no student should be paid for his athletics."

Market forces prevailed, however, giving college football its first cheating scandal just one year after the Brown conference gave it a rule book: desperate to beat rival school Yale, and unable to find eleven "men of weight and muscle" among his university's 2,100 male students, Columbia's head football coach, George Foster Sanford, resorted to hiring ringers. The university tried to pin the scandal on a departing assistant coach, but years later Sanford would blame his unprecedented $5,000 coaching salary. The lure of quick money, the unexpected pressure that came with it, and "the virus of the game," he said, had nearly destroyed him.

That scandal at Columbia did little to contain the "virus." Just six years after Oregon's Civil War football rivalry began, the sport had grown to be immensely popular, with forty-three schools throughout the country fielding teams. And though the sport was still in its infancy, athletics departments at America's growing number of "football schools" were already becoming practiced in the art of managing college football's image problems in an effort to shield the teams from outside interference or regulation. Its worst image problem was one that spread along with the game's popularity, as legions of new fans witnessed the brutality of helmetless young men getting their skulls fractured, their spinal cords twisted, and their lungs punctured by broken ribs. In 1904, there were 18 deaths and 159 serious injuries recorded at football games around the United States—a toll high enough that that the following year saw President Theodore Roosevelt, a sportsman in his own right, summon football coaches from 62 schools to visit the White House for a discussion on curbing widespread violence and cheating in the sport. The death toll nevertheless rose to 19 casualties in 1905, which led to the formation of a new organization called the National Collegiate Athletic Association (NCAA) in 1906. Miraculously, the NCAA managed to swiftly accomplish what the president could not, and in a few short years college football was demonstrably safer thanks to the introduction of widely enforced rules of play. The new organization did little, however, to allay concerns about the quality of education and the specter of corruption at America's football schools.

As intercollegiate football continued to spread, new divisions and conferences emerged, and with them a growing competition between schools. Local rivalries became regional, and regional rivalries became bitter interconference feuds. Football schools increasingly sought to distinguish themselves on the field, where the public, the media, and alumni could see the schools' efforts and applaud them. This proved to be an easier path to demonstrating excellence than most schools had ever had access to, even if the kind of excellence being demonstrated had nothing to do with the prestige of an institution or the quality of the education it promised. It was visceral and immediate, primal and popular.

The University of Oregon's transformation into a football school began immediately after its stinging loss to Oregon Agricultural College in the first Civil War game. The turnaround was so swift and absolute that from 1895 to 1922, the University of Oregon Webfoots lost just three more Civil War matches to the Hayseeds from Oregon Agricultural College, which was eventually rechristened Oregon State University. It remained, however, a rural agricultural college, the kind of place where farmers sent their sons, if their sons were lucky enough to go to college at all. The University of Oregon, meanwhile, was from the beginning the very model of an urban liberal arts college, producing lawyers, scientists, journalists, and professionals of all sorts. As the decades passed, the annual Civil War game came to highlight, if not deepen, the state of Oregon's profound cultural and economic divisions: the game was, increasingly, a performative battle between educated, wealthier urban liberals and poor, rural working-class conservatives. For the Hayseeds, and the rural Oregonians they represented, there was a great deal of pride on the line each time their team took to the field against the University of Oregon.

Over the course of the next several decades, Oregon State managed to even the scorecard until the rivalry reached a point where victory often went to the team with home-field advantage. The Oregon Webfoots became the Ducks, and the OSU Hayseeds became the Beavers, but the intense social and economic divisions between the teams and their fans remained: Beavers became farmers, or maybe engineers, while Ducks became novelists, like Chuck Palahniuk and Ken Kesey, journalists like Ann Curry, or U.S. Senators like Ron Wyden.

There was much more than pride on the line for Oregon head coach Rich Brooks when he arrived in Corvallis on a rainy Saturday afternoon in November 1994. One hundred years had passed since Oregon lost its first Civil War match against Oregon State, and eighteen years had gone by since Brooks began coaching the Ducks. His team had struggled for the past decade to keep its head above water in the increasingly competitive Pac-10 conference, and the last two seasons had been particularly bad, capped by humiliating Civil War losses. Brooks had managed to right the ship midway through the 1994 season, however, winning five consecutive games leading up to the Civil War, including a 55–21 rout of Stanford. But he still felt his job was on the line when he walked onto the damp grass of Parker Stadium, where 37,000 college football fans had gathered on that chilly November afternoon.

A win for his team would send the Ducks to their first Rose Bowl since 1958.

"This is what I've wanted ever since I've been at Oregon,"

Brooks said before the start. "It's down to one game now, and it's great that there will be national attention on the Civil War."

A good amount of that attention fell on Danny O'Neil, a senior who had been a starting quarterback for the Ducks since he'd chosen Oregon over big football schools in Southern California and Alabama. O'Neil was coming into the game with a mixed Civil War record: as a freshman, an injury had forced him to watch from the sidelines as a winless Oregon State team trounced the Ducks 14–3 at Autzen Stadium in Eugene; a year later, he endured stinging rain and powerful winds to throw the only touchdown pass in a 7–0 Ducks victory over the Beavers; and in 1993, he completed just fifteen of thirty-four passes through a dense fog that descended on Autzen Stadium as Oregon State beat the Ducks 15–12.

For his final and most important Civil War game, there was rain, which O'Neil had already proved he could handle. And there was tremendous pressure, which he'd struggled to cope with throughout his college football career.

"The value of my life was directly related to my performance on the football field," O'Neil recalled. "That's a tough way to live. Especially when you're not doing well."

On game day, it seemed that his composure had failed him. Midway through the fourth quarter, the Beavers held a three-point lead over the Ducks, and were steadily driving toward a game-clinching touchdown. Then Oregon State coach Jerry Pettibone made a critical error, opting to charge ahead for a touchdown attempt rather than take a 31-yard field goal. The Beavers blew the play, returning possession to Oregon, who moved the ball steadily downfield with a series of first-down passes from O'Neil to Cristin McLemore, who had returned to the game with a badly injured hand after being carted off the field during the third quarter. In less than a minute, O'Neil had managed to move the ball more than 70 yards toward the Beavers' goal. With just under four minutes left to play, Cory Huot blitzed O'Neil—a moment after the quarterback completed a short flip to his running back, who ran the ball in for a touchdown that gave the Ducks a 17–13 lead with just 3:43 left on the game clock.

The momentum of the game had reversed, and when Oregon regained possession with their lead intact and just 36 seconds until time ran out, Ducks fans began celebrating. Up in the stands, a fan named Tucker Davies rose to his feet and flipped over his Nike-branded seat cushion. The warm side of the cushion carried the athletic company's slogan, "Just Do It," while the cool side, which Davies revealed only when the game clock had run out, carried a variation that punctuated his team's victory: "Just Did It."

"For the first time in 37 years we can hold our finger in the air and say, 'We're number one,' and it's for real," Davies said. "It's for real."

Stanford and Michigan contested the first Rose Bowl on New Year's Day in 1902, as part of a publicity stunt meant to lure tourists from colder climates to a recently incorporated California town called Pasadena. The annual parade and college football game grew, over the course of a few decades, into one of the country's best-known sporting events, and by 1952 the "Granddaddy of Them All" was an institution of such value that NBC decided to make it America's first nationally broadcast college football game.

Six years later, when Oregon faced Ohio State in the 1958 Rose Bowl, the black-and-white television broadcast opened with jaunty marching band music and a title card proclaiming the game a presentation of the Gillette safety-razor company's Cavalcade of Sports. Gillette's advertising dollars, and the broadcasting fees paid by NBC, were not yet hefty enough to trickle down to Oregon's football program in any significant way. But over time, the NCAA leveraged its considerable clout to extract juicier broadcast fees from television stations, which then raised advertising fees for increasingly popular college football games. By 1983, NBC was paying $7 million to air the Rose Bowl.

What it meant for a college football team to play in the Rose Bowl had changed considerably in the thirty-seven years leading up to Oregon's unexpected return to Pasadena on January 2, 1995. Broadcast rights, sponsorships, and ticket and concession sales guaranteed each team more than $6 million just for showing up and playing ball. This was an eye-opening development for University of Oregon President Dave Frohnmayer, who traveled to Pasadena that year with no grander plan than to extract a generous donation from his guests, Beverly and Robert Lewis, two Oregon alumni who had met on the Eugene campus, married, and made a small fortune in beverage distribution. Oregon's football program, Frohnmayer realized, might offer multiple avenues for raising the funds he would need in order to save the school from an increasingly ruinous financial situation.

When Frohnmayer took over as president of the university in 1994, the school was already in dire need of alternative funding thanks to a piece of state legislation known as Ballot Measure 5. The measure, which was narrowly passed by Oregon voters in 1990, severely cut the property-tax revenues that Oregon schools relied on for most of the state funding they received; Oregon's K–12 schools were effectively pitted against the state's public universities by the tax cuts, which forced educators from both groups to compete for support from the same general fund. During Frohnmayer's first two years as president of the University of Oregon, the state cut its support for higher education by a whopping 10.5 percent, making Oregon the only state to scale back funding for its public universities by double-digit percentages in those years. From his earliest days as interim president of the school, Frohnmayer knew that the University of Oregon would need to look elsewhere for funding if it were to survive. He told his faculty in October 1994 that outside fundraising would be his priority, and a year later he'd secured pledges of nearly $100 million in gifts. But these hard-won donations came mostly from local business owners like Tom and Carol Williams, who ran bakeries in Eugene, and from local mutual-fund managers like Jim Rippey. Frohnmayer's herculean fundraising efforts were barely enough to stanch the bleeding caused by five years of Measure 5 cuts, which had forced the university to raise its tuition by 72 percent. With deeper cuts still to come, Frohnmayer would need to court a different class of donor if he wanted to do more than tread water—the kind of donor who could afford to give more than a few million dollars once or twice a decade. A better football program, he realized, might help the school raise cash while also adding enough shine to attract the one corporate sponsor within his reach: Nike. Phil Knight remained close with Bill Bowerman, after all, and Bowerman was close with Frohnmayer, who he called "one of the great men of our times."

Frohnmayer had other reasons for pinning his hopes on college football as a means of luring a corporate sponsor. The NCAA had just instituted new limits on athletic scholarships for Division I football programs, capping them at eighty-five per school per academic year, which effectively ended the monopoly that USC and UCLA had held on attracting the West Coast's top high school football prospects. This left just one other obstacle to building a competitive football program in Oregon, and it was an obstacle that no NCAA rule could affect: Oregon weather. The school's recruiters would never be able to convince top prospects to come play ball in rainy Eugene as long as the University of Oregon lacked an indoor training facility for its football team to use.

The University of Oregon's most prominent alumnus graduated from the school in 1959, then spent a year with the U.S. Army reserves before deciding his future was best prepared for at Stanford University's Graduate School of Business. On his way to Palo Alto, Phil Knight stopped in Eugene to see his old coach. He wanted to make sure Bowerman understood how much his guidance and leadership had meant to him, but when it came time to deliver the speech he'd prepared, he choked up. The visit ended up being one last occasion for Bowerman to give Knight a pep talk, which he later considered to be his "true commencement ceremony."

"Never underestimate yourself," Bowerman told him.

Herbert Hoover founded Stanford Graduate School of Business in 1925, hoping that it would act as a bulwark against the spread of Ivy League liberalism by offering promising West Coast minds an alternative to the elite schools of the Eastern seaboard. In this respect, the school was remarkably successful, and in the postwar years it became a breeding ground for precisely the kind of professionals Hoover had imagined: well-educated young men who could be slotted into the managerial ranks of any one of America's top companies, which had by the 1950s become responsible for half the world's manufacturing and one-third of its exported goods.

Knight's roommate at Stanford was William "Reed" Jenney, who recalled him as "a little on the wimpy side at first glance," but quiet and kind. His future success, Jenney said, "was amazing to me, really." Most of Knight's friends from this time recall him as shy, not particularly ambitious, and an average student at best.

"Now that I think about it, it was unclear whether he did have goals," one classmate recalled.

Whether or not he had ambition while studying at Stanford, Knight did have one of his most important ideas there. It came to him while taking a small-business class taught by Frank Shallenberger, who asked his students to imagine a new business and write a term paper outlining the venture and its marketing plan. The assignment proved challenging for Knight, who turned ideas over in his head in his bedroom until his eyes landed on a new box of Adidas running shoes that had cost him $30.

The German-made running shoes were the best on the market, but they were only available in the U.S. as costly imports.

"American running shoes were still made by offshoots of the tire companies, cheap and terrible," Knight said. "They cost five bucks and gave you blood blisters after five miles. Adidas was taking advantage."

Knight's paper outlined how an American business could use the German company's own greed against it by focusing on athletes who were being ignored twice over: first by athletic equipment and apparel manufacturers, who felt it wasn't worth making gear for an equipment-light sport that required only shoes, shorts, and a T-shirt; and also by retailers, who had long held runners in contempt, like the Eugene sporting goods shop owner who had called Bowerman's runners "sissies."

Knowing how much better American running shoes could be, and how little interest the industry took in improving them, Knight focused on the key problem: how to improve the quality of running shoes available in America without making them so costly that consumers decided to spend a few extra dollars for the superior Adidas imports. He was reminded of something that had happened in the camera market a decade earlier, when increasingly prominent photographers began trading in their expensive German Leica cameras for more affordable Nikons, made in Japan. In just under ten years, Japanese camera-makers had gone from virtually no presence in the U.S. market to selling more than $6 million of merchandise there annually. And they were able to do it because of Japan's substantially lower labor costs. So, Knight reasoned, there must be room in the U.S. track and field market for an American distributor selling Japanese running shoes at prices that undercut the costly German-made imports sold by Adidas. In his term paper, Knight theorized that a U.S. distributor could, within three years of opening its doors, sell 20,000 pairs of running shoes a year to track-team members at high schools and colleges in California, Oregon, and Washington alone.

After finishing his MBA, Knight sold his car, borrowed some money from his father, and boarded a plane bound for Japan on Thanksgiving Day in 1962. He visited the track at the University of Tokyo, where he watched young athletes exhaust themselves, paying close attention to what kind of shoes the fastest runners were wearing. He found that the majority of student-athletes were wearing Japanese brands, and among those, one struck the best balance between quality and price: the Onitsuka Tiger. Some might have considered the Onitsuka Tiger an Adidas knockoff, right down to a familiar-looking set of stripes running down the side of each shoe, but the design differed from the famed Adidas stripes just slightly, with a downward curve that caused the individual lines to come together and collide in an inverted swoosh near the front of the shoe.

Early in 1963, Knight hopped on a train to the port city of Kobe, where Onitsuka's headquarters were located. He didn't have an appointment, and during the train ride, he realized he didn't have a company, either. He scanned the passing billboards, which were incomprehensible to him, then caught a glimpse of some Suntory Blue Ribbon among the bottles of booze being sold on the train. When he arrived at the three-story wooden building where Onitsuka's headquarters were housed, he introduced himself as a representative of Blue Ribbon Sports, while mentioning that he'd run track at the University of Oregon alongside Dyrol Burleson, who was considered a strong contender for 1500 meters at the upcoming Tokyo Olympics. When Knight was shown to a conference room and joined by six Onitsuka executives, he told them his college running coach, Bill Bowerman, had taught him everything he knew about designing shoes—and from what he'd seen, Onitsuka's shoes were of the highest quality.

Blue Ribbon Sports, Knight told the executives, could sell many pairs of their shoes in America, as long as the price was right and the quality was adequate. But instead of a deal, Knight left only with Onitsuka's assurance that he would receive samples of their latest line of running shoes, made from leather rather than canvas, just as soon as he sent them a check for $37.

In a travel diary entry, Knight wrote frankly about his own deal-making prowess: "Faked out Tiger Shoe Co.," he wrote, mistaking the name of the company for the name of its line of sixty-six different athletic shoes. He penned a letter to his father, asking to borrow enough money to pay Onitsuka for a set of samples.

The man Knight felt he'd "faked out" was Kihachiro Onitsuka, who had founded the eponymous company fourteen years earlier.

At the time of Knight's first visit to Kobe, Onitsuka's company was selling $8 million worth of athletic shoes each year. Still, he was flattered that Knight had chosen to distribute his company's shoes rather than those made by Mizuno, which was then a much more popular brand in Japan. Onitsuka and his executives had recently traveled to the United States, so they knew that Knight wasn't lying to them about the spectacular market potential there. Onitsuka was also intrigued by the fact that Knight had run for Bowerman, because the company was then pushing to develop lighter, faster track shoes ahead of the 1964 Tokyo Olympics, which were less than two years away. Bowerman's feedback, Onitsuka felt, could be invaluable in the research-and-development phase.

Knight received his first shipment of samples from Kobe three weeks after the Kennedy assassination: five pairs of Onitsuka Tiger Limber Ups, made from blue and white leather. Knight had to make an unexpected promise in order to get them: if he still wanted to partner with Onitsuka, he would have to content himself with distributing the company's shoes only on the West Coast of the United States; the East Coast would remain exclusive territory for a New York wrestling coach who had been Onitsuka's sole U.S. distributor since 1959.

The arrangement Onitsuka proposed would give Knight exactly the distribution network he'd imagined while writing his accounting term paper at Stanford's Graduate School of Business. But Buck's world had grown larger in the two years that had passed since then, and he considered it a concession when he reluctantly promised not to distribute Onitsuka's shoes on the East Coast "at this time." Knight's first business partnership was, in a sense, his first rivalry as well. Still, he was impressed with the samples Onitsuka had sent him—so impressed that he sent two pairs to Bowerman, hoping his old coach would like them enough to become his first customer.

"Here is a sample of the hot new shoes coming out of Japan," Knight wrote. "If you feel the shoes are of reasonable quality, you could probably save a little money, since I wouldn't make a profit on shoes sold to you."

Instead, Bowerman offered Knight $500 to become his partner. The men shook hands on the deal, and Knight used the fresh capital to place his first order with Onitsuka: three hundred pairs of Tiger running shoes for Blue Ribbon Sports, an imaginary company made real at last.

In the fall of 1967, Bowerman pulled aside Geoff Hollister, one of his junior runners.

"There's someone I want you to meet," Bowerman told him. "He's from Portland, one of my former half-milers, Buck Knight."

Hollister's family had moved to Eugene around the time Knight was leaving for Stanford. The family home was just a few blocks from Hayward Field, where Hollister would retreat to watch Dyrol Burleson train for the 1964 Tokyo Olympics after coming home from high school each day. His parents had both gone to Oregon State University, and they wanted the same for their son. In 1964, Hollister turned down a generous scholarship to Oregon State, feeling that only Bowerman could train him to run the best mile he had in him.

The coach's growing dynasty had added significantly to the brand value of the Onitsuka shoes his runners had been wearing since '64, and Bowerman continued to give valuable feedback that aided in developing lighter, faster designs. Bowerman's endorsement was crucial for Onitsuka, which awarded more territory to Knight in part because Onitsuka so feared losing the coach's seal of approval. But Bowerman also helped Knight by acting as an informal recruiter for Blue Ribbon Sports.

Hollister's first meeting with Knight took place over cheeseburgers and milk shakes at a Dairy Queen restaurant that still sits at the edge of the University of Oregon's sprawling, tree-lined campus in Eugene. Knight offered Hollister a job selling Onitsuka Tigers out of the trunk of his car for a commission of $2 per pair. His territory, Knight said, would be all of Oregon, but he'd have to pay for his own gas and other travel expenses. Hollister accepted the job, then paid his new boss's lunch tab.

"Buck forgot his wallet," Hollister said.

Blue Ribbon Sports was founded on Knight's insights about the untapped potential for affordable running shoes in the U.S. market, but the company only survived its early years because of dedicated sales representatives like Jeff Johnson, who began selling Tigers for Knight on commission in 1965. Johnson met Knight at Stanford, where he was an undergraduate studying anthropology while Knight was there earning his MBA. By the time Johnson became the first Blue Ribbon Sports employee, he was raising a family in Los Angeles. Johnson proved to be a tireless multitasker, with unpaid duties that included snapping photographs for the company's catalogs, developing its first marketing materials, and establishing its mail-order business. He even designed a few of the company's early shoes, and in 1967 he opened the first Blue Ribbon Sports retail location at 3107 Pico Boulevard in Santa Monica, California.

When Knight added Hollister to his stable, he gained more than a new salesman and a free lunch at Dairy Queen. The Hollister family home also became the unofficial Eugene headquarters for Blue Ribbon Sports, which had grown to become Onitsuka's most important U.S. distributor. Like Johnson, Hollister proved to be a generator of keen business insights as well as labor. It was clear to Hollister, for instance, that as an Oregon company, Blue Ribbon Sports should have its own dedicated retail shop in Oregon. Knight felt that this was an extravagance the company could not afford; the Los Angeles outlet, after all, served as a warehouse as much as a retail space. So Hollister took it upon himself to find an empty, narrow brick storefront in downtown Eugene, where he negotiated a rental agreement that would cost the company just $50 each month. He thought his boss would jump at the chance to have such an affordable storefront, but Knight still hesitated.

"You'd think I was bleeding Buck dry to get the fifty dollars a month rent," Hollister recalled.

When Hollister finally convinced his boss to part with enough money to open the shop, it proved so successful that the company soon opened retail outlets in Portland, Oregon, and Natick, Massachusetts. It wasn't long before Blue Ribbon Sports had trouble keeping shoes on its shelves, in part because of consistently late deliveries from Onitsuka, which insisted on prioritizing its domestic customers. Onitsuka's executives, meanwhile, had doubts about the size of Knight's operation. When he sent John Bork to Mexico City for the 1968 Olympic Games, Knight was careful to brief the Blue Ribbon Sports employee on how to deal with any Onitsuka executives he met there. If they asked him about the number of Blue Ribbon Staff, Knight said, he should include part-time employees in order to inflate the tally.

"Get it as high as you can without lying," Knight told him.

Onitsuka's suspicions turned out to be both well founded and utterly naïve: while Onitsuka executives nagged Blue Ribbon Sports employees for hints about the number of staff the company employed, Knight was cultivating a spy deep within the ranks of the Japanese company. Knight told his staff about the mole in a 1968 memo that focused on "two clouds on the horizon" at Onitsuka. The first cloud, according to Knight's spy, was a price increase that would make its shoes more expensive for Blue Ribbon Sports starting in January 1970.

"The other cloud," Knight wrote, "is the illogical Japanese mind which may decide that there should be two dealers in the U.S." rather than an exclusive arrangement with Blue Ribbon Sports.

Knight justified putting a corporate spy on the company payroll by telling his employees, falsely, that corporate espionage was so common in Japan that "they actually have schools for industrial spies much the same as we have commercial schools for typists and stenographers." Then he outlined what would prove to be a blueprint for his company's future: the spy, Knight wrote, could reveal the names of Onitsuka's subcontractors, which would allow Blue Ribbon Sports to cut its partner out of the relationship and go directly to the manufacturers it used to produce its shoes. They would get the same shoes at a cheaper price, but without the Tiger brand name.

"While it is somewhat remote that we might ever have to go direct to the subcontractor, even the slightest possibility dictates a change in emphasis in our ads and promotions," Knight wrote. "We keep the name TIGER before the public but we do not understate our role in the scheme of things."

The situation was made worse by growing pains on both sides of the Pacific: after struggling to produce all the shoes Blue Ribbon Sports needed, Onitsuka opened two new factories, which pushed its productivity beyond what Knight's letters of credit could finance. Blue Ribbon Sports was forecasting strong sales for 1970, but a "great glob of liabilities" nevertheless caused the company to miss a bank-imposed sales quota, which hurt Knight's ability to get new letters of credit to finance the larger orders Onitsuka was prepared to send. With his own bank turning him away, Knight met with Nissho Iwai, a Japanese trading company with offices in Portland, which offered to finance a $350,000 shoe order in exchange for a 2 percent commission.

Knight still had other worries on his mind. His spy had told him that Onitsuka would be meeting with another distributor who was interested in selling its track shoes in the United States, which made him wonder whether Onitsuka would renew his exclusive contract after it expired in 1972. With a little more than a year left on the contract, Knight moved forward with the plan he'd once called a remote possibility: with financing from Nissho Iwai and factory intelligence from his spy at Onitsuka, Knight would manufacture his own shoes.

The result was the birth of a shadow brand called Nike, on June 18, 1971, when the Cortez went on sale at each of America's Blue Ribbon Sports retail shops. The all-leather football and soccer shoes bore a new swoosh logo that had been designed by Carolyn Davidson, a student at Portland State University, where Knight had taught accounting classes as an adjunct professor until 1969. Knight paid Davidson $35 for the logo design, telling her "I don't love it, but it will grow on me." (It did; in 1995, Knight had the logo tattooed just above the sock line on his left calf.)

Like the logo, the name Nike came from someone other than the company's founder: one night in 1971, Johnson had a dream about the Greek goddess of victory, called Nike, and became convinced that this should be the next iteration of Blue Ribbon Sports. Eventually, Johnson's dream was chosen over Knight's proposal to call the company's first independent shoe design the Dimension 6.

After eight years at the helm of a successful shoe distribution company, Knight unveiled the newly christened Nike brand at the 1972 National Sporting Goods Association show in Chicago, where Blue Ribbon Sports brochures described the Cortez as "a parallel development to our Tiger line." When the 1972 U.S. men's track and field Olympic trials came to Eugene, the Nike team showed off the new brand, and began to realize what distinguished them among competitors like Adidas and Puma: while these other companies were networking at industry trade shows and negotiating deals in hotel conference rooms, Nike's employees made their inroads after closing the Eugene retail store early so they could hang out with the athletes during track events at Hayward Field. Hollister, Johnson, and Knight were all runners themselves, after all, and when Hayward Field hosted national championship qualifiers or Olympic trials, athletes from around the country would gather at Hollister's home for cold beers and hot home-made food.

Nike's first shoe was made in Mexico, along with a Nike-branded T-shirt that came free with each of the ten thousand pairs that were made. But only one thousand pairs of the shoes sold at the full retail price before Knight was forced to discount the shoes to just $7.95 a pair in order to unload them. When the company made a second attempt at the Cortez, in 1974, Knight chose to have them manufactured in Exeter, New Hampshire, but not because of quality concerns.

Knight's relationship with Onitsuka had gone from bad to worse. Blue Ribbon Sports had potentially violated its contract with Onitsuka by secretly producing its own shoes, while the Japanese company had flirted with violating its commitment to Blue Ribbon Sports by talking with other U.S. distributors. Knight used this as a pretext for deepening his partnership with Nissho Iwai, which offered him a $650,000 line of credit that he used to order Nikes from factories in Japan and Mexico, with each sale generating a commission for the trading company.

The partnership with Onitsuka dissolved into acrimony that culminated with a 1973 lawsuit which ended up hinging on whether an Oregon judge felt Knight was more or less trustworthy than an Onitsuka executive named Shoji Kitami. The judge sided with Knight, despite the fact that he admitted to acts of corporate espionage, including the theft of a file that he secretly stole, photocopied, and then returned during a meeting with Kitami. His reason for taking the file was the same as his reason for inflating the size of his company: he was worried, he said in a deposition, that Onitsuka was trying to cut them loose. By the time the lawsuit was resolved, in 1974, Knight had already decided on measures that would allow him to stay one step ahead of Japanese backers at Nissho Iwai, just in case. Nike's first American-made shoes came from Exeter simply because Knight could more easily hide the New England factory from his own Japanese partners.

Steve Prefontaine discovered his love for running through a kind of Darwinian selection that began when he was a freshman at Marshfield High School, which sits atop a steep hill overlooking a beautiful stretch of Oregon coastline and a blue-collar mill town called Coos Bay, where his father worked as a carpenter, his mother as a seamstress.

"Coos Bay is a sports-minded town. You had to be an athlete to be somebody," Prefontaine said. "I knew I had to show everybody that I could excel at something. But I didn't know what."

Prefontaine rode the bench during basketball season because he was too short, and again during football season, because he was too slight. But in gym class he ran the mile faster than all but one other student, and without even trying too hard. He joined Marshfield's cross-country team as a freshman, but didn't really impress coach Walt McClure until his sophomore season. His results were unspectacular, but he was beginning to show signs of the maniacal determination so common among champion athletes.

"I decided that if I was going to continue in track, that I didn't want to lose," Prefontaine said. "That I wasn't going to lose."

He flogged himself throughout summer training, stubbornly refusing to let anyone finish ahead of him, no matter how casual the pace. When the next year's cross-country season arrived, it seemed as though some mysterious fission had released all the energy Prefontaine had been forced to hold back while riding benches in other sports. He won his first state championship and ended the cross-country season undefeated.

McClure had a reputation for treating all of his runners the same, which he signaled by wearing a stopwatch for each of them around his neck. But in the winter of 1968 he put Prefontaine on a special thirty-week training program that focused heavily on interval training. The workload was so intense that McClure had to rotate Prefontaine's training partners to keep them from slowing the distance prodigy down, or injuring themselves, but it paid dividends in Prefontaine's junior track season, when he set a new two-mile state record of 9:01.3. His confidence soared to meet his blossoming talent. As a sixteen-year-old, he promised his mother he'd run in the Olympics one day; as a senior, he set a national two-mile record of 8:41.5, bringing recruiters from forty different colleges to his doorstep, begging him to sign a letter of intent. Bowerman wasn't among them. Instead, he sent two of his best distance runners to Coos Bay for a ten-mile practice run with Prefontaine. When they returned to Eugene, they told their coach the kid was fast, but cocky. So Bowerman appealed to that cockiness in a short recruiting letter, which immediately won Prefontaine over.

"If you want to come to Oregon," the letter read, "there is no doubt in my mind you'll be the greatest distance runner in the world."

Bowerman wasn't the only one expecting greatness from Prefontaine. As a University of Oregon freshman, he appeared on the cover of the June 1970 issue of *Sports Illustrated* magazine, dressed in a yellow Oregon jersey pulled over a green T-shirt, with his neatly trimmed hair blowing in the wind as he cut a path across a bluff overlooking the pine-stippled shores of the Willamette River. By then, anyone in the world who knew a thing about running knew about the young man they called Pre.

The caption that appeared alongside the cover photograph of Prefontaine read "America's Distance Prodigy," and the story inside the magazine outlined Bowerman's plans for the wunderkind, who was "only a freshman, but the best prospect in the world at two miles, three miles, and 5,000 meters." The kid would train for good results in the 1972 Munich Olympics, Bowerman said, and for peak results in the 1976 Montreal Olympics.

These great expectations were not misplaced: by the time he was nineteen, Pre had beaten his idol, Gerry Lindgren, by a whopping twenty-seven seconds in a six-mile cross-country race, and he had run a faster three miles than any other runner on earth had managed that year. He was a genuine prodigy, and with Bowerman as his coach, there was no telling how far he might go.

Bowerman was obsessed with every aspect of running. Years earlier, he had become fascinated with the mechanics of footwear, and began spending time with a local cobbler, who taught him the basics of how shoes are made. At first he experimented with trying to make shoes lighter; then he worked on developing a new sole to improve his runners' traction in the rain. But his most radical experiment with footwear began around the time Pre arrived in Eugene. It started with an idea for a shoe with rubber spikes but was transformed by the experience of Bowerman watching his wife make waffles one morning. The resulting design was called "the waffle," because he'd made them by pouring a rubber compound into a mold he produced using his wife's waffle iron, then affixing the flap of hardened rubber onto whatever leather uppers Knight sent to him. Hollister ran the fastest mile of his life (4:09) while wearing a pair of

Bowerman's waffles during Hayward Field's annual Twilight track meet in 1972. Another Bowerman runner, Kenny Moore, ran the mile six seconds faster than Hollister in his pair of waffles. But none of them could match Prefontaine, who ran a remarkable 3:56.7 mile. His blistering performance couldn't have been more heartening for Bowerman as a coach, or more devastating for him as a cofounder of Nike, as Prefontaine had run his mile wearing a pair of Adidas spikes.

The sensational young runner usually wore Onitsuka Tigers while working out, and sometimes wore Nike flats after Knight and Bowerman began making their own shoes under Onitsuka's nose. In competition, however, he always wore Adidas, because Nike didn't yet make a spiked running shoe suitable for the track. "When you're going to run 57 seconds for your last lap," Prefontaine said, "you have to have spikes on your feet."

By the time the Olympic trials came to Eugene in 1972, Prefontaine's boyish, clean-shaven look had been replaced by a more rugged, iconoclastic image—long, unkempt hair and a thick mustache. The cult of Pre, which was outgrowing the sport of running itself, helped draw 23,000 fans to Hayward Field on the final day of trials for the Munich games.

"I've seen four Olympics," one biographer wrote. "But I've never seen anything like when Pre ran in Eugene."

His running style, as much as his rock-star looks, contributed to the atavistic frenzy Pre inspired in his fans. While other contenders of his generation tucked themselves in the slipstream of the race leader to remain fresh for the closing sprint, Pre went to the front of the pack and set the most blistering pace he could manage. His lack of guile was a constant source of frustration for Bowerman, who sometimes called Pre a "rube" for refusing to hold anything back until the finish line was behind him. But for Pre, any other way of running was "chickenshit."

On the final day of the 1972 Olympic trials, the crowd at Hayward Field rose to its feet as Pre broke free from the field in the 5,000-meter qualifier. In the last mile, he slipped away from his final challenger, George Young, with lap times that got faster and faster—63.4 seconds, 61.5 seconds, and 58.7 seconds—until Young, a three-time Olympian, could no longer stand Pre's relentless effort. Pre crossed the finish line alone, then celebrated qualifying for the Munich games by running a sixty-nine-second victory lap while wearing the "Stop Pre" shirt Gerry Lindgren had worn during his warm-up. (Lindgren, who was booed for wearing the T-shirt, failed to qualify.)

Pre was in peak physical condition when he arrived in Munich for the Olympics. Bowerman, who was coaching Team U.S.A., watched his runner clock a new two-mile American record of 8:19.4 in his final practice run before the 5,000-meter semifinal. But his concentration and his drive were shattered by the tragedy that unfolded just a few days before the biggest race of his life. Shortly before five o'clock on the morning of September 4, Bowerman was awakened by a loud knock on his door. When he answered, Bowerman found Israeli racewalker Shaul Ladany standing in the hallway.

"The Arabs are in our building," he said. "They've shot some of our people."

Bowerman ushered Ladany into his room and called the U.S. Consulate to report the incident, which turned out to be the work of a Palestinian terror group called Black September. He asked that Marines be sent to guard the quarters of swimmer Mark Spitz and javelin-thrower Bill Schmidt, both Jewish Americans. The hostage crisis that played out ended on the morning of September 6, when the Olympic village woke up to German newspaper headlines reading "Sixteen Dead." Devastated, Pre retreated to the Austrian countryside, where he considered withdrawing from the Olympics altogether.

"If they loaded us all into a plane right now to take us home," Pre said, "I'd go."

Instead, he returned to Munich, where he gave everything in the 5,000-meter final, running at the front until he began to fade within sight of the finish line. He finished fourth, just a stride out of contention for the bronze medal, and returned to the United States filled with self-doubt and self-pity. For weeks, he locked himself away in his trailer.

"They'll name a street after me in Coos Bay," he said. "Fourth Street."

Nike had grown to forty-five employees, and was poised to pass the million-dollar sales mark just a few years into the new decade. The company signed its first endorsement deal with Romanian tennis star Ilie Năstase, who was paid $10,000 to wear a pair of Nike Match Point shoes in competition. Hollister, meanwhile, convinced the University of Oregon's head football coach to outfit the Ducks in Nike's new waffle-soled shoes for the 1972 Civil War game, which they won for the first time in nearly a decade.

"I always called them 'my Ducks,' but now they really were," Knight said. "They were in my shoes."

Knight was beginning to think more seriously about the value of finding a truly iconoclastic athlete to wear his company's shoes in competition, and the pairing of Nike and Pre seemed inevitable: Nike made running shoes, after all, and Pre was as big a star as running had ever produced, not to mention the protégé of Nike's cofounder. The timing was ideal for Pre as well. He'd emerged from his funk with redemption on his mind, but was inching closer toward graduation, which meant the end of the scholarship funds that had sustained him from 1970 through 1973. He would need to find a job to support himself, and build his grueling training schedule around it, which would put him a step behind strong rivals from Finland, who were secretly experimenting with blood doping, and from Eastern-bloc countries that lavished government support on their Olympians. All Pre had was Bowerman and a small community of running geeks back in Eugene.

The coach had set to work on a special pair of racing spikes for his young prodigy. They bore gold Nike swooshes cut from gold tape, rather than nylon or leather, to make them lighter. And because Bowerman's shoes were effectively prototypes, cobbled together from his own soles and nylon uppers from Japan, they were glued, not stitched.

"I build these shoes to last one race," Bowerman told Pre. But the truth was that sometimes they couldn't even make it through a training run. Hollister once watched a pair of swoosh logos fly off Pre's shoes during a warm-up run through a Eugene park. Eventually, Bowerman was forced to eliminate some of his weight-saving techniques for the sake of the brand, affixing heavier, sturdier swooshes to Pre's shoes. After all, Knight argued, what good was it to have the world's best-known distance runner wearing your shoes if no one could tell he was wearing them? Makers of athletic apparel often claim to be uncompromising, but in truth compromise is the very essence of the business: a 175-pound jogger requires a very different shoe than a 138-pound elite athlete like Pre, and convincing the jogger otherwise is simply a matter of marketing.

Pre's performance was uncompromised by the slightly heavier shoe. In 1973, while wearing the heavier Nike spikes Bowerman had made him, Pre ran some of the best races of his life, finishing the Oregon Twilight mile in 3:55 flat—the third-fastest mile ever run by an American.

Bowerman and Knight were determined to do everything they could to ensure that Pre trained for the '76 Olympics unburdened by the demands of a day job. So Knight decided to give him a job that wouldn't interfere with his training. He gave Pre a yearly salary of $5,000 and a business card identifying him as Nike's National Director of Public Affairs. It was enough money for Pre to buy himself a British sports car and trade the trailer he'd been living in for a house. When Pre wasn't training or recovering, he hung out at the Eugene Nike store and helped put on clinics for younger athletes. Sometimes he and Hollister would drive a van to meets around the country, with Pre acting as a brand ambassador for Nike. Because of Olympic rules preventing sponsored professionals from competing in the games, this was a job, not a sponsorship, which helped Pre remain an amateur on paper.

A year ahead of the Montreal Olympics, Pre's training was on course. On May 29, 1975, after winning a 5,000-meter race at Hayward Field, he made his way across town as daylight faded and the clear spring air turned cool, bound for a post-race party at Geoff Hollister's house. The NCAA meet had attracted elite runners like Frank Shorter and the Olympian Jon Anderson, who had won the Boston Marathon two years earlier. Bowerman protégé Kenny Moore was also at the party, along with Pre's parents, who drove up from Coos Bay that afternoon. Around midnight, Pre said goodbye to Hollister and the others, climbed into his MG convertible, and dropped one of the visiting runners off at Moore's house, where he was staying. Finally alone, Pre headed home with the top down, his blood alcohol level still above the legal limit. Just after midnight, he swerved into a cliff in the hills above Eugene, flipping his small sports car, which landed on top of his lithe body, crushing him to death. He was twenty-four.

When Knight first launched the Nike brand in 1972, he claimed that he could convince the world to buy his shoes if only he could first get them on the feet of "five cool guys." But it really took just two cool guys to transform Nike into one of the world's most iconic brands. The first was Pre, whose early death rooted his legend, and his unrealized potential, firmly in the soil of Nike's origin story. A decade after Pre's death, a new wunderkind reintroduced the Nike brand to millions of Americans in a thirty-second television commercial.

It opened with a shot of a basketball rolling across the rough pavement of an outdoor court, where it collided with a pair of red-and-black high-top sneakers worn by an NBA rookie named Michael Jordan. He kicked the ball up into his hands using the tip of his shoe and drove toward the basket, in slow motion, while the sound of a jet engine roaring to life played in the background. After dunking the ball, Jordan's voice asked: "Who says man was not meant to fly?"

When the commercial first aired, in early 1985, only dedicated college basketball fans would have recognized Jordan from his time at the University of North Carolina, but that quickly changed during his electrifying rookie season with the Chicago Bulls. The NBA gave Nike's new pitchman added publicity by banning his prototype red-and-black Air Jordan shoes for violating the league's "uniformity of uniform rule." Nike paid the $5,000 fine Jordan incurred for wearing different shoes from his teammates, then aired a second commercial advertising the league's ban on his controversial kicks. In time, few could claim not to recognize his unmistakable Jumpman silhouette rising from the earth, arm outstretched toward the basket as he prepared to dunk the ball.

It took Knight ten years to reach his first million dollars in sales, which he did with Pre at his side. A decade later, his company's annual revenues were nearly $700 million, while its staff swelled from 45 to 3,600 employees. Jordan came along just in time to save the company from the disaster that was waiting at the tail end of the jogging boom. By marketing the sense of awe that great athletes like Jordan inspired, Knight was able to transform his cash-strapped shoe company into an aspirational brand. No longer a mere shoemaker, Knight was now the owner of the hottest apparel company in the world. But the transformation went deeper: in 1981, Nike helped upend the manufacturing world by using factories in China to exploit the country's cheaper labor, freeing up immense cash reserves that were then poured into advertising and marketing. Over the course of eight years, Nike's annual advertising budget exploded from $20 million to more than $150 million.

"What Phil and Nike have done," Jordan said, "is turn me into a dream."

The dream business turned out to be much more profitable than the shoe business. Two years after Jordan's debut commercial for Nike, the company surpassed a billion dollars in annual sales. Five years into the partnership, Nike was raking in $2.2 billion in sales annually, and by 1993 that figure climbed to almost $4 billion. Profits soared nearly 1,000 percent during Nike's peak Jordan era, when one out of every three pairs of shoes sold in America were Nikes. Adidas, once an unimaginably powerful foe, was all but vanquished, along with newcomer Reebok. Then, in the midst of a year when Nike sold two hundred pairs of shoes each minute, every single day, Jordan brought the company back down to earth with a sobering announcement.

It began with an unexpected phone call Knight got from Jordan in the fall of 1993. The basketball legend had won a third title with the Chicago Bulls and had helped the U.S. Dream Team win gold at the Olympics, and he was ready to retire. A few weeks later, Knight and the small team who had built the Jordan brand gathered on the second floor of the basketball legend's restaurant in Chicago, where they watched local television stations break the news as they drank and wished him well.

Air Jordan merchandise accounted for just 5 percent of Nike's $4 billion revenue, but the brand awareness Jordan brought to Nike helped prop up every other sale the company made. Jordan was the most famous athlete in the world, and probably the most famous person in the world—at the time of his retirement, schoolchildren in China ranked him as more recognizable than most of the revolutionary heroes they'd been taught to revere.

It was through Jordan that Knight realized the extent to which nonathletic people would buy his athletic apparel, if only the marketing budget was significant enough to convince them to pay for what Jordan had called "the dream." Nike's customer base was no longer athletes but, to paraphrase Bowerman, "anyone with a body." Jordan's retirement meant that Nike might need to find new dreams to sell.

Still, Knight knew that there were billions of dollars waiting in untapped corners of the athletic apparel market, just as there had been in the running shoe market when he'd written his accounting term paper at Stanford's business school. A few cool guys had helped make Nike the most valuable shoe company in history, but to stay on top, the company would need to move beyond amateur runners and professional basketball stars.

—

When Ballot Measure 5 passed in 1990, it was in part because Oregonians who had once thought of themselves as citizens were convinced to see themselves instead as overburdened taxpayers. Rural Oregonians, in particular, began to view their relationship with the state's public institutions as transactional, even adversarial. This was especially true in cases where the taxpayer could be convinced that institutions working for the public good were, implicitly, more onerous for private citizens. Oregonians did not come to believe these things on their own. They were convinced by a dedicated group of deeply conservative anti-tax activists like Don McIntire.

McIntire was born in Tacoma, Washington, in 1938, and worked for years at Boeing before moving to Alaska, where he took a low-level administrative job in state government. In 1970, he moved to a suburb of Portland, Oregon, where he used the money he'd saved while working in government to open a health club. As years passed, he became increasingly active in the right-wing political scene. Twice each month, for years, McIntire met with other conservative activists at a hotel near the Portland airport, where they would eat a buffet-style dinner, smoke cigars, and fume over the city's largely liberal political representation.

In the 1980s, McIntire recognized an opportunity to use the momentum of Reaganomics and Thatcherism to push for changes in state tax laws that would favor wealthy property and business owners like himself. Oregon, he realized, was unusually fertile soil for nurturing this kind of effort, in part because of the ease with which activists could propose ballot initiatives for consideration. Oregon requires very few signatures to get an initiative on the ballot, and unlike most states, there is no requirement that signatures be gathered across a wide distribution of different counties. By canvassing rural, sparsely populated areas of the state, conservative operatives could force voters to consider far-right initiatives that wouldn't even make it to committee through ordinary legislative procedures.

The first such ballot initiatives were considered in 1904, and since then Oregonians have voted on several hundred popular referenda; only California comes close to matching Oregon in its use of this kind of direct democratic action, which was called "the Oregon System" by political reformers in the early years of the twentieth century.

The so-called Oregon System had spread to nineteen states by 1918, but broader enthusiasm for this brand of direct democracy dimmed once people realized how easily it could be hijacked by special-interest groups. The initiative and referendum system was overused and abused by a host of different interest groups, which became practiced in the art of using ballot initiatives to secretly benefit wealthy, anonymous political benefactors. Initiative campaigns were not, for example, required to reveal to the public how much money they had received or from what groups they had accepted funding. Prior to 1913, the Oregon public didn't even have the right to know who had initially filed a ballot initiative, much less who was bankrolling the effort. Corruption and fraud were particularly rampant in the ballot-initiative system used in Oregon, where one infamous case decided by the circuit court found that a 1912 public referendum to overturn the state legislature's appropriation for the University of Oregon had been propped up by more than seven thousand forged or fabricated signatures—60 percent of the total number of signatures the ballot initiative received.

These kinds of ballot initiatives remain an institutional force in Oregon state politics, driven not by the will of the public but by skilled, experienced activists like McIntire. These activists are aided not only by political tradition, but also by the deep cultural and economic divisions between rural and urban Oregonians, which conservative operatives exploit to their own ends in order to get divisive, partisan initiatives on the ballot, over and over, until they can be pushed through. In testimony before the state legislature, one prominent conservative operative said it was often just a matter of finding the right title necessary to sell voters on a ballot initiative—a brand of direct democracy not unlike the process of screen-testing a Hollywood film to get a sense of what audiences are willing to sit through.

When McIntire convinced Oregonians to pass Ballot Measure 5, in 1990, no other state in America was seeking to significantly reduce its level of financial support for colleges and universities. These institutions had, after all, proved to be as important for state and local economies as they were for individual social mobility, allowing residents to increase their earning power with relatively affordable degrees. This social mobility was among the first casualties of Measure 5's deep cuts to higher-education funding in Oregon.

When Myles Brand became the University of Oregon's president in 1989, the school was receiving nearly half of its funding from state coffers. After Ballot Measure 5 passed, the impact was swift enough that Brand almost immediately began urging faculty members to speak at high schools whenever they traveled out of state, in order to increase the proportion of students paying the school's higher out-of-state tuition. For every hundred students paying out-of-state tuition, Brand told his faculty, the school would rake in a million dollars. This extra money would be crucial for keeping the school afloat in the wake of deep funding cuts brought on by Ballot Measure 5, even if it would deprive many Oregon students from access to an affordable higher education. And it did just that: within a few short years, Oregon universities enrolled about 10,000 fewer students who had graduated from Oregon high schools.

Oregon's tax revolt did not end with McIntire's Ballot Measure 5. As the head of conservative group Oregon Taxpayers United, Bill Sizemore championed more than a dozen ballot initiatives aimed at slashing property taxes, hamstringing labor unions, reducing pensions for public employees, and linking teacher pay to performance. In 1997, Sizemore started his own signature-gathering firm, I&R Petition Services, allowing him to qualify the initiatives he proposed, while also profiting from other interest groups active in Oregon. Sizemore's clients included Lon Mabon and the Oregon Citizens Alliance (OCA), which managed to qualify several anti-gay initiatives that would have been impossible to put before voters through any other means. These included multiple attempts to deny legal protections to gay and lesbian citizens, and an attempt to prevent even the mention of homosexuals or homosexuality in Oregon schools. The anti-gay initiatives proposed by the OCA always failed, but not without exposing generations of Oregonians to discriminatory political rhetoric and radio and television ads aimed as much at promoting hate as changing laws.

As the University of Oregon began to feel the painful effects of Ballot Measure 5, Nike was soaring to heights previously unimagined, surpassing $2 billion in annual sales. When Jordan announced his retirement, Nike's annual revenues had climbed above $4 billion, just as state funding for Oregon universities dropped to a level about 20 percent lower than when Ballot Measure 5 went before Oregon voters. The same political winds that were hurting Oregon schools were helping Knight: throughout the next decade and a half, conservative groups like Taxpayers United would help Nike and other Oregon corporations win some two dozen different tax breaks.

It was confluence, not conspiracy, that Knight went looking to invest in a university just as one of Oregon's oldest and most prestigious liberal arts institutions found itself in need of a wealthy benefactor. But it was hardly an accident of history given that Nike's rise was aided by the same small group of conservatives who engineered the University of Oregon's decline. Could the end result of sowing boundless contempt for public institutions be anything but unchecked dependence on private institutions?

Knight bought his own suite at Eugene's Autzen Stadium in 1991, but the steady chaos of Nike's ascent often kept him from enjoying it. When the Ducks reached the Rose Bowl in 1995, Knight took notice, and even caught himself thinking about how much he'd like the team to do it again in his lifetime.

Up until then, Nike's forays into college athletics apparel had been sporadic and largely focused on basketball. But the shock of Jordan's retirement had forced the company into a period of self-reflection that yielded broader, fresher thinking about Nike's future. One idea that emerged from this moment of clarity was the potential for Nike to cut deals to outfit NFL teams. To get there, the company would follow the path that had helped it gain a dominant position as a sponsor of NBA athletes: outfit college teams, develop new shoes and apparel for them, and aggressively brand and market the results to ordinary sports fans. Access to college football programs would be a boon for Nike's research-and-development department, while access to the student body would offer affordable, unprecedented advertising possibilities.

Knight presented his first major gift to the University of Oregon in the midst of the football team's turnaround 1994 season: $27.4 million to renovate and expand a library that was rechristened in his honor. Knight's philanthropy put him in close touch with the school's new president, Dave Frohnmayer, and with the football team's new coach, Mike Bellotti. Rich Brooks, who had led the Ducks to their first Rose Bowl in thirty-seven years, was rewarded with an NFL job as head coach of the St. Louis Rams, which led to considerable anxiety about whether Oregon could repeat its miracle '94–'95 season.

Knight made better use of his Autzen Stadium suite during Bellotti's first year at the helm, which was successful enough to end with a trip to the Cotton Bowl, where the Ducks lost to Colorado, 38–6.

The day after Oregon's drubbing in the Cotton Bowl, Knight met for drinks with Bellotti and his offensive coordinator, Al Borges.

"What would it take to get to the next level?" Knight asked Bellotti.

"Well," the Ducks head coach said, "if we had an indoor facility that we could use to practice in the fall, we could raise ourselves considerably."

Knight told Bellotti he might be able to find a way to help him.

Two

Outside Money

Throughout 1987, a team of eighteen volunteers gathered regularly in a dusty office in downtown Halifax, where they worked for months on a centuries-old puzzle. Church and cemetery records dating back two hundred years filled boxes and filing cabinets, and tables and desks were strewn with piles of documents from Nova Scotia's public archives. Spread across the floor, one hundred feet of paper charted the branches of a family tree tracing twenty-four distinct surnames, each stretching back across five generations to John Braden and Elizabeth Scott, who were married in the tiny village of Middle Musquodoboit in the eighteenth century.

Among the Logans, Archibalds, Leeks, and twenty-one other families that sprang from the Braden-Scott marriage, the amateur sleuths hoped to find two long-lost relatives of Kirsten Frohnmayer, who was fourteen, and her sister Katie, who was nine. The young girls lived on the opposite end of the continent, in Eugene, Oregon, and they would soon die without bone marrow transplants from a donor whose branches intersected with theirs on that dusty floor in Halifax.

Dave and Lynn Frohnmayer first suspected something was wrong when they noticed how easily their oldest daughter, Kirsten, became bruised or fatigued. When she collapsed on July 4, 1983, the worrisome mystery unraveled over the course of a single night that never seemed to end. When it did, the results of a battery of medical tests revealed that Kirsten, who was ten, suffered from a rare and fatal disease called Fanconi anemia (FA). Doctors told her parents it would kill her before she was twenty. Even worse, it was a genetic disorder, so the Frohnmayers needed to bring their two other children in for testing as well. Katie, who was four, was given the same diagnosis as her older sister, while her brother Mark tested negative for the disease.

"I was raised to believe that if you do the right things, certain things happen," Lynn said at the time. "We thought we had these perfect children. Life was just swimming along. It was a staggering blow to find it wasn't so."

When Lynn became pregnant again in 1986, the genetic math said her new child, like the rest of Dave and Lynn's children, would have a one-in-four chance of being born with FA, which is so rare that it typically afflicts just one child out of every 350,000 births, with a higher frequency among Ashkenazi Jews and the Afrikaners of South Africa. The disease results from a genetic defect in a cluster of proteins responsible for repairing DNA, which leads most sufferers to die after developing some form of cancer, often leukemia. Ninety percent of all FA patients would develop bone marrow failure before the age of forty, though few lived that long; 50 percent didn't reach the age of ten, and most of the rest were dead before they were twenty. Roughly three-fourths of all FA patients suffered from endocrine problems and congenital defects, including short stature and abnormalities of the skin, arms, head, eyes, or ears. Many also faced developmental limitations. But against almost astronomical odds, the Frohnmayer children suffered none of these abnormalities—just the promise of a frail life and an early death.

In 1985, feeling "isolated and alone," Dave and Lynn decided to start a support group for the parents of children with FA. They penned an open letter and asked an FA researcher to forward it to the families listed in his private registry. Responses came from nineteen different families, which became the basis of a newsletter the

Frohnmayer family began sending out with the latest information on the disease. The mailing list quickly grew to dozens of families, then hundreds, from nearly every state in America and twenty-one foreign countries. In 1989, they registered the Fanconi Anemia Research Fund as a nonprofit organization, realizing that it had become much more than a support group for grieving families. Gradually, the focus had shifted from coping with FA to raising much-needed money to fund grants for the small number of scientific researchers who dedicated themselves to learning more about the disease and investigating treatments. In its first five years as a nonprofit, the group was able to fund fifteen grants for researchers studying FA, making the Frohnmayers the foremost backers of global efforts to isolate the gene responsible for the disease.

In 1986, the available research told Dave and Lynn that their daughters' best hope for a full life was through a radical bone marrow transplant requiring a donor whose tissue was a nearly identical genetic match. And because Kirsten and Katie had inherited their father's extremely rare tissue type, a national database of 300,000 potential donors turned up zero matches. So Dave began tracing his mother's lineage, following each branch of the family tree until one led him to a stack of old letters that placed the family's first American homestead in Wayzata, Minnesota. In the Wayzata phone book, he found someone sharing his mother's maiden name, Braden, and after placing just a few phone calls he found himself speaking with a third cousin he'd never known about. Soon Dave and Lynn were arranging for medical examinations and testing for fifty long-lost Minnesota cousins, none of whom proved to be a close enough match to provide bone marrow for the girls. But one of these cousins, Shirley Braden Hedican, revealed that Frohnmayer's maternal great-grandfather had come to Minnesota from Nova Scotia in 1868.

"We knew the next step was to go to Canada," Lynn said. "But we didn't know how we'd find the money to do it."

Alexis de Tocqueville argued in his 1835 introduction to *Democracy in America* that, through education, "every fresh truth and every new idea became a germ of power placed within the reach of the people," and that the "conquests" of democracy "spread, therefore, with those of civilization and knowledge." The story of Otto Frohnmayer and his descendants eloquently bears this truth out, while testifying equally to the effectiveness of the public university as a tool of social mobility in America.

The Frohnmayer family fled Germany just before the outbreak of the First World War and settled in Medford, Oregon, near the California border, when Otto was still a young boy. In 1925, he moved to Eugene and enrolled at the University of Oregon, where he paid his tuition by working as a bellboy at a local hotel. Otto graduated with the class of 1929, then enrolled at the University of Oregon's law school, where he studied alongside William Knight, who would leave with his law degree a year earlier than Frohnmayer, in 1932. When Frohnmayer returned to Medford after several years in Eugene, he rented a home with two other bachelors, one of whom was a high school football coach named Bill Bowerman. Frohnmayer started a thriving small-town law practice, married, and bought a house on several acres of property at the northern edge of town, where he and his wife started a family.

Otto's son, David Braden Frohnmayer, was born in the summer of 1940 and from an early age began making good on the implicit promise that an immigrant's child should take every opportunity to strive for more than their parents achieved, even when a parent had achieved as much as Otto Frohnmayer had. David entered Harvard College in 1958, graduated four years later, and was chosen for a Rhodes Scholarship to Oxford, where he earned a second undergraduate degree, in philosophy. In 1967, Frohnmayer earned his law degree at Berkeley, then worked for a short time at a tony law firm in San Francisco before his career unexpectedly veered into politics. President Nixon appointed as his Secretary of Health, Education, and Welfare a California Republican named Robert Finch, who hired Frohnmayer to be his speechwriter and special assistant. Within just two generations of American life, the Frohnmayers had proven, in a very literal sense, Tocqueville's assertions about education and democracy in America.

Frohnmayer was twenty-nine and living in Washington, D.C., when his parents called to tell him that Lynn Johnson, the daughter of a local family back in Jackson County, Oregon, was also living in the nation's capital, where she was a social worker. Frohnmayer called Lynn and asked her to coffee, and the two began dating in 1969. They married the next year and spent their four-day honeymoon skiing at Mount Hood before driving through a record rainstorm to Eugene, where Frohnmayer had accepted a position as a professor at the law school where his father once studied. They decided to start a family together in Eugene, unaware that each of them carried an extremely rare recessive gene that causes FA when two carriers have children together.

Politics and public service soon came calling again, and in 1975 Frohnmayer began the first of three consecutive two-year terms representing south Eugene in the Oregon House of Representatives. When he left the legislature in 1981, it was only to continue his climb up the ladder of political power, as Oregon's attorney general. His decade-long stint as Oregon's chief legal officer involved two unusually important religious-freedom cases, each full of high-stakes legal drama of the sort rarely associated with the Pacific Northwest. One of these cases was a six-year argument against First Amendment protections for Native Americans who wished to incorporate the psychoactive peyote plant into their religious practice. It ended with a Supreme Court victory so controversial that it was disavowed by Congress and by Frohnmayer's own state legislature. The other case emerged from a strange series of events that began in 1981, when the Bhagwan Shree Rajneesh, an Indian guru, paid $5.75 million for a 64,000-acre ranch along the John Day River, in eastern Oregon.

Bill Bowerman's oldest son, Jon, lived on the other side of the river, where he watched a religious colony take shape over the course of the summer of 1981. The guru's secretary, Ma Anand

Sheela, arrived with a small group of disciples, and told the mayor of nearby Antelope, Oregon, that they would employ no more than forty people on their ranch. In reality, they had plans to establish a city called Rajneeshpuram, where 50,000 of the Bhagwan's 200,000 global followers would settle. What ensued was more than just a clash between local ranchers, who were conservative Christians, and Rajneesh's disciples, who were mostly young white hippies; it was also a battle over land use in a state where open grazing was protected against urban sprawl; and it was a battle over whether the citizens of Antelope might end up footing the bill for the infrastructure needed to support a tax-exempt city with 50,000 residents.

In 1982, Bill Bowerman cofounded a nonprofit group to stop Rajneeshpuram, and he moved to Antelope in order to establish voting rights in the community, which was home to fewer than a hundred residents.

"Citizens for Constitutional Cities," Bowerman wrote, "is going to monitor the activities of the Rajneeshee and challenge them in court if necessary to avoid the creation of unlawful cities in this state and protect our citizens from harassment and intimidation in violation of the Oregon and United States Constitutions."

The Bhagwan Rajneesh had taken a vow of silence, and he was rarely seen outside the Rolls Royce that carried him slowly through the commune once each day. The work of defending the group fell to his secretary, Sheela, who claimed they were victims of religious persecution and bigotry. But Jon Bowerman had bigger concerns than the strange red-and-orange clothing the Rajneeshee wore, or the ecstatic chanting and singing they practiced. What worried the former Marine was what he saw going on across the river from his home, where armed guards used spotting scopes to surveil the surrounding landscape. At night, they used searchlights to keep outsiders away from Rajneeshpuram, and they sometimes aimed them at Bowerman's home, flooding it with light while the family slept. Bill Bowerman, frustrated and furious, turned to Dave Frohnmayer, the son of his former roommate, Otto Frohnmayer. Oregon's new attorney general advised the Bowerman family to tread lightly.

"I remember hearing Jon Bowerman mention how easy it'd be to take down the power lines to the ranch," Frohnmayer recalled. "I said that'd be the worst thing anybody could possibly do."

In September of 1983, an Oregon legislator asked Frohnmayer to look into any potential conflicts between First Amendment religious protections and the establishment of Rajneeshpuram as a city. It was then that he realized, after exhaustive research, that the Rajneeshee had made one critical error.

"They stopped busing the Antelope-area farm kids to [the nearby town of] Madras and forced them to go to the Rajneeshpuram school," Frohnmayer said. In a legal opinion issued on October 6, 1983, he called Rajneeshpuram "the functional equivalent of a religious commune," making it unconstitutional, as a city, for as long as its governance was enmeshed with a religion.

Sheela issued a statement saying she was "outraged beyond words" over Frohnmayer's "bigotry." But the extent of her outrage would only become clear after a series of failed plots to seize control of the Wasco County elections in the fall of 1984. Hoping to install two county judges and win control of the sheriff's office, Sheela brought some 1,500 homeless men to Rajneeshpuram for a "share-a-home program" that was meant to increase the commune's voting power. When they remained far short of enough people to challenge the 12,000 voters living in the county seat, in the Dalles, Sheela instead sought to incapacitate voters there by poisoning the town's water supply with *Salmonella enterica* on election day. She and a small group of followers rehearsed the attack by infecting ten restaurant salad bars in the Dalles, which led 751 people to get sick. Remarkably, no deaths resulted from the outbreak, which remains the largest biological attack to take place on U.S. soil. It could have been far worse: a year later, after Sheela fled to Europe, Frohnmayer put together an interagency task force that found, beneath her cabin, *Salmonella* cultures and evidence of an attempt to weaponize the AIDS virus.

The task force also found evidence of aborted assassination plots against Frohnmayer and a U.S. district attorney, as well as an extensive wiretapping operation run by Sheela. Rajneesh was deported, and Sheela was arrested in Germany, along with a disciple named Puja. They were both extradited and prosecuted, but served less than three years in prison.

The Rajneeshpuram affair demanded a lot of Frohnmayer, who was later credited with helping to prevent a disaster of the sort that took place in Jonestown, Guyana, and Waco, Texas. When he wasn't advising Jon Bowerman against cutting the power to Rajneeshpuram, he was getting commune leaders on the phone, telling them, "you know above all, we've got to keep the peace in this and keep the lines open."

However strenuous, the professional drama of those years would prove to be a relatively minor challenge when compared with the personal difficulties Dave and Lynn Frohnmayer faced after July 4, 1983.

The problem of getting to Canada, where there seemed to be hope of finding bone marrow donors for Kirsten and Katie, was a financial one. The Frohnmayers had exhausted their medical insurance by 1987, which put the family in serious financial difficulty for the first time. So they turned to private fundraising to cover the cost of the research trip to Canada, and found a benefactor in Elmo Zumwalt, Jr., a retired admiral whose son was fighting leukemia, a disease faced by many FA patients. Zumwalt quickly raised $50,000 from a small group of private donors and foundations, which was enough money to send the Frohnmayers to Nova Scotia and to pay for the costly medical testing that needed to be done there. The experience proved to be a turning point both for the Frohnmayers and for FA research. Almost overnight, the focus of the FA support group they'd founded shifted from newsletters and coping to fundraising and organizing.

In Canada, Dave and Lynn held press conferences, gave radio

interviews, and interviewed more than one hundred potential relatives who turned up to meet them at a community theater in Middle Musquodoboit.

"It made you feel as though you'd come to a family reunion just a little too late," Dave said of the community's support.

In Halifax, volunteer efforts were being led by Allan Marble, a genealogist who had spent three decades investigating provincial bloodlines throughout Nova Scotia. His offices filled with boxes of church and cemetery records, and with a growing staff of volunteers to catalog them. It quickly turned into a sort of war room for the effort to trace the twenty-four branches of the family tree that sprouted from the eighteenth-century union of John Braden and Elizabeth Scott. Meanwhile, small victories came in from the field as well, often from unexpected places. Red Cross officials had told Dave and Lynn they would probably need to identify 1,500 relatives before they could expect to find tissue matches for Kirsten and Katie, which made surnames a kind of currency that Dave collected with steadfast vigilance. He made it a habit to introduce himself to nearly everyone he met during this period, and questioned people with certain surnames more deeply than others. Once, while stopping at a gas station, Dave introduced himself to the owner, who he learned was named Tom Parker, just like a long-lost fifth cousin from the family tree that spread itself across the floor of Allan Marble's office in Halifax. The filling station owner turned out to be the same Tom Parker they'd been trying for weeks to find.

Before Amy Frohnmayer was born, in February 1987, Lynn decided to confront her dread head-on by having a prenatal test to determine whether her third daughter would be born with FA. She felt relief, for the first time in a long time, when the test came back negative.

"I thought I won the lottery," Lynn said.

In Halifax, the race to find a suitable donor continued, and new help arrived later that year after a national registry for bone marrow donors opened in Minnesota. Back in Eugene, the Frohnmayers did their best to let their children lead normal lives. Kirsten was elected freshman class president at South Eugene High School, while her younger sister learned to play the piano and celebrated her ninth birthday with a slumber party.

Kirsten was pathologically determined to lead a normal, productive life, often reminding herself that "a lot of people have bad things happen to them." But the truth was that her condition was dire, and worsening every day. Her blood counts eventually sank so low that Lynn and Dave took her to Harvard Medical School to explore a radical treatment that other doctors had advised against. It involved treating Kirsten with a male hormone called oxymethalone, and it was particularly controversial because Kirsten was thirteen, which meant she would be taking male hormones while going through puberty.

"It was a horrible thing to do, but we felt that our backs were completely against the wall," Lynn said. Kirsten's bravery was rewarded when her blood counts improved as a result of the treatment, and they remained steady as long as she continued taking the hormones. At the same time, her younger sister Katie began showing her first serious symptoms. Dave and Lynn responded by doubling down on their efforts with the FA group they'd founded. In 1988, they raised $50,000 for Dr. Arleen Auerbach, a geneticist at Rockefeller University, and the following year they assembled a formal review board to assess the value of the research being proposed by each potential grantee who approached them. The FA support group formally became the Fanconi Anemia Research Fund in 1989, and the Frohnmayers hosted their first scientific symposium later that same year. Eighteen FA researchers and a number of patients took part in the symposium. After it was over, Lynn found one of the eighteen researchers crying in the bathroom.

"I have been working with cells under a microscope," the woman told her. "I have never ever seen a person with this disease."

One branch of the family tree after another turned out to be fruitless when it came to the search for a bone marrow donor, and it soon became clear that significant advances in medical research would be Kirsten's and Katie's only hope for survival. Advances in gene therapy showed promise, but research required money. Dave put more of his time and effort into fundraising, not only from foundations but from corporate donors. He and Lynn began to gain traction, but learned early on not to let their hope grow into full-blown optimism. Another setback was always around the corner.

A few weeks after Amy was born, Lynn got a call from the family's pediatrician. The blood sample they'd taken from Amy had clotted, he said, so they'd need another one.

"I already knew the real reason they wanted a retest," Lynn said. "Mother's intuition."

Amy's prenatal test had produced a false negative. Suddenly they had a third daughter suffering with FA.

Dave Frohnmayer never allowed personal struggles to blunt his professional ambitions. If anything, his family's misfortunes only sharpened his desire for higher political office, which invariably put him in a better position to raise money for the research that might save the lives of his daughters. In the fall of 1989, when the Fanconi Anemia Research Fund first began raising money as a registered nonprofit, Frohnmayer announced his decision to run for governor against a popular incumbent named Neil Goldschmidt.

Frohnmayer had accomplished much during his decade as Oregon's U.S. attorney general, but his political bona fides paled in comparison to Goldschmidt's three decades of public service in local, state, and federal politics. When Goldschmidt was elected mayor of Portland in 1972, he was the youngest mayor any major American city had seen. He helped revitalize downtown Portland's ailing business district, and his efforts to improve the city's transportation infrastructure were so successful that President Carter appointed him U.S. Secretary of Transportation in 1979. After Carter left office in 1981, Goldschmidt spent several years as a senior executive for Nike before becoming Oregon's thirty-third governor in 1986. He was considered a heavy favorite to win reelection in 1990, so Oregonians were mystified when August 1989 arrived without any campaign announcement from Goldschmidt.

Behind Goldschmidt's reticence was a rape trial that was quietly unfolding in a Seattle courtroom late in the summer of 1989. While Goldschmidt was weighing whether to seek reelection, the trial's judge was considering whether to unseal counseling records that an accused rapist claimed would exonerate him by showing the woman was simply reliving sexual abuse she'd suffered between the ages of fourteen and seventeen. Governor Goldschmidt didn't need any court order to know what lay behind those hours of counseling sessions: he was the man who had sexually abused the young girl, who had been his family's babysitter during the late 1970s.

Adding to his worries was the possibility that Dave Frohnmayer might be among the Oregon political insiders who had heard about Goldschmidt's dark secret—a concern that was exacerbated by a pointed statement Frohnmayer's campaign manager, Donna Zajonc, had made during his August kickoff rally.

"I gotta believe the best family will win," Zajonc said of the campaign against Goldschmidt.

The fact that Goldschmidt's secret remained hidden for another decade and a half probably owed a lot to his decision not to seek reelection in 1990. Instead, Frohnmayer would run against Oregon's fifty-three-year-old Secretary of State, Barbara Roberts, who was experienced and charismatic, but lagged behind when it came to raising campaign funds.

Frohnmayer, meanwhile, had in a few short years become as skilled at raising money as anything else he'd ever tried his hand at. He was a strong Republican contender for the governorship of a traditionally blue state, with the support of powerful friends like President George Bush, who helped Frohnmayer's campaign raise $800,000 by appearing at a fundraising breakfast in May of 1990.

"Dave Frohnmayer is a man of integrity, achievement, and honor," Bush said at the breakfast. "A man who will leave Oregon an even mightier heritage than the one left to him. I'm proud to say that he's got a good friend in Washington pulling for him on election night."

By the time election night arrived, Frohnmayer had raised almost $3.5 million in total—more than any other gubernatorial candidate in Oregon's history. But in the end, it was Oregon's increasingly fractured Republican base that lost Frohnmayer the election.

Frohnmayer had come from a long tradition of Oregon Republicans who were very moderate compared with the party's national representatives: he was pro-choice and fervently against any measures that limited the rights of gays and lesbians, which put him at odds with the same conservative groups responsible for pushing initiatives like Measure 5. With ballot day approaching, the Oregon Citizens Alliance came to Frohnmayer with an ultimatum: they would support him only if he reversed his stance on abortion, came out against gay rights, and agreed to hear the far-right group's input before choosing his Cabinet members. Frohnmayer refused all of the group's demands, leading it to endorse a third-party candidate. His sizeable lead in the polls began to slip.

Stiffer than any political headwinds were the ones blowing at home. Just weeks after Frohnmayer announced his candidacy for governor, Katie began complaining of pains in her side, which ultimately led to an operation to remove her spleen. In just over a year, she was hospitalized eighteen times with a host of new symptoms, including a narrowing of the carotid artery, which caused her to have a stroke in June of 1990.

Frohnmayer's lead over Roberts dwindled a bit more each week as the race dragged on, and when the ballots were counted on election day, he came up 67,000 votes short of the Democratic contender.

Katie's stroke prompted doctors to begin a new course of treatment using gamma globulin injections, which revitalized her enough that she was able to join the family for a summer skiing trip to Utah in 1991. But she began experiencing shortness of breath after taking a ski lift to the top of a mountain to enjoy the view with her father, and a few days later her sister Kirsten found her on the floor in their hotel room, unable to move half her body after suffering a second stroke. She spent a month in a hospital in Salt Lake City, unable to speak or move.

"She was trapped inside," Dave said. "But she could still blink and she could smile."

Months earlier, after suffering her first stroke, Katie had grown reflective, as though she knew she was going to die soon. After she lost her ability to speak, Lynn recalled conversations during which her young daughter had prepared her for what was to come.

"Mom, I'm just so glad that I have had these years," she said to Lynn.

On September 26, 1991, Katie died at a hospital in Eugene. She was twelve years old. Just weeks later, her sister Kirsten started school at Stanford, and a short while after that the first FA gene was identified by one of the research teams the Frohnmayers had helped fund. Before Katie's funeral, Dave gave the pastor strict instructions that forbid him from making any statements that might imply Katie's death had been some part of God's plan.

"It's not a time for comfort," Dave Frohnmayer said. "It's an occasion of deep anger that this thing should be visited upon our child. If there is a God, why should this happen?"

Frohnmayer left public service after Katie's death, resigning his position as Oregon's attorney general, and on the first day of January in 1992, he became dean of the law school at the University of Oregon. From the beginning, he could sense that the school was already feeling the strain of the budget cuts imposed by Ballot Measure 5. Frohnmayer possessed a talented legal mind, but he distinguished himself most as an administrator, and in 1994, when the school's president, Myles Brand, left the school to take charge of the NCAA, Frohnmayer was appointed interim president. He ended up keeping the job for the next fifteen years, and often referred to himself as the University of Oregon's "accidental president."

On October 5, 1994, Frohnmayer opened his first academic year as the university's president with a speech extolling the virtues of the public research university.

"Our research universities made the United States the technological and scientific leader of the world," Frohnmayer said. "On a more jarring note of reality, they helped win the Cold War. Our humanists, artists, and professional scholars add discipline and understanding to every endeavor of value."

A state's public universities also carried a burden of public service, he argued, because the students they educated and the research they performed were inextricably linked with the success of the state and society. The work done at the University of Oregon must be shared, he said, not only because it was the societal duty of a public institution, but also because any region that did not nurture a major research university in its midst was, in his view, a region that would "doom itself and its people to economic servitude."

Economic servitude was, by then, more than an abstract fear for an increasing number of Oregon high school graduates who could no longer afford tuition at their state's flagship university—in the years since Measure 5 took effect, the University of Oregon had raised in-state tuition by more than 60 percent, and applications from graduates of Oregon high schools subsequently dropped by several thousand. Things were only going to get worse: Governor John Kitzhaber's budget proposal for 1995 called for a 14.4-percent decline in state support for higher education, making Oregon the only state in America to send its legislature a proposal asking for less money to support its public universities and colleges. Disinvestment in higher education was, in essence, a matter of policy in Oregon.

In the face of this, Frohnmayer told his faculty and administrators, they must reconsider the University of Oregon's funding model.

"We must raise more outside money," he said in October 1994. "One way we are changing is in an increased reliance on private funds."

A year later, Frohnmayer's focus on bringing in more outside money had helped the school gain pledges of nearly $100 million from private and corporate donors. But the fundraising never seemed to stop for Frohnmayer, who had dodged one form of economic servitude only to stumble across another.

After Bellotti told Knight that he needed an indoor practice facility to convince top high school prospects to come play ball in rainy Oregon rather than sunny California, Knight committed to giving the school $8 million to help build it.

When the 117,000-square-foot Moshofsky Center opened less than two years later, it made the University of Oregon the only school on the West Coast with its own indoor practice facility. The sparkling edifice featured a full-length artificial field with ceilings that reached seventy feet high at their tallest point. Four lanes of synthetic indoor running track stretched 120 meters across an area adjacent to its football field. There was even an indoor retail outlet for selling Oregon Ducks merchandise and apparel.

Knight proved from the beginning to be a more hands-on booster than college athletics had ever seen. He treated his philanthropic endeavors like he treated any other business investment. Rather than paying for building projects outright, he invested in them, paying half of the $16 million required to build the Moshofsky Center, leaving the school to raise the remainder of the funds from other private donors, or through tuition increases or bond initiatives. Knight, as the principal donor, always maintains the naming rights for the university buildings he invests in, but often forgoes the option. (The Moshofsky Center is named for Ed and Elaine Moshofsky, who also donated to its construction; on other occasions, Knight has paid for buildings and had them named after family members or early Nike employees.) The Nike CEO also found creative ways of ensuring that his dealings with the public university were handled like private business deals.

"In higher education you have more hoops to jump through and policies, you can't move as fast as corporate America," said Bill Moos, Oregon's athletic director. This proved to be a constant source of frustration for Knight. He could attribute much of his success as a businessman to finding ways of coloring outside the lines—Nike had circumvented U.S. minimum-wage laws by using factories based in countries where wages were much lower; it avoided paying international tariffs on some of the foreign-made shoes it then imported back to the U.S. by classifying them as slippers rather than shoes; and it had end-run its own partners through corporate espionage and cutting secret deals on the side.

Knight did things "the Nike way" in his dealings with the University of Oregon as well. When giving the school money for a building or athletic facility, Knight circumvented many of the processes public universities are expected to go through with such undertakings. Instead of handing over the money to the school, for instance, Knight often took charge himself. He opened limited-liability corporations controlled by himself and his wife, Penny Knight, using names like "Penny and I, LLC" or "PHIGHT, LLC." Through the relevant LLC, Knight would pay for the design of the building, lease the land it would go on from the university, and then proceed with construction on his own. Once completed, the facility would be handed back to the school as a finished product, having relieved it of responsibilities like a public bidding process with construction firms, negotiations with union laborers, and an open dialogue with the campus community and other Eugene stakeholders. This proved to be an endless source of frustration for labor unions like UA Local 290 Plumbers and Steamfitters, which claimed that the university prevented scrutiny of Knight's projects by blocking access to records that were supposed to be public.

By the end of 1996, it was clear that Knight was precisely the corporate super-booster Frohnmayer had been hoping for when he told his faculty that the school was going to need to embrace change and seek out more private funding. In less than two years, the Nike CEO had committed to giving some $35 million for various building renovations, athletics facilities, and endowed chairs and professorships. He had also given Oregon's football team a new look to go along with its new facilities.

In 1986, the University of Oklahoma spent more than $2 million on its championship football team. There were rich budget lines for travel, recruitment, and scholarship costs, but also a significant budget for athletic apparel and equipment: $6,000 for helmets made by the Bike Athletic Company, $10,000 for jerseys made by MacGregor, and $5,400 for 200 pairs of Nike shoes, with variations meant for artificial turf, grass, and playing in wet conditions. Oklahoma was just one of many schools spending this kind of money on college football.

The market for supplying and outfitting America's college football teams was worth hundreds of millions of dollars, and Nike was on course to dominate it, with Adidas trailing just behind. But Knight had learned some valuable lessons in the two years since he'd started working with Michael Jordan; he'd learned to sell the dream rather than the product, and he knew that there were not just millions but billions of dollars in dreams to be sold on America's football fields and blacktop basketball courts. Everyday consumers spent $14 billion each year on sporting goods and equipment—ordinary people who wanted to be convinced that they were athletes simply because, as Bill Bowerman once said, they had a body. To reach these consumers, Nike, Adidas, and other shoe companies sought exclusive deals to ensure that college athletes wore their shoes each time they stepped in front of the tens of thousands of fans who came out to see them play, and the millions of fans who watched the games live on television. The problem was that there were no such deals to be had under NCAA rules, which barred companies from forging direct relationships with college teams and players. So the shoe companies got creative, starting with Nike.

In 1977, Knight's company began sending Nike sales representatives to meet directly with college coaches, who were allowed to cut their own personal deals through an NCAA loophole. Nike's college basketball dealmaker was Sonny Vaccaro, the son of a steel-mill worker who grew up east of Pittsburgh, in Trafford, Pennsylvania, a small town that he escaped with the help of a football scholarship to Youngstown State, where he was a star running back. Vaccaro had olive skin and thick, curly hair that he grew into an afro, with bug eyes that made him look perpetually surprised.

In college, Vaccaro met Dom Rosselli, the school's head basketball coach, who asked if he thought he could convince some decent basketball players from Pittsburgh high schools to come to Youngstown State.

"That's how my basketball life started," Vaccaro recalled.

In 1964, Vaccaro had an idea that would change college basketball recruiting forever: an all-star game that gathered the best high school players from around the country to compete against the best players in Pennsylvania. The inaugural Dapper Dan Roundball Classic was held at Pittsburgh's Civic Arena on March 26, 1965, and in subsequent years would draw coaches like UNLV's Jerry Tarkanian and Notre Dame's Digger Phelps, who came, along with the University of Maryland's Lefty Driesell, to find college basketball's next great talent. If it wasn't the beginning of the arms race in college athletics recruiting, it was at least the start of its nuclear era. And Sonny Vaccaro had played the role of J. Robert Oppenheimer.

Vaccaro was a natural showman. At courtside, dressed in white suits and gaudy jewelry, he could be seen talking with coaches, who were anxious to learn about recruitment from the man who was reinventing it as an art form right in front of their eyes. His success stemmed from the fact that he always spent most of his time getting to know the players.

"He wasn't hesitant to tell you: 'Well, you're not gonna get that guy, but you might have a chance with this guy,'" said Steve Fisher, the head coach at San Diego State University. "Because he knows this guy is already gonna go here, or that guy there."

The Dapper Dan Classic also gave Sonny Vaccaro a training ground for the backroom deals that would make him one of the most influential people in the shoe industry. Vaccaro arranged private rooms for coaches like Tarkanian and Driesell, where they met with some of the high school players and their parents, often with Vaccaro himself acting as a broker for whatever deals got made.

After graduating from Youngstown State, Vaccaro became a middle-school teacher in Trafford, where he felt increasingly trapped and isolated from the jet-setting coaches he'd befriended courtside at the Civic Arena. One day in 1976, he had an idea that he hoped might help launch him back into the glamorous world of sports: an odd hybrid of a basketball shoe and a sandal, meant for kids to wear in the summer. He drew up designs for a few different shoes and brought them to a local Trafford shoemaker to have prototypes made. When the samples were finished, he tossed them into a burlap potato sack and boarded a plane bound for Portland, Oregon, where a friend had helped him get a meeting at Nike's Beaverton, Oregon, headquarters.

A Nike executive named Rob Strasser looked at Vaccaro's shoes and said there was no way the company could buy them—but he was curious to know whether Sonny might be able to use his connections from the Dapper Dan Classic to help Nike make inroads with college basketball players.

Strasser knew that basketball could be the sport to help Nike outgrow the market limitations it was encountering as a running shoe company, and he sensed that Sonny Vaccaro was the man to help the company get there. He sent him a few boxes of shoes to hand out to high school players around Pittsburgh. But Vaccaro had a different strategy in mind:

"I looked him in the eye and I said: 'You wanna get involved in college basketball? Pay the coaches, give free shoes to all the teams, and the kids will wear the shoes.'"

In 1978, college basketball coaches began hearing about the "sneaker money" Vaccaro had been spreading around the country. He had packed up his car and driven cross-country to Las Vegas, where he gave his friend Jerry Tarkanian a check for $10,000 and promised him free Nike shoes for any of his players who wanted to wear them. NCAA rules banned Tarkanian from guaranteeing that his players would all wear Nikes, so Vaccaro had to settle for his winking promise—which in reality was as good as a contractual guarantee, Sonny knew, because Tarkanian would receive another $10,000 the following year only if Nike felt the money was buying complete fealty from the team as well as the coach. It was a major turning point for college athletics programs that had always bought their own equipment and apparel, and it was immediately clear that there would be no going back.

"I was charmed by Sonny," Knight said. "We had been beating our brains in trying to get a foot in the door in this game. Then this little portly Italian fellow comes around and says he's going to burn down the walls for us."

After charming Knight with his connections, Vaccaro impressed his Nike boss with the massive shoe orders that began pouring in once he'd seeded half the country with sneaker money. In the early years, the average coach cost Nike $5,000, which represented about one-fifth of what most colleges then paid their basketball coaches during their first year. The going rate for someone of Tarkanian's caliber was $10,000. By 1986, Vaccaro was cutting $100,000 deals with coaches at schools like Georgetown, Kentucky, and St. John's, making Nike the primary source of income for many college basketball coaches, whose contracts earned them far less than they made from "sneaker money." Nike's methods soon spread to competitors like Adidas, which managed to sign Indiana basketball coach Bobby Knight, and Puma, which cut a deal with Larry Brown at Kansas.

At Nike, backroom deals with coaches gradually evolved into an enterprise called College Colors, which marketed a full line of athletic apparel and shoes designed by Nike, using the logos and colors of different universities. "Sneaker money" and a few boxes of free shoes turned out to be a small price to pay for the chance to have Nike's logo seen on television by millions of college sports fans each week.

It also helped them reach significantly more consumers. Until then, the battleground for the shoe wars being waged by Nike, Reebok, and Adidas were department stores and brick-and-mortar shops like Foot Locker. The competition for wall space at dedicated sneaker shops was especially ruthless, and pushed Nike designers to constantly come up with new innovations and branding tricks. The College Colors program helped Nike gain a foothold at university bookstores around the country, where millions of students would see Nike apparel whenever they went to buy textbooks or supplies. Having an edge at a particular college also landed the company access to every serious sports fan among its student body, who could be counted on to buy things like branded T-shirts and sweatpants, and jerseys to wear to home games.

Sonny Vaccaro emerged as more than a backroom deal maker in 1984, when he played an instrumental role in signing Michael Jordan. Nike executives had planned to sign three athletes coming out of the NBA draft that year: Hakeem Olajuwon, Charles Barkley, and John Stockton. But Vaccaro had seen Jordan play against Georgetown with the North Carolina Tar Heels, and couldn't shake the feeling that he'd seen a singular athlete coming into his own. He convinced Knight to give just one athlete all the sponsorship money Nike had in its budget, and he convinced him that athlete should be Jordan.

"You gotta give the kid everything you got," Vaccaro said.

After Knight agreed, Vaccaro called his friend George Raveling, who knew Jordan, and helped arrange a meeting at Tony Roma's restaurant in Santa Monica, California. Jordan had been wearing Converse as a college player, and he'd expressed an interest in wearing Adidas as a professional. But Vaccaro helped convince him to become a Nike athlete by promising to name a shoe after him.

Nike's Air Jordan brand generated $100 million in sales during its first year, on its own, and it helped turn Jordan into an icon overnight. Vaccaro decided to capitalize on the success of his latest good idea by reviving his first good idea, this time by bringing America's most promising high school basketball talent directly to Nike for a basketball camp. For three days each summer, the world's biggest athletic shoe and apparel company had the country's most promising college basketball prospects locked away on a private campus, wearing Nike gear while they played pickup games and ran drills in front of any college basketball coach Phil Knight decided to invite. Coaches who didn't play ball with Vaccaro, or who worked at schools that didn't have a good relationship with Nike, were excluded from the summer basketball camp, giving their rivals an edge when it came to recruiting future stars like Alonzo Mourning and Joakim Noah.

In May 1986, an NCAA committee met to begin drafting new rules governing contracts and other financial agreements between coaches and companies like Nike. The president of the NCAA, John R. Davis, said the rules were aimed at preventing "the properties of the institution" from being marketed by coaches alone.

"We're wondering if the property of the institution shouldn't be marketed by the coach and the institution together," Davis said. And that's exactly what began to happen under a new set of rules that allowed Nike to make its first all-school deal with the University of Miami in 1987.

This new kind of deal allowed Nike to "own the school," Vaccaro said, because it formalized what backroom deals had long sought to accomplish by making Nike the only athletic apparel company allowed at the University of Miami's retail outlets. In a pre-Internet retail climate marked by fierce competition for wall space at brick-and-mortar stores, this exclusivity gave Nike a huge advantage. In the two years following Nike's first all-school deal with an American university, the company's revenues doubled and its profits quadrupled.

Within the span of a few years, Nike managed to fundamentally change the way college athletics programs functioned behind the scenes. For decades, equipment buyers at American universities had approached their jobs as an accountant might, buying enough gear and apparel, of the best quality possible, without exceeding their budget. Nike taught these administrative factotums to behave like businessmen rather than stewards of public funds and tuition dollars. Bidding processes and local wholesalers were replaced by one-on-one meetings with sales representatives like Vaccaro, who cut private deals with both coaches and administrators. Sports equipment that had once cost colleges money instead generated it, in great sums, by transforming unpaid amateur athletes into walking billboards. And it became the job of athletic department business managers, like Robert Smith at Oklahoma, to decide whether those walking billboards would be wearing Nike or Adidas.

"The athletes are considered; we put them first and foremost, academically as well as athletically," Smith said in 1986. "But in terms of purchasing and marketing our products, we do conduct it as a business."

It was the beginning of a new era—an era of outright corporatization of the public university in which Phil Knight would teach America's college football and basketball powerhouses what it really meant to play ball. But first he would cut ties with the man who had made it all possible. Even when he was brokering backroom deals, Sonny Vaccaro had always been honest about who he was and what he did; he spoke plainly, even proudly, about things that Knight would rather have left unsaid—like the fact that Nike had so deliberately commercialized college sports.

"We were the first corporate entity to be involved with a coach or a university," Vaccaro said of his days with Nike.

On August 15, 1991, Knight summoned Vaccaro to his office at Nike's campus in Beaverton and told him his time with the company was over. Vaccaro was shocked. He told his boss that he felt like a gunslinger from an old Western film who had been hired to clean up a one-horse town only to be chased out once the dirty work was finished.

"Yeah," Knight said. "Basically that's probably true."

In 1993, with Jordan's retirement looming, Nike began a two-year push to sell more licensed apparel for college teams. It was fertile territory: the NBA and the NFL were each selling about $3 billion worth of apparel and merchandise annually through licensing arrangements with big brands like Nike, Adidas, and Reebok, while U.S. colleges were bringing in $2.5 billion each year through licensing deals with smaller local and regional companies. Using its College Colors program as a blueprint, Nike moved into the fractured market for college athletics apparel, which was earning the company an extra $50 million each year by the end of 1995.

College athletics promised much more room for growth than the nearly saturated market for professional apparel. It also gave Nike the chance to expand its influence in the world of college football, which would help the company as it sought more licensing deals with NFL teams. In the mid-1990s, Nike signed a slew of all-school apparel deals like the one it had made with the University of Miami in 1987, hoping to do for college football what it had done so well, and so profitably, with college basketball. And though Sonny Vaccaro was no longer with Nike, his chief strategy for cutting deals with universities remained: pay the coach. As part of its $6.2-million deal with Florida State, Nike agreed to pay $225,000 per year to head football coach Bobby Bowden, on top of his salary. The company inked a six-year $8-million deal with the University of Michigan and paid Penn State $2.6 million over three years. Nike also signed North Carolina, Miami, Colorado, Southern Cal, and Illinois, but the most enduring of its all-school deals proved to be the one Knight cut with the Oregon Ducks, who took to the gridiron in 1996 wearing a simple green-and-yellow jersey, with Nike's swoosh logo printed on the left shoulder. Aside from the logo, they didn't look much different from any other school's uniforms, but that would soon change. Nike's research-and-development unit had decided to use the University of Oregon as a testing ground for developing new football gear it might later sell to other schools and to NFL teams.

It made sense: Knight's philanthropic gifts and his long

association with the university meant that Oregon's athletic department was more likely to protect his company's secrets; and since Eugene was just a short flight from Nike's Beaverton headquarters, the company's executives, designers, and marketing team members could spend all the time they needed evaluating a product with players on the field—new gloves, cleats, and proprietary fabrics could be tested on short notice during practices, and could be tinkered with throughout the season in order to get them ready for market.

One prototype tested by the Ducks was a type of Lycra made with Cordura, a proprietary fabric owned by the Koch brothers. After being fine-tuned by the Ducks, this new type of Lycra was used to make uniforms for other college and NFL teams. Years later, it would be used to make a successful line of base layers and performance underwear that played an instrumental role in helping Nike stave off a ferocious challenge from apparel upstart Under Armour.

Two decades after Knight outfitted the Ducks in waffles for the Civil War game, Nike's efforts to get its gear on more college football fields proved to be much more than an exercise in nostalgia: in 1996, the company's U.S. apparel sales had risen by 99 percent, and Knight attributed this largely to "getting our apparel products on the playing fields of the world."

It was, Knight said, the year that Nike moved past being a shoe company or even a shoe and apparel company, and instead became "a total brand."

The company was flush with cash and eager to get its gear on more soccer players in Europe and more college football players in the United States, both of which Knight saw as central to keeping Nike in the realm of the "total brand." But in 1998, Nike's tailwind was suddenly slowed by a major financial crisis in Asia, where demand for Nike products dried up almost overnight. As orders were canceled throughout the troubled region, Nike slashed retail prices in the United States in a desperate bid to unload its massive inventory surplus. Profits plummeted and Nike laid off hundreds of workers overseas and hundreds more at its Beaverton headquarters, where it had already lost five of its most important executives to retirement and resignation. Worst of all, Knight's company was suffering a public-relations crisis unlike anything it had faced before as media reports revealed the unsettling conditions Nike's overseas laborers were working in, and the meager wages they were being paid to do so.

Despite the setbacks Nike was facing, Knight continued to invest in the University of Oregon, where he committed to spending another $30 million on a renovation that would, among other things, expand the number of seats at Autzen Stadium in Eugene. He also made a much smaller, more unusual investment at the school, which went largely unnoticed. On top of endowing professorships, Knight began personally contributing $40,000 toward President Dave Frohnmayer's annual salary through a supplemental payment approved by the board of higher education. Behind the scenes, the Nike CEO quietly invested himself even more deeply, and more personally, in Frohnmayer's affairs by becoming the Fanconi Anemia Research Fund's single largest donor with an annual gift of $1 million. This gave Knight an unusual amount of leverage over the University of Oregon and its president, particularly in light of the Frohnmayer family's most recent tragedy.

Just days after Frohnmayer returned home from Pasadena following the Ducks' devastating loss in the 1995 Rose Bowl, his oldest daughter, Kirsten, noticed a bruise that she couldn't explain. A blood test revealed values consistent with leukemia, which was especially tragic because it disqualified her from participating in clinical trials for a gene-replacement therapy that doctors at the National Institutes of Health (NIH) hoped might end FA by making it possible to replace the defective inherited gene with one that does not have the defect.

In February 1995, Kirsten traveled to the University of

Minnesota for a bone-marrow transplant, which was considered a long shot since the donor was not a close relative. Miraculously, the transplant seemed to be a success, and Kirsten was well in time to attend her graduation ceremony at Stanford University. Then, late in the summer of 1995, her leukemia returned. Increasingly desperate for a remedy, Lynn brought her daughter to Milan, Italy, for an experimental treatment in which doctors administered genetically altered T cells—a treatment that was not yet approved in the United States. Her leukemia went into remission, briefly, but returned in April of 1996. On June 20, 1997, Kirsten Frohnmayer died of complications from FA at the same Eugene hospital where her younger sister had died. She was twenty-four.

Amy, who was ten, was suddenly the only daughter Dave and Lynn had left. And Phil Knight's money was the only thing that seemed like it might save her.

Three

We Don't Make Shoes

Jonah Peretti made his first piece of viral content four years before cofounding the *Huffington Post*, and five years before he launched BuzzFeed, a Web site that would make him among the richest and most powerful figures in the media world. It began one day in January of 2001, when he visited Nike's Web site while trying to put off work on his Master's thesis at the Massachusetts Institute of Technology (MIT) Media Lab.

"They had just launched NikeiD, which was a service where you could customize your shoes and put a word on the side of the shoes," Peretti recalled. "I customized a pair of shoes with the word 'sweatshop,' cause I thought, oh, is Nike going to send me a pair of shoes that says 'sweatshop' under the swoosh?"

Instead of sending him shoes, Nike sent Peretti an email saying his order was canceled. He sent the following email in reply:

> From: "Jonah H. Peretti" peretti@media.mit.edu
> To: "Personalize, NIKE iD" nikeid_personalize@nike.com
> Subject: RE: Your NIKE iD order o16468000
>
> Greetings,
>
> My order was canceled but my personal NIKE iD does not violate any of the criteria outlined in your message. The Personal

> iD on my custom ZOOM XC USA running shoes was the word "sweatshop."
>
> Sweatshop is not: 1) another's [sic] party's trademark, 2) the name of an athlete, 3) blank, or 4) profanity.
>
> I choose the iD because I wanted to remember the toil and labor of the children that made my shoes. Could you please ship them to me immediately.
>
> Thanks and Happy New Year, Jonah Peretti

The email chain continued, with Nike arguing that Peretti's order contained "inappropriate slang," which he countered by pointing out that *Webster's Dictionary* did not categorize "sweatshop" as a slang term. In his final email, Peretti relented, saying he would order the shoes with a different iD if Nike would fulfill "one small request," writing:

"Could you please send me a color snapshot of the ten-year-old Vietnamese girl who makes my shoes?"

Peretti posted the entire email chain to the Web site shey.net, and it spread quickly across the Internet before being picked up by newspapers like the *Guardian*. He was then surprised to be asked to appear on *The Today Show* with Katie Couric, where he sparred with a Nike executive as though he were an expert on labor issues or global manufacturing. Peretti has called the NikeiD stunt the genesis of his fascination with how things go viral on the Web, but the reason behind his post's success is clear: for years, Nike's overseas factories had been subject to increasingly critical media coverage, and more recently activists on college campuses around the country had been organizing to bring the company's alleged abuse of its labor force into closer focus. Peretti had simply found a clever way of using the Internet to capitalize on the momentum of work that activists and journalists had been doing for years.

At the time of Peretti's stunt, Nike's manufacturing operations consisted of more than 500 different shoe and apparel factories around the globe, all operating as independent contractors, with Nike technicians on-site to act as advisors. Knight had been exploiting Asia's cheap labor market from Nike's very inception—it was, in fact, one of the company's founding principles, laid out in his assignment at Stanford Graduate School of Business. But things had been different when Nike was a start-up partnering with a Japanese firm to take advantage of the country's cheap labor market as it rose from the ravages of war, during the 1960s and 1970s; decades later, it was a mature company seeking out the poorest nations, with the weakest labor laws, in order to maximize already stunning profits. By 1982, Nike was importing 70 percent of its shoes from South Korea, 16 percent from Taiwan, and another 7 percent from Thailand, Hong Kong, and the Philippines. The 7 percent of Nike's shoe production that had been based in a secret New England factory was soon moved offshore as well.

Nike was pioneering in its use of offshore manufacturing, which proved to be immensely profitable for the company: a single factory like the one run by South Korea's Samyang Tongsang could produce up to 4 million pairs of Nike shoes each year, for lower wages than Knight could legally pay workers in the United States, and without any big investments in construction, raw materials, or training of a labor force. Contractors also proved useful when Knight sought to distance his brand from the problems that arise when manufacturing in countries with weak or absent laws to ensure worker safety.

Knight had many such problems to distance himself from. Throughout the 1980s and 1990s, underage workers toiled in the company's plants in Indonesia; at factories in China, workers claimed that they were coerced into putting in excessive overtime in order to meet Nike's demanding production schedule; and in Vietnamese factories, workers faced dangerous conditions. As Nike spent many tens of millions of dollars on marketing to associate its shoes with luxury and performance, news reports told the American public that they were cheaply made by laborers dwelling in poverty.

Just outside of Jakarta, Indonesia, a slum the size of a small city grew up around the 50 buildings it took to house 22,500 workers making Nikes on behalf of Taiwan's Pou Chen Corporation, the largest manufacturer of shoes in the world. In the August 1992 issue of *Harper's*, union activist Jeff Ballinger documented wages as low as $0.14 per hour for a factory worker named Sadisah, despite Indonesia's minimum wage of $1.24. An annotated pay stub published with the report showed that it would take a worker like Sadisah 44,492 years to earn the equivalent of Michael Jordan's endorsement contract. Abuses these workers suffered at the hands of management often went unpunished thanks to rampant corruption and bribery among the country's 700 labor inspectors, who prosecuted as few as 7 reports of abuse in a year when 7,000 such reports were filed.

Nike's general manager in Jakarta maintained that neither the company nor its executives should be held responsible for poor labor conditions in the factories they contracted. "I don't know that I need to know [about what's going on in the factories]," he said.

Later that year, Knight took action—not by raising wages or instituting rules against child labor, but by tasking Dusty Kidd, a member of Nike's public relations department, to draft a series of new regulations for its contractors to follow. It was highly unusual for a corporation to use its public relations department to craft policy, rather than to spin policy, so there was little surprise when Kidd's efforts failed. Several months later, a group of Indonesian factory workers making shoes for Nike told *CBS News* that they were being paid just $0.19 an hour. Then, in 1996, Knight's public relations nightmare approached its crescendo after *Life* magazine published a photograph of a twelve-year-old boy stitching a Nike soccer ball in Pakistan, prompting daytime talk show host Kathie Lee Gifford to call on Michael Jordan himself to investigate the issue.

Near the end of 1996, an editorial in *BusinessWeek* called on American corporations to do more to prevent the exploitation of its overseas labor force, suggesting that even Wall Street was beginning to turn a corner on the issue.

"They have protested, disingenuously, that conditions at factories run by subcontractors are beyond their control," Mark L. Clifford wrote in *BusinessWeek*. "Such attitudes won't wash anymore. As the industry gropes for solutions, Nike will be a key company to watch."

Those who did watch saw things go from bad to worse in the months that followed.

—

The shoes that Nguyen Thi Thu Phuong died making were designed at Nike's headquarters in Beaverton, Oregon. The plans for the shoes were then relayed by satellite to a computer-aided manufacturing desk in Taiwan, where prototypes were developed and tested. Once the shoe's blueprints were approved, they were sent by fax to the factory where Phuong worked, in Bien Hoa, northeast of Ho Chi Minh City. There the shoe's three main parts—the outsole, the midsole, and the upper—were produced individually, then assembled in a labor-intensive process that was difficult to automate, and therefore relied on manual labor.

It was a summer day in 1997 and Phuong was making midsoles, carefully trimming away the excess synthetic material overflowing from molds that had just come out of an oven. Nearby, a coworker's sewing machine suddenly broke down, spraying metal parts across the factory floor. A piece of shrapnel pierced Phuong's heart, killing her instantly. She was twenty-three.

Nike's response to the young woman's death was to boldly claim: "We don't make shoes."

Knight and his team of self-proclaimed "shoe dogs," whose origin story was tied to making prototype soles in Bill Bowerman's waffle iron, now claimed they were little more than the designers and marketers of shoes made by other companies.

The backlash against Nike amplified just as the company was expanding its retail operations by opening its upscale Niketown retail outlets around the country. Picketers and news cameras showed up at store openings, including one in San Francisco, where NFL wide receiver Jerry Rice was assailed with questions about sweatshops and child labor. This was a major problem for Knight, who planned to open three more Niketown shops in 1998; they weren't just retail outlets, but brand-awareness generators that helped increase Nike's sales at other retailers, like Foot Locker. And key Niketown locations, like the one in London, would help give the company the foothold it needed as it sought to make inroads into the European soccer market.

Michael Jordan faced his own tough questions about Nike sweatshops during a press conference, but even worse things were in store for Knight, who learned that documentary filmmaker Michael Moore was set to release a new film, *The Big One*, focused on Nike's misadventures in offshore manufacturing.

Wall Street took notice, and throughout 1997 it was not uncommon to find stock analyst reports filled with summaries of the latest news reports on the condition of Nike's factories throughout Asia, and the extent to which the company and its shareholders were exposed. For the first time in years, analysts began downgrading Nike's stock and lowering its expectations for the company's outlook.

When Knight at last looked outside his company for help, he turned to a firm called GoodWorks International, owned by Andrew Young, a former mayor of Atlanta who had also been the U.S. ambassador to the United Nations. He hired GoodWorks to evaluate Nike's operations in 1997, and Young himself went to Asia to meet with some of Nike's suppliers and contractors there. When Young issued his report on Nike's use of overseas labor, it was hard to imagine that Dusty Kidd and the rest of Nike's public relations staff could have done more to polish what was clearly a rotten apple. Knight was so pleased with Young's conclusions that he took out full-page newspaper advertisements highlighting them.

"It is my sincere belief that Nike is doing a good job," one advertisement in *The New York Times* read. "But Nike can and should do better."

Knight was also pleased with another aspect of Young's evaluation: while third-party monitoring of Nike's overseas factories was a good idea, it should be left to a company like his own firm,

GoodWorks, Young felt, and not to global labor and human rights organizations. The benefits of this approach for Nike were evident from the amount of control the company was able to exert over the Young report, which completely ignored the key issue of wages for factory workers. Young had also relied entirely on Nike interpreters during his ten days of interviews with the workers making Nike shoes at factories in Asia.

The widely criticized Andrew Young report was further undermined in November 1997, when a disgruntled Nike employee leaked some highlights from a series of formal audits Nike had commissioned Ernst & Young to prepare. The accounting firm had, in fact, been auditing Nike factories in Indonesia since 1994, but Knight had managed to keep these less-forgiving assessments quiet up until the November 1997 leak of an Ernst & Young report recommending improvements to a factory just northeast of Ho Chi Minh City in Vietnam. The factory where Nguyen Thi Thu Phuong died making Nike shoes, Ernst & Young found, did not have safety equipment or training for its workers, who were forced to work more hours than allowed by law, making them more likely to become injured or killed on the job. For months, Nike had known exactly which measures needed to be taken to prevent others from dying like Phuong had; but instead of focusing on solutions for the problems Ernst & Young had found at its factories in Asia, Nike instead promoted the much rosier portrait that Andrew Young had painted in his report, which was conducted the same summer that Phuong died—a picture of a company doing its best and coming up a little short, as even the best athletes sometimes do. A story rather than a solution, or, as Jordan might say, a "dream" to be sold, rather than a problem to be fixed.

On the afternoon of April 4, 2000, six University of Oregon students locked arms and blocked the entrance to Johnson Hall, a stately one-hundred-year-old building that housed the offices of the school's top administrators. A heaving mass of protesters came with them, swarming the six stone columns framing the entrance to the redbrick façade, which sits on 295 immaculately kept acres of campus, bordered by the Willamette River and stippled with some 3,000 trees. From the window of his third-floor office, Dave Frohnmayer could see the message his students had written to him, spelled out on the sidewalk in bright pink chalk: "TAKE A HIKE NIKE," with the company's signature swoosh logo standing in for its name.

It was the University of Oregon's first major student sit-in since the anti-war demonstrations that began in 1969 and carried on into the following year, when four members of a self-described student women's militia hurled buckets of fresh animal blood on army recruiters while chanting slogans of protest against the My Lai massacre in Vietnam. Oregon's campus protests against the war in Vietnam intensified just as Frohnmayer arrived at the university as a law professor and legal counsel to then-president Robert D. Clark. In many ways, Clark had had it easier than Frohnmayer. Had he sided with protesters and kicked recruiters off his campus, he'd only have angered the U.S. Army. Frohnmayer, on the other hand, had to worry about angering Phil Knight.

In the three decades since Frohnmayer had moved to Eugene, the college by the river had grown to become Eugene's largest employer, with 10,000 Oregonians depending on the school for their livelihood. And in the handful of years since Knight had begun paying for new buildings on campus, he'd become more than just an important booster for Oregon athletics; he was the school's most important benefactor, which made him, in a sense, the town's most important benefactor. On campus, not everyone was comfortable with the influence Knight seemed to have, or the school's renewed focus on athletics over academics.

These developments coincided with a moment in which student activism was regaining its voice, particularly when it came to labor and human rights issues. And Nike—which was facing intensifying calls for independent monitoring at its overseas factories—had a target on its back. It was a major problem for Knight's company, which was losing ground to Adidas and couldn't afford to give up its position as the shoe and apparel supplier to America's top universities.

Nike's war to maintain its grip on America's college campuses began in earnest late in 1997, when students at the University of North Carolina protested the company's $7.2-million endorsement deal with the school. In early 1998, the movement gained a powerful voice in Jim Keady, an assistant soccer coach at St. John's University, who decided to publicly quit his job rather than wear the Nike gear his school's contract demanded.

"I don't want to be a billboard for a company that would do these things," Keady said of Nike's overseas labor practices.

In 1999, the pressure on Nike intensified after student activists took over buildings at Duke, Georgetown, the University of Michigan, and the University of Wisconsin, and staged sit-ins at many other schools. Just before Christmas in 2000, student carolers strode through the halls of Harvard University's administrative buildings singing "Away in a Sweatshop." It was becoming more than just an image problem for Nike. When a factory worker was fired by one of Nike's contractors in Honduras, student activists organized such effective protests that the company was forced to rehire the woman.

Nike's university shoe and apparel contracts became the common battleground shared by activists concerned over issues ranging from sweatshop labor and China trade policy to college athletics, which increasingly took precedence over academic excellence at schools around the country. And it wasn't just contracts with athletic departments that were under fire. Nike was facing significant backlash over the branded apparel it had so successfully marketed to ordinary university students through its College Colors program.

"It really is quite sick," said Tom Wheatley, a student and organizer at the University of Wisconsin. "Fourteen-year-old girls are working one-hundred-hour weeks and earning poverty-level wages to make my college T-shirts. That's unconscionable."

At a growing number of campuses around the country, organizations like United Students Against Sweatshops (USAS) and the Movement for Democracy and Education collaborated with the National Labor Committee and the Worker Rights Consortium (WRC). The student-led WRC proved to be especially effective at recruiting universities to the cause, first by protesting and then by lobbying students, faculty, and university presidents to sign its pledge censuring corporations using sweatshop labor to produce athletic apparel and shoes. By April 2000, the months-old organization had already gained the backing of 45 different universities around the country, which frustrated and angered Knight because joining the WRC meant publicly criticizing Nike for failing to allow, among other things, surprise inspections at the overseas factories where its shoes were made. Knight, meanwhile, was trying to pressure Nike's partner schools into ignoring the WRC, steering them toward the relatively toothless Fair Labor Association (FLA), which had executives from various apparel companies sitting on its board.

The campus wars came to a head in April of 2000, when Knight abruptly ended negotiations to renew his company's sports equipment contract with the University of Michigan—a deal that would have been worth as much as $26 million, making it the largest of its kind up until that point. Michigan's administrators and athletics department stood firm, issuing an unusually pointed statement aimed at Nike's retaliatory tactics.

"Nike has chosen to strike out at universities committed to finding appropriate ways to safeguard and respect human rights," the school said.

Sarah Jacobson made her way through the crowd as Eugene police officers handcuffed the six students who had blocked the entrance to Johnson Hall, the student body vice president and president-elect among them. When Frohnmayer finally left the building, Jacobson, a senior and anti-sweatshop activist, blocked the path police had cleared for him.

"We've got the votes we need in the faculty senate and we've got the support of all these students and more," she said to him. "You might as well sign on to the WRC right now."

Frohnmayer had done his best to delay the issue, but by March of 2000, there was no longer any question about what the campus community wanted: a referendum sponsored by the student government yielded a majority vote in support of WRC membership, followed by an affirmative vote from a committee made up of students, faculty, alumni, and administrators. The faculty senate vote was coming, and early indications were that Jacobson was right about where the votes would fall.

A number of faculty members, like biology professor Nathan Tublitz, had actively pressed for the school's membership in the WRC, and they had the support of more moderate professors. Jim Earl, who led the faculty senate, saw it as a "standard protest issue."

"The idea of academics even thinking twice about upsetting a corporation that gave the school money frankly didn't occur to us," he said.

It had occurred to Frohnmayer, who was left with nothing but bad options. As much as he wanted to side firmly with Knight, the situation on campus had deteriorated to the point where he couldn't even leave his office without having student protestors arrested. The day after his encounter with Jacobson, who police had to remove from his path, Frohnmayer faced more protestors. Six of them were arrested and charged with trespassing, but more showed up the following morning, ready to do it all over again. The local media breathlessly covered the showdown, and national activists descended on Eugene in solidarity, including Bobby Seale, a cofounder of the Black Panthers. Frohnmayer left town on business, and when he returned, the activists were waiting for him.

On April 7, the sit-in moved from the lawn to the hallway outside the president's office, and the following morning Frohnmayer and two mediators met with Jacobson and seven other students. One of them was a senior named Melissa Unger, who had been involved in campus labor politics since her freshman year. She knew it was only a matter of time before Frohnmayer would be forced to sign on with the WRC, but she also knew the terms of that deal still left room for concessions to Nike—concessions that could cost the protestors everything they'd fought for if they were to underestimate Frohnmayer.

"We want you to sign on with the WRC for a term of five years," Unger said.

Across the table from her, Frohnmayer just smiled. On April 12, he signed the WRC's members document, making the University of Oregon "a fully committed member" in the "effort to take a socially responsible stand on sweatshops and child labor," for a term of one year, rather than five.

Knight did not appreciate the lengths his friend of more than two decades had gone to in order to seek compromise. He was incensed by the fact that his alma mater had signed on to join the WRC rather than the industry-friendly FLA. He was livid that the school, which had been happy enough to accept tens of millions of dollars that had been generated by Nike's labor practices, now had the gall to criticize them. And he would be damned if he was going to give them the $30 million he'd pledged for the renovation of Autzen Stadium.

In a statement sent to the media on April 24, Knight said the school had "inserted itself into the new global economy where I make my living. And inserted itself on the wrong side, fumbling a teachable moment." He left no room for doubt about who he felt had quarterbacked that fumble: "Ask University of Oregon President Dave Frohnmayer one question," Knight wrote. "Ask him if he will sign a pledge that all contractors and sub-contractors of the University of Oregon as well as University itself [*sic*] meet the WRC's 'living wage' provision."

Nike profits paid for a significant chunk of Frohnmayer's salary, not to mention Knight's enormous financial contributions to the Fanconi Anemia Research Fund. Knight was interested in results, not the efforts Frohnmayer had made. And the results were bad enough that on April 24, Knight publicly withdrew his outstanding $30 million donation to the University of Oregon. Privately, he resorted to even more brutal means of punishing Frohnmayer.

In the six months leading up to the WRC protests, Frohnmayer was recovering from a full cardiac arrest that might have killed him if his heart hadn't stopped while he was surrounded by doctors at a meeting at the NIH, in Bethesda, Maryland. When he regained consciousness the next day, all he remembered was slipping away during his talk and waking up on a table surrounded by doctors in scrubs and green masks. The first thing he remembered thinking was that he couldn't die until they'd found a cure for Amy.

It was a week before he was breathing on his own and some days after that before he could talk, hoarsely, and with difficulty. He underwent surgery to implant an electronic defibrillator to jump-start his heart in case he suffered another arrhythmia, and Lynn made him give up the coffee, scotch, and cheap cigars he loved so much. He also exercised more, walking two miles each day, but there was nothing he could do to avoid the stress of the WRC protests, the pressure from Knight, or the strain of fighting to save his daughter's life.

In the days after Knight withdrew his $30 million gift, Frohnmayer and Knight talked personally and "soul-searchingly" about resolving the issue. The best that Frohnmayer could offer was his assurance that he would do his best to see that the university didn't extend its agreement with the WRC beyond the one-year agreement he'd already signed. This seemed not to be good enough for Knight. The angry letters Frohnmayer received each day from the university's more pro-business alums compounded the stress of these secret talks with Knight.

Some letters, like the one John S. McGowan wrote to Frohnmayer on April 28, 2000, were angry but fairly harmless, harsh words from small-time donors with no influence on campus or civic affairs. McGowan accused Frohnmayer of betraying and alienating the university's largest benefactor, and defended Knight's spiteful response, writing in his letter that "virtually any CEO placed in that position would respond the same way." He also criticized the WRC, calling it "a front organization for organized labor" that had no place on a college campus where taxpayers and alumni should be calling the shots.

Other letter writers demanded to be taken more seriously. Jane Moshofsky and her husband Arthur had donated millions of dollars to the University of Oregon, and the school's Moshofsky Center was named for Arthur's brother Ed, and his wife Elaine. In her letter to Frohnmayer, Jane Moshofsky said the University of Oregon's membership in the WRC "shouts 'antibusiness!'" She also gave him a list of donations that she and her husband had "seriously discussed" before being put off by the school's membership in the WRC—money for the Autzen Stadium expansion that Knight had withdrawn from, and for establishing "a scholarship fund for young people from small towns." It was the school's duty, she added, to "support all legitimate business in Oregon" and "promote the free enterprise system."

The University of Oregon should teach that corporations are not evil, she argued, adding that Oregon businesses had every right to enrich their own enterprises through investment in the school. Students, she said, should work as apprentices at Oregon businesses, while representatives from the business world should be welcomed in classrooms to "edify the curriculum." Frohnmayer, she wrote, had dealt "an unfair blow to Phil Knight and 'Nike,' a business started in Oregon by a U of O alumni," provoking "irreversible consequences for our University of Oregon."

She could not have possibly known how closely her wish list aligned with the immediate future at Oregon's oldest and most prestigious public university.

When the Second World War began, in 1939, the self-help organization Alcoholics Anonymous (AA) had just one hundred members. Over the course of the following decade, its ranks swelled, partly because of men like Arthur Golden, who returned from battle with a drinking problem. He got sober in 1953, built a successful career in real estate, and raised a family in Utica, New York, before moving to Eugene upon retirement in 1980.

Golden's experiences with AA left him deeply committed to helping others, and he spent his twilight years volunteering at Eugene public schools, where he enjoyed reading to young children. When he heard about the Frohnmayer family's fight against FA, he volunteered to help out with the Fanconi Anemia Research Fund. He also became a trusted babysitter for the Frohnmayer kids, someone Lynn and Dave could count on when they needed an extra hand around the house. As the years passed, he became a close friend to the family and something of a caretaker for the girls, who he loved as if they were his own grandkids.

"Arthur was a wonderful, kind, honest man," Lynn Frohnmayer recalled.

As a close member of the Frohnmayer family's inner circle, and a regular presence in the household, Golden shared in the good times and the bad. In 2000, there were good and bad times in the Frohnmayer household. Amy Frohnmayer—Lynn and David's last surviving child to inherit FA—was in the seventh grade during the spring of 2000, thirteen years old, with long blond hair and blue eyes. She could play Vivaldi on the violin and loved to run, like Knight had when he was her age. She exhibited no outward signs of the toxic blood cells coursing through her veins, allowing her parents to practice what Dave sometimes called "functional denial" about the reality of their situation. Unlike her sisters, she managed to reach her teen years without any serious health problems. But Lynn and

Dave had already seen how quickly the end could come once the bruising and fainting spells begin. They knew a cure was the only way to make sure their daughter had a long, full life. And thanks to advances in gene therapy, they had reason to hope that a cure might be found in Amy's lifetime.

The first attempt at gene therapy was made in September 1990, when doctors at the NIH treated a four-year-old Cleveland girl named Ashanthi DeSilva, whose immune system was crippled by a genetic disease called adenosine deaminase deficiency, or ADA. It worked well as an experiment in a petri dish, but DeSilva's treatment led to only a partial correction of the defective gene. Repeated and refined over a period of two years, the girl's genes were tricked into producing about a quarter of the normal amount of ADA. The problem was an inefficient delivery system for getting corrective genes into the nuclei of thousands or millions of defective cells. Eventually, with more funding for more researchers, scientists found better ways of delivering the corrective genes through viral carriers. The crucial advancements came when private companies began human trials for gene-therapy treatments aimed at diseases like melanoma and hemophilia.

These breakthroughs gave the Frohnmayers reason to believe that the disease etched into Amy's genes, which was barely understood by doctors when she was born, might soon be something they could scrub from her DNA completely. Thanks to research made possible by the Fanconi Anemia Research Fund, the gene responsible for causing the disease had been identified. Now all they needed to do was raise the massive amounts of money researchers would need to proceed with human trials for genetic therapies aimed at curing FA.

Phil Knight's money had brought that goal within reach. Each year, around Christmas time, the Nike billionaire added to the Frohnmayer family's holiday cheer with a gift of $1 million to the Fanconi Anemia Research Fund; some years, he even gave $2 million. Things were different, however, in the final months of 2000. Even as Frohnmayer worked tirelessly to repair the damaged relationship between Nike and the University of Oregon, Knight made it clear that he would not be making his annual contribution to the Fanconi Anemia Research Fund. A dark, distressed mood fell over the Frohnmayer household, according to Golden, who was so shocked by Knight's cruelty that he wrote a letter to a University of Oregon faculty member who had been openly critical of the school's relationship with Nike. Early in 2001, over coffee, Golden unburdened himself: Dave was distressed, he said, and Lynn seemed to be on the verge of a nervous breakdown.

Four

Severed Ties

In more than two decades of friendship, Frohnmayer had never seen such cold, calculated wrath from Knight. The extent of the personal considerations Knight seemed to expect in exchange for his financial gifts to the University of Oregon also surprised Frohnmayer. The disastrous fallout from the signing of the WRC agreement was, in many ways, a wake-up call for the university president, who suddenly realized he'd been laboring for years under some serious delusions about the nature of the bargain he'd made by taking Knight's money.

One of these delusions, he later wrote, was believing that Knight was someone who wanted merely to be informed on university matters, rather than to be consulted on them. Throughout the protests and negotiations surrounding the school's WRC membership, there had been communication between staff at the university and staff at Nike, and this, Frohnmayer assumed, was as much as any booster, however generous, could expect from a university president. But Knight turned out to be less a booster than a businessman in his dealings with the university, with expectations commensurate to the scale of the investments he'd made in his alma mater.

"If I had to do it over, I would have given him a courtesy call to make sure he knew how things were proceeding," Frohnmayer said. "I did not do that, and my regret is enormous."

Equally enormous was the scale of panic spreading through the campus community and every other corner of Eugene, a town reliant on the university, more than any other institution or industry, for jobs. Knight's cancellation of a $30 million gift toward a planned renovation of Autzen Stadium was disastrous, but the prospect of losing his patronage completely was nothing short of an existential dilemma for the school: since the 1995 Rose Bowl, Knight had funded not only athletics facilities but also renovations and expansions of libraries and other crumbling buildings on campus, as well as scholarships, professorships, and endowed chairs of departments. Meanwhile, the average student-loan debt and tuition were rising each year, while enrollment and funding from the state continued to plummet. The University of Oregon had come to depend on Uncle Phil, and without him the school's future seemed bleak.

The prospects for finding an FA cure within Amy Frohnmayer's lifetime were also much dimmer without Knight's millions of dollars in gifts, the absence of which meant the Fanconi Anemia Research Fund would only raise half the money in 2000 that it had the previous year. Golden was so angry over Knight's decision, which seemed to him needlessly cruel, that he couldn't resist going behind Dave and Lynn's back to reveal the Nike billionaire's secret. Dave, however, did his best to remain composed and think strategically. Whatever happened, he would be called on to make a number of tough decisions regarding the school's future.

The first decision Frohnmayer needed to make was the one that was on the minds of anyone even remotely involved with the university, the anti-sweatshop movement, or the Nike corporation: Was it time for the school to sever ties with Knight and build an alternative funding model? Or was it time to send the Nike CEO a clear message that he would get nothing less than exactly what he wanted out of his relationship with the University of Oregon from now on? Compromise was impossible.

The piles of letters Frohnmayer received from Oregon alumni made it clear to him that there was a deep political and cultural divide on the matter. Some alumni applauded Frohnmayer's courage for signing the WRC agreement, calling Knight everything from a "horse's ass" to an abuser of human rights. But more still wrote in support of Knight, casting the billionaire CEO as a "disenfranchised" victim of radical politics. Other Nike supporters went even further, calling the signing of the WRC agreement "reprehensible and morally wrong," the work of student protesters who were "smug," "puerile," and "arrogant." Many letters accused Frohnmayer of playing politics, which he hadn't even begun to do, aside from slowing down the process in order to delay signing with the WRC for as long as possible. When Frohnmayer did at last apply his considerable political acumen to repairing the school's relationship with Knight, he did so with a delicate touch.

It began in the weeks and months after the fallout of the WRC agreement, as Frohnmayer and Knight conversed "soul-searchingly," if sporadically, about what had happened and what could be done about it. "The bonds of trust" between the University of Oregon and Nike, Knight said, had been "shredded." But Frohnmayer felt, after a few conversations with Knight, that they could be repaired in time. There was no turning back the clock on the signing of the WRC agreement, but with some help from a Nike insider, Frohnmayer thought he might be able to find some way of doing the next best thing.

Prominent labor activists like Jeff Ballinger had been after Nike for years, but in the end it was a daytime television star who finally forced Phil Knight to acknowledge the issue of sweatshop labor. The turning point came on April 29, 1996, when a representative from a human-rights organization told Congress that Kathie Lee Gifford's Wal-Mart clothing line was being made by thirteen- and fourteen-year-old children who worked twenty-hour days at factories in Honduras. Rather than declining to discuss the issue, as Knight had done, Gifford seized what she called a "unique opportunity to make a difference" by stopping "the horrible practices of some of these manufacturers." She also seized the opportunity to call out other celebrities who endorsed apparel made using sweatshop labor, including Michael Jordan, who proved to be a chink in Nike's armor when he deflected Gifford's criticisms by saying it wasn't his job to "know the complete situation" surrounding Nike's labor practices.

"Hopefully," Jordan said. "Nike will do the right thing."

The leadership at Knight's company already had a good idea of what it would mean to "do the right thing" for the foreign workers making Nike shoes and apparel: the Ernst & Young audit had made a number of detailed recommendations about how to improve the working conditions in the Asian factories Nike used to produce its goods. But instead of focusing on these recommendations, Knight chose to run a full-court press on the public relations front, with an assist from President Bill Clinton, who invited Nike to be a part of an advisory committee that would tackle the issue of sweatshop labor. It was an opportunity for Knight to present himself as a proactive labor reformer, rather than the villain human-rights and labor activists had made him out to be.

On August 2, 1996, Knight joined President Clinton and Kathie Lee Gifford in the White House Rose Garden for a press conference, where the president announced that Nike, Reebok, Liz Claiborne, and other companies on the advisory committee had pledged to "take additional steps to ensure that the products they make and sell are manufactured under decent and humane working conditions." These companies also agreed to report back to the president on their progress within six months. After Clinton finished speaking, and the secretary of labor after him, Knight was invited to the podium, where he thanked the president "for inviting Nike to be a part of this coalition," as though it was the company's prominence, rather than its transgressions, that had brought him to the Rose Garden that morning. He also mentioned Nike's "code of conduct," which he said had been in place for five years in order "to ensure that subcontractors follow fair labor practices in good quality conditions," despite the fact that Ernst & Young's audit had demonstrated the code's utter ineffectiveness.

Among those watching Knight's speech as it aired live on C-SPAN was Silas Trim Bissell, a former college English professor and activist with the national Campaign for Labor Rights (CLR). Bissell had sacrificed a great deal by choosing the same life of protest as his mother, Hillary, who had been a prominent civil rights activist: for refusing to go into the family business, Bissell was disowned by his father, Wadsworth, who had founded the Bissell carpet sweeper company; and for his involvement with the radical Weathermen group, he once spent seventeen years living as a fugitive before being arrested in Eugene, where he settled once again after serving eighteen months in federal prison for planting a bomb in the stairwell of the ROTC center at the University of Washington. Prison had mellowed him, and in 1996 he helped form CLR, and began writing letters to Phil Knight in an effort to persuade Nike to become the first major apparel brand to allow independent monitoring for its factories. When his letters went unanswered for months, he wrote to Robert Reich, Clinton's secretary of labor, to express his concern that "Nike could use its position on the Clinton administration's advisory committee to evade issues relating to its contractors in Indonesia." Bissell's letter promised further action from a coalition of labor and human rights organizations if Nike and the Clinton administration continued to ignore the movement's calls for independent monitoring and proper investigation into the abuse of overseas factory workers. It was no idle threat: throughout the summer, a series of fact-finding missions to Indonesia produced extensive interviews with workers who went on the record about the poor conditions they endured while producing Nike shoes. When Nike's next shareholders meeting arrived on September 16, 1996, the report was released as part of an anti-marketing blitz orchestrated by a coalition of protest groups ranging from radical Marxist organizations to conservative church groups. The report angered Knight, who felt that Nike was being unfairly singled out, and in his anger he made what would prove to be a major tactical error in dealing with the anti-sweatshop movement. He had Nike's board vote down, without discussion, a shareholder resolution for independent factory monitoring that had been brought by the United Methodist General Board of Pension and Health Benefits, and in the process he angered the most conservative members of the anti-sweatshop movement—people who might have been brought over to his side through dialogue and compromise. Knight was more even-tempered, however, when it came to dealing with a group of labor activists who stormed Nike's September 1996 shareholders meeting. Even-tempered enough to realize that it was best if he handed the meeting over to someone who had more experience dealing with a protest head-on.

———

Jill Ker Conway joined Nike's board of directors in 1987 after being recruited by Knight himself, making her one of two board members who weren't, in her words, "either relatives of Phil's or people who had helped him sell things out of the back of his father's car to get the company going." It was the tail end of Nike's start-up years, when the company's revenues were soaring higher with each passing financial quarter, and Ker Conway proved to be a valuable, proactive member of the team, a corporate insider who could see the company with the discerning gaze of an outsider. This proved to be especially useful when international news organizations began documenting and widely publicizing the abhorrent conditions faced by workers making Nike shoes in factories based in Indonesia and Vietnam.

Nike's strategy for dealing with the controversy surrounding its use of so-called "sweatshop labor" had been to ignore it when possible and disavow it when absolutely necessary. Ker Conway took a different approach by volunteering to visit some of the factories herself—three in Indonesia, three in Vietnam, and one in Hong Kong. And unlike other members of Nike's board and its executive ranks, Ker Conway could claim to have started working as young as many of the women she met while touring the factories where Nikes were made, having grown up on 32,000 acres of harsh, windswept terrain in Australia's outback, where she and her two brothers helped herd sheep until the death of their father and seven years of drought forced their mother to send them off to Sydney for schooling. Her fortuitous path from there to Harvard, and from Harvard to the boardrooms of corporations like Merrill Lynch, Colgate-Palmolive, and Nike, seemed like it had as much to do with fate as any unlucky bend in the road that might lead a fourteen-year-old girl to end up gluing Nikes together for twenty hours a day. But it wasn't oral histories and empathy Knight expected Conway to bring back from Indonesia and Vietnam. The material she brought back from her fact-finding missions was usually just enough for Nike's public relations team to weave into vague initiatives on "corporate responsibility."

Ker Conway's other great strength came from her distinguished academic career, which saw her spend nine years as vice president at the University of Toronto before becoming the first woman ever to serve as president of Smith College in 1975.

"Both places had very active radical student movements, and I was used to a demonstration a day, if not two or three," Ker Conway said. "I had a lot of experience with this kind of problem."

This made her the perfect person for Knight to turn to when labor protestors interrupted Nike's September 1996 shareholders meeting. She had so much experience dealing with protestors, in fact, that she almost completely ignored them in favor of keeping the Nike executives from shooting themselves in the foot on September 16, 1996.

"My worry was that this wonderful Nike team might lose it, especially if Phil was called nasty things," she said. "So I thought my role was to keep everybody on the platform quiet and let the labor group, and anybody else who wanted to, ask their questions."

Knight and the Nike shareholders were incensed by the protestors, and repeatedly urged Ker Conway to declare their questions unfair or out of order. The Nike boardroom was not a place of dissent, after all.

"What I did at the meeting was totally alien to the way people on the Nike team thought of dealing with problems like that," Ker Conway said. "So I had to keep calming everyone down and saying 'Leave it be, because these people came to cause a confrontation. If you don't give them one, they'll get tired and go away,' and indeed, that's what happened."

Frohnmayer knew how much Knight had relied on Ker Conway's advice when it came to issues like sweatshop labor and the student protest movement. So when he found himself wanting to get back in Knight's good graces, while also getting out of the WRC agreement he'd signed, he felt she was the best person to advise him. Knight agreed, and asked Ker Conway to become an "unofficial liaison" between Nike and the University of Oregon, "to keep the lines of communications open." After meeting with Frohnmayer in person for the first time, she told her colleagues on the Nike board that she liked him very much, and intended to further the dialogue with him and the University of Oregon. Finally, after several months of brainstorming, an idea came to Frohnmayer after he discovered a newspaper article in the October 3, 2000, edition of the *Eugene Register-Guard*: "MILLER QUITS WORKERS RIGHTS BOARD," the headline read, with the following summary just below it: "California lawmaker says the potential for ethical conflicts led him to step down, though he supports the group."

Frohnmayer clipped the article, which reported U.S. Representative George Miller's decision to step down as chairman of the WRC, citing House ethics rules that complicated his relationship with the group. In the article, Miller reiterated his support of the WRC and its mission, signaling his full support for human rights even as he disassociated himself with the organization. It was just the kind of tightrope Frohnmayer had been looking to walk across.

He had his secretary fax the newspaper clipping to Ker Conway, made some phone calls to his friends at the Oregon State Board of Higher Education, and spoke to the university's general counsel, Melinda Grier. It took less than a week for Grier to produce the document Frohnmayer had asked for, in part because he'd been specific enough that he could have easily authored it himself, had the appearance of propriety not been so important. It was a simple letter of opinion raising a number of legal questions about the university's agreement with the WRC and formally advising the president not to pay any further dues it owed the labor organization. On October 25, Frohnmayer made the decision public, saying that the school would no longer pay the dues necessary for membership in the WRC.

For months, the University of Oregon faculty senate committees examined WRC and FLA membership from every conceivable angle, while the university's general counsel produced further letters of opinion. Chaos reigned, which played to Frohnmayer's advantage. He was, essentially, biding time until the Oregon State Board of Higher Education could take action on his recommendation. Finally, on February 16, 2001, the board passed the motion Frohnmayer had been quietly lobbying for since drawing inspiration from the *Register-Guard* article he'd faxed to Ker Conway in early October. It read:

> "Consistent with [the Oregon University System's] OUS's commitment to the free flow of commerce and efficient business practices, OUS institutions shall not adopt limits on eligibility to enter business agreements or otherwise conduct business unless based on the ability to perform, evidence of illegal activities or other criteria required or allowed by statute or Board rule. OUS institutions shall report compliance with this policy no later than December 31, 2001."

It came just in time for those who wanted the University of Oregon to leave the WRC: a faculty senate ad hoc committee on trademark licensing and monitoring of factories was leaning toward recommending further research on Nike's use of overseas labor, which might have led to a longer relationship with the WRC. Instead, the University of Oregon's general counsel confirmed that the motion prevented the school from having an agreement with either the WRC or even the less stringent Nike-affiliated FLA. A few weeks later, on March 6, 2001, Frohnmayer clipped another

Register-Guard article and faxed it to Ker Conway: "UO WILL BREAK TIES WITH WRC," read the headline, beneath which an article cited a state policy prohibiting the school's membership in the anti-sweatshop group. The article cast Frohnmayer as a passive participant who did little more than accept general counsel Melinda Grier's determinations, which, in reality, he had conceived and all but drafted, along with the Oregon State Board of Higher Education's motion.

Before faxing the article to Ker Conway, Frohnmayer scrawled a personal note across the top of the page, thanking the Nike insider for her "wise counsel."

Five

Industrial Education

The legislation that would end up helping generations of young Americans escape lives of plowing, planting, and picking, originally grew out of a movement to establish the nation's first agricultural colleges. The progenitor of this movement was a professor named Jonathan Baldwin Turner, who had moved to Jacksonville, Illinois, in 1833, after earning a degree in classical literature at Yale. Turner was a deeply religious man who hoped to become a missionary out on the great frontier of the American West, among the Native Americans. But after seeing Potawatomi Indians suffering with cholera they'd contracted from white men like himself, he turned to another of his era's great race-based injustices by becoming the editor of a Jacksonville abolitionist newspaper, an operative on the underground railroad, and, in his classroom at Illinois College, an outspoken critic of slavery.

Turner was keenly interested in agriculture. In the late 1830s, he spent much of his time outside of the classroom searching for a plant that might be used as a hedge to divide large expanses of open prairie for tilling and cultivation. Eventually he settled on the Osage orange plant, which worked so well that he began selling the seeds to Illinois farmers, who used it widely as a precursor to barbed wire, which wouldn't be developed until a few decades later. Turner's interest in agriculture deepened after 1848, when he was pressured to resign from his teaching post by colleagues and school administrators who disapproved of his abolitionist activism. It was then that he established the Illinois Industrial League, an organization dedicated to advocating for a publicly funded system of higher education aimed at the "industrial," or working classes.

Turner unveiled his vision of a public university at the Putnam County Farmers' Convention, held at the Granville Presbyterian Church on November 18, 1851, where he had been invited to speak by a group of local reformers called the Buel Institute. The group wanted Turner to discuss taking "steps toward the establishment of an agricultural university," but for him it was a chance not only to publicize his new ideas about education, but also to sharpen his carefully prepared remarks on the establishment of colleges focused on agriculture and industry and open to all. As he became a recognizable figure, associated once more with what some considered to be radical ideas, Turner again paid a steep personal cost for his activism: in 1853, his farm was burned to the ground by activists who felt America's educational system was better left alone, to carry on in the model of religious colleges and the aristocratic academic institutions of Europe.

Turner was not without influence, however, and a good number of powerful people admired his ideas. In February of 1853, the Illinois legislature adopted a resolution, drafted by Turner, calling for the state's congressman to push for the establishment of a land-grant bill to fund a national system of industrial and agricultural colleges, with one in each state. Illinois Senator Lyman Trumbull thought Turner's idea was too important to fail and too radical to succeed if not properly executed. It stood a much better chance, he thought, if it were introduced by a congressman from an Eastern state, rather than one from the west, which was still an untamed and uncivilized frontier in the minds of many Americans. He convinced Justin Smith Morrill of Vermont to introduce the bill.

Morrill did not share Turner's vision of an equal grant for each state to start its own industrial college. Instead, he opted for a bill that allocated land based on the number of senators and representatives each state had in congress, giving an advantage to more populous Eastern states like his own. It took years for the Morrill Act to wind its way through the corridors of Washington politics, and in the meantime Michigan Governor Kinsley Scott Bingham seized the initiative in 1855, signing a bill establishing the Agricultural College of the State of Michigan, now known as Michigan State University, as the first so-called "industrial college" in the nation.

The Morrill Act was finally introduced to Congress in 1857, and it passed in 1859, but was vetoed by President James Buchanan, a northern Democrat who sided with Southern Democrats on the issue of education, which, along with slavery, they contended was a state matter, not a federal one. It was reintroduced in 1862, with amendments guaranteeing that public colleges would teach military tactics, engineering, and agriculture, but more than any of these amendments, the new iteration of the bill was helped by the fact that the states opposing its passage most vehemently had seceded from the Union by the time it crossed Lincoln's desk on July 2, 1862. It was the last of three laws he signed that day, after one banning polygamy in the territories and another requiring a loyalty oath for government officials, and it followed just a day after he scrawled his signature on the land-grant bill that funded the transcontinental railroads.

As much as the railroads, America's public university system generated immense wealth and economic opportunity. Very much unlike the railroads, which reproduced inequality by generating wealth for the wealthy first, public universities helped transform the poor, serf-like taxpayer into a better educated, more empowered citizen. And so these universities would also help pave the way for a growing American middle class, creating the country's most stable and enduring model for social mobility simply by building colleges meant for people from all walks of life.

By 1867, twenty-two states had accepted the federal grant of thirty thousand acres of land per congressman for the endowment of a public college built "upon a sure and perpetual foundation, accessible to all, but especially to sons of toil." These schools, focused on "agriculture and the mechanic arts," included Kansas State Agricultural College, Illinois Industrial University at Urbana–Champaign, the Agricultural College of Minnesota, and Cornell

University. Existing schools, like Brown University, gained agricultural or industrial programs because of the Morrill Act.

Engineering and agriculture were, at the time, cutting-edge fields, making land-grant universities as trailblazing as the first colleges to offer computer science courses; they were also radical in terms of admissions, not only for educating people who previously didn't go to college, but also because many of them admitted women on an equal basis with men, though they would not be required to do so until many decades later; and by admitting nearly any student who earned good marks in state schools, they established a pipeline that allowed non-elites and the nonreligious to think constructively about an education beyond their immediate circumstances.

President Franklin D. Roosevelt invested anew in the possibility of an egalitarian and meritocratic higher education system, first with New Deal programs giving public universities the funds to build six hundred new campus buildings, then with the Servicemen's Readjustment Act of 1944, better known as the G.I. Bill. This bill offered Americans returning from the Second World War benefits like cut-rate mortgages, health care, and money for college, which proved to be such an effective tool for rebuilding American society in the aftermath of the war that it led to more government programs aimed at building up the country's higher education system. The U.S. government got into the student loan business with the National Defense Act of 1958 and the Higher Education Act of 1965, which extended student loan programs while adding work-study programs and federal grants to the aid options available to students. These programs especially benefited non-legacy and first-generation college students, who enrolled in far greater numbers after all land-grant colleges were at last forced to become racially integrated.

In the wake of the Second World War, the public university became a primary instrument for reconnecting American society with the idea that democracy was firmly rooted in a kind of meritocracy that flourished with greater access to higher education. The movements for civil rights and women's liberation added to this rising pressure for a truly equal university system, giving more

Americans access to the "germ of power" described by Tocqueville.

With the Cold War, however, came a new set of imperatives—from various branches of the U.S. government, its military, and its intelligence apparatus—for funding America's public universities. Transformed into the world's best research institutions by millions of dollars in government funding, some of it covert, America's universities became instruments of empire. In the process, a terrifying truth came to light: America's public universities are fundamentally weak at an institutional level, open to virtually any kind of corruption and influence from outside forces, especially when those outside forces were allowed to obscure their influence. Throughout the Cold War, at the level of the institution, the administration, the academic department, and the individual scholar, America's universities proved themselves willing to do virtually anything for money, especially when they were allowed to operate in the shadows.

The Central Intelligence Agency (CIA) began partnering with American universities as early as 1950, with a series of psychological experiments that were eventually brought under the umbrella of one many-tendrilled program called MK-Ultra. The MK-Ultra program is largely remembered for the many failures of its first phase, which lasted between 1953 and 1956: a bizarre hodgepodge of esoteric experiments involving hallucinogenic drugs, hypnosis, and suggestion, with results that ran the gamut from the hilarious to the morbid—from CIA experiments at Stanford that administered LSD to Ken Kesey to former tennis pro Harold Blauer dying at the age of forty-two in a New York State psychiatric ward after being used, in the words of a federal judge, "as a guinea pig in an experiment to test potential chemical warfare agents for the U.S. Army."

This first phase of MK-Ultra was also memorable for its immeasurable cruelty. When experiments called for what CIA

Director Allen Dulles deemed "extraordinary techniques," unwitting or unwilling human subjects were obtained using a vast array of methods ranging from random to exceptionally strategic. North Korean prisoners were used as unconsenting test subjects for injectable drugs, for instance, while hallucinogens, which could be more easily administered to unsuspecting targets, were used on private U.S. citizens ranging from a summer camp full of children to men who had been lured into a CIA safe house by prostitutes who had been paid to dose them with LSD.

What is often forgotten about MK-Ultra is that its second, less spectacular phase, which ran from 1956 until 1963, became the basis for the CIA's first manual for interrogation and torture. This was, in many ways, a logical progression considering the fact that an MK-Ultra precursor, called Project Bluebird, used as its starting point Nazi interrogation techniques. In fact, the CIA might have arrived at the study of torture sooner if not for an almost pathological early obsession with LSD experiments, which one MK-Ultra scientist later testified was based on rumors that the Soviet Union had secured a massive supply of the drug. When the second phase of MK-Ultra did arrive, the psychology and human behavior research developed from it turned out to be far more consequential than the dark comedy of the program's first act.

The CIA's accomplice in its MK-Ultra research was America's university system. Between 1953 and 1963, MK-Ultra and related programs paid out $25 million for human experiments performed at eighty different institutions, including twelve hospitals and forty-four universities. The academics and medical researchers who participated in MK-Ultra experiments, and who received covert CIA funding for their efforts, seemed to know what kind of devil's bargain they were making: Richard Helms, who oversaw the project, convinced CIA director Dulles that the Agency's university contractors should be allowed to work without signing formal contracts.

Helms recognized that academics and researchers were "most reluctant to enter into signed agreements of any sort which connect them with this activity since such a connection would jeopardize their professional reputations."

Some of the results from these experiments were also secret, known only to the government agencies that funded them. Experiments conducted at Columbia University, for example, produced both secret results that were reported only to the CIA, and public results that were published widely in medical journals, with key facts about methodology obfuscated for obvious reasons. Consequently, it's anyone's guess how reliable any research study funded by MK-Ultra might prove to be if repeated under intellectually honest conditions.

When the CIA's years-long obsession with LSD and other hallucinogens came to an end, the agency began building more formal relationships with universities, often through intermediaries like the Office of Naval Research (ONR), which had become an early patron of experimental psychology starting in 1950. Within just a few years, the ONR was sponsoring psychological research at fifty-eight universities, in close collaboration with the CIA, with an end goal of developing more effective methods of interrogation and torture. This research was often funded through a system of philanthropic money-laundering that funneled CIA funds through private foundations, like the Ford Foundation and the Rockefeller Foundation. In this way, somewhere between $7 million and $13 million flowed into universities each year for research on behavioral science. The Agency also funded this kind of research through slightly more direct channels. In 1950, the U.S. government established the Bureau of Social Science Research (BSSR) at American University, which was used to underwrite studies on the effects of torture on prisoners of war, under the guise of social-psychology research. Among the BSSR studies conducted at American University was an Air Force–funded experiment aimed at determining the relative utility of drugs and violence for the purposes of interrogating prisoners.

Some of the most important psychological studies of the century were conducted at research universities funded by the CIA, including Yale psychologist Stanley Milgram's controversial experiments, which concluded that virtually any person could be made to torture another human being. The eminent psychologist Albert Biderman, whose experiments were funded by the CIA both directly and indirectly, accidentally revealed in a widely published study on isolation the sinister aim of the experiment. Psychological torture, Biderman concluded, was "the ideal way of 'breaking down' a prisoner," and isolation produced a similar effect to being beaten, starved, or forced to endure sleep deprivation.

University psychology departments were especially easy targets for government intelligence agencies to infiltrate because so many psychology professors had served in the military during the war. Even those who hadn't were likely to have done contract research for the Pentagon, which had spent broadly on research aimed at understanding what might happen to its soldiers in various phases of combat. The CIA sent operatives each year to the American Psychological Association (APA) conference, with orders to build relationships and report back on people who were doing particularly relevant or interesting research. Such close ties were developed with so many professionals in the field that the CIA sometimes used government aircraft or chartered planes to transport groups of psychology researchers and professors to conferences. And however outlandish that may sound, these were far from the boldest or most visible partnerships between the U.S. government and the public universities it sought to co-opt through investing in research projects.

In April 1965, a University of Pittsburgh anthropology professor named Hugo Nutini traveled to Chile to recruit scholars for a research project focused on counterinsurgency measures and the process of political revolutions in the developing world. Nutini was born in Italy but grew up in Chile. He began working at the University of Pittsburgh in 1963, just as the university was expanding its social science programs, like many other schools around the country. Behind this rapid expansion of interdisciplinary university programs was a U.S. Department of Defense (DOD) program called Project Camelot.

Launched in 1963, Project Camelot sought to predict and control revolutionary political movements in third-world nations through the use of advanced research on group psychology and behavior—the winning of "hearts and minds" through psychological warfare, marketing, and manipulation. The project emerged from the Army Office of Research and Development's growing worries over "wars of national liberation" in countries like the Belgian Congo, Cuba, and Yemen. But the program itself spiraled out of control in the spring of 1965, when Nutini began telling Chilean scholars about his research project, which he claimed was funded by civilian agencies like the National Science Foundation.

What Nutini didn't know was that the scholars he was trying to recruit knew that he was working as an advisor for the U.S. government, and that his research projects were, in reality, being funded by Project Camelot. The secret program had been quietly undone by a Norwegian sociologist named Johan Galtung, who had seen Project Camelot's preliminary research design, including its military sponsorship, and leaked the information to his Chilean colleagues. The whistleblower exposed Nutini, who was not only disgraced but banned from ever returning to the country where he was raised. Project Camelot was canceled by Secretary of Defense Robert McNamara on July 8, 1965.

The widespread media coverage that exposed Project Camelot forever changed attitudes toward U.S. academics in the developing world, where professors could now face credible accusations of collaborating with the CIA or other U.S. government agencies. It also marked a shift in attitudes at home: these alliances were not anything like Princeton University's Listening Center, which had been established in 1939 to monitor Axis broadcasts before this task was handed over to the Federal Communications Commission (FCC); there was no war effort to support and there was no clear division between civilian academic consultants like Nutini and CIA or DOD operatives. Project Camelot was a dubious exercise in empire building, crafted by architects with no regard for academic objectivity or the sovereignty of other nations, and undertaken by a mix of covert professionals, covert amateurs, and unwitting academic accomplices.

Government funding for projects like Camelot continued despite the controversy. And just two years after the operation's scandalous end, Arthur H. Brayfield, the director of the APA, once again rubber-stamped defense research of the sort that had dragged the field into such murky territory through operations like MK-Ultra and Project Camelot.

"I think the military should be free to use all reasonable, ethical, and competent tools at its command to help carry out its mission," Brayfrield said. "And I would say strongly that the use of behavioral science and behavioral scientists is one of those useful tools."

An important shift came in 1967, when federal expenditures on what the government called the "psychological sciences" peaked at $158 million; after nearly two decades of covert, unethical, and occasionally incompetent employment of behavioral scientists, the DOD sought to improve its image and repair its damaged relationships with academics by openly spreading funds for social science research through Project THEMIS. In its first year, Project THEMIS distributed $20 million to schools around the United States, and two years later its budget had swelled to nearly $60 million—about one- third of the total annual budget for Pentagon programs funneling cash to American universities. One reason behind the success of Project THEMIS, which came along just two years after the public-relations nightmare of the Camelot scandal, was a calculated adjustment the DOD made to the types of academic institutions it funded. Instead of Yale, where Milgram studied the psychology of torturers, or MIT, where the DOD held early conferences to recruit behavioral scientists, THEMIS specifically targeted schools and departments that were underdeveloped and underfunded—a key insight that would later work to the advantage of corporations once the U.S. government began abandoning the universities that had by then reshaped entire departments and disciplines to suit the research appetites of the Cold War.

The social sciences flourished in the years after the end of the Second World War, but the intense existential competition of the Cold War also produced incredible advances in physics, chemistry, biology, and engineering, as government grants funded the development of bacterial weapons, ballistics, computers and communications, and radioactivity. Universities expanded and enrollments increased an incredible 122 percent between 1960 and 1970, the year when subsidies and grants finally began to slow as the government started relying more on think tanks than colleges. University administrators were forced to look elsewhere for patrons, and it wasn't long before they found them in America's corporate boardrooms.

This shift took place at an ideal moment for the American tobacco industry, which was then grappling with growing scientific evidence that smoking could cause cancer and other serious health problems. In a 1969 memo, an executive from tobacco giant Brown & Williamson spelled out the industry's strategy for weakening the scientific consensus over whether smoking was harmful to your health.

"Doubt is our product, since it is the best means of competing with the 'body of fact' that exists in the mind of the general public," the memo read. "It is also the means of establishing controversy."

The tobacco industry's methodology was later identified by researcher Lisa Bero, who outlined the industry template:

1. Fund research that supports the interest group position.
2. Hide industry involvement in research.
3. Publish research that supports the interest group position.
4. Suppress research that does not support the interest group position.
5. Criticize research that does not support the interest group position.
6. Change scientific standards.
7. Disseminate interest group data or interpretation of risk in the lay press.

8. Disseminate interest group data or interpretation of risk directly to policy makers.

This methodology, according to Bero's research, was dangerously effective. Studies on secondhand smoke, when conducted by researchers with ties to the tobacco industry, were nearly 90 percent more likely to find no harm. By funding research, tobacco companies were able to control the research agenda, influence the design and methodology of studies, and build, through financial patronage, the kind of relationships necessary to help suppress research that might damage cigarette sales. Tobacco industry lawyers, in particular, were deeply involved in the design and execution of studies funded through the tobacco industry's philanthropic bodies and its trade association. In some cases, industry-funded research was made to appear independent from tobacco companies by funneling payments through law firms like Covington & Burling, which represented Philip Morris. (Covington & Burling's other clients included Halliburton, Blackwater Worldwide, and Chiquita Brands International, the last of which became the first U.S. corporation convicted of financing terrorism for paying protection money to the United Self-Defense Forces of Colombia, a paramilitary organization.) At tobacco companies like Brown & Williamson, lawyers were even responsible for disseminating the results of any scientific research and studies funded or carried out by the company.

One of the tobacco industry's main vehicles for undermining the scientific consensus on smoking's harmful effects was the Council for Tobacco Research (CTR), which was founded in 1954 as part of an industry-wide public relations effort. In the 1970s, as universities and other research institutions began to feel the effects of shrinking government investment, the function of the CTR evolved into something much more proactive, according to an internal 1978 Brown & Williamson memo.

"Recently it has been suggested that CTR or industry research should enable us to give quick responses to new developments in the propaganda of the avid anti-smoking groups," Brown & Williamson vice president Ernest Pepples wrote. "The industry research effort has included special projects designed to find scientists and medical doctors who might serve as industry witnesses in lawsuits or in a legislative forum."

Another tobacco industry group, called the Center for Indoor Air Research (CIAR), was founded in 1988 specifically to combat the growing scientific consensus that secondhand smoke was harmful. Between 1989 and 1993, the group spent more than $11 million funding mainstream peer-reviewed research projects, most of which examined indoor pollutants other than tobacco smoke. This served not only to divert attention away from tobacco but also to build up the reputation of the CIAR by associating it with respected research universities and peer-reviewed results. During those same years, the group quietly spent $4 million on non-peer-reviewed research projects that relied instead on "special-review" by a board of directors consisting of tobacco company executives. These studies focused mostly on undermining research on the harmful effects of secondhand smoke, and while they were less rigorous and relied on methodologies crafted by industry lawyers rather than scientists, they benefitted by association from the fact that CIAR funded so much high-quality peer-reviewed research. This means that even universities and professors who accepted tobacco industry funding only on the condition that it went toward conducting sound research unwittingly aided the industry's efforts to undermine good science.

Tobacco companies were far from the only beneficiaries of the research-funding model that the Cold War helped create. In the 1970s, the University of Wisconsin made an agreement with the Kimberly-Clark paper company and the manufacturing corporation Kohler, among others, to conduct research that was either "too basic or costly for the companies to conduct themselves," in exchange for financial backing from those companies. Similarly, Harvard Medical School received $23.5 million from Monsanto to perform cancer research. The Hammermill Paper Company not only funded but designed courses in economics at Gannon University in Pennsylvania and Springfield College in Massachusetts. They weren't ordinary economics classes, but training courses for high school teachers, meaning that the curriculum designed by Hammermill Paper would trickle down to teenagers throughout the region. The aim of the course was to present a pro-business view of economics. Throughout the 1980s and 1990s, arrangements like these gave corporations and their broader networks undue influence on any number of academic institutions. They also gave conservative activists the opportunity to colonize young minds.

In the fall of 1993, Republican congressman Newt Gingrich taught a course called "Renewing American Civilization" at Kennesaw State University in Georgia, for which he solicited contributions from Republican donors and corporations. His goal, he wrote in letters soliciting funds for the course, was to use class lectures as a means of recruiting Republican activists ahead of the 1996 presidential campaign. The House ethics committee later found Gingrich in violation of campaign financing laws because the courses were aimed at indoctrination rather than education, and had been funded using tax-deductible donations from wealthy Republicans and corporations like Hewlett-Packard. In exchange for Hewlett-Packard's financial support, Gingrich described the corporation in lectures as "one of the great companies in American history." Corporate donors were also given the opportunity to present promotional videos for viewing in class.

Other aspects of corporate intrusion into the American classroom have taken hold so deeply that it requires some effort to imagine a time when things were different. There was a time, for instance, before the recession of the 1990s, when American universities did not have exclusive beverage partnerships with Coca-Cola or Pepsi, and did not host campus events like the University of Minnesota's Diet Coke Classic volleyball tournament.

The 1996 Minnesota–Coke deal, which was among the earliest of its kind, was heralded by university administrators as "a national model for beverage partnering in higher education." And it was only appropriate that Coke and Pepsi should head to college, because they had already graduated from America's public elementary schools, middle schools, and high schools.

It was no accident of history that the first corporations to advertise inside America's public schools did so in Colorado Springs. In 1989, when Kenneth Burnley took over as the superintendent of the city's largest school district, the dozens of schools he was charged with overseeing were running a collective deficit of about $12 million. Classes were overcrowded, teachers were overworked, and facilities were rotting away faster each year as the district fell deeper into the red. By 1993, it had been nearly two decades since voters approved a tax increase to help fund public schools in Colorado Springs, and Superintendent Burnley knew that wasn't likely to change in the near future. He decided he'd need to turn to someone other than the voters if he wanted to get more money for the schools in his district.

"This was the first school district in the nation to offer advertising opportunities," he boasted. "Our taxpayers have challenged us to be more creative and businesslike in how we finance the schools, so we decided to take a page out of business's book. I realized we could sell for cash something we always had, but never knew we had."

What Burnley had was access to students, whose undivided attention he sold to some fifty different corporate clients for rates ranging from $1,500 to $12,000—advertisements on school benches and buses, loudspeaker announcements at football and basketball games, and, most important, an exclusive contract with Coca-Cola paying the school district $8.4 million over the course of ten years. The decade-long contract with Coke meant that District 11 students who entered the first grade in 1993 would make it halfway through high school before the deal expired, spending several hours of each day, for nine months out of each year, surrounded by Coke products and advertisements. Many of them would have no idea that schools had not always been this way, or that other schools were any different. It was not only a grand marketing experiment, but an experiment in sales techniques, with contractual incentives intended to push district officials to see that their schools sold as many Coke products as possible. These incentives worked.

During the fall of 1998, John Bushey, who oversaw the school district's contract with Coke, wrote a letter to school administrators urging them to move vending machines to areas where they would be "accessible to the students all day."

"Research shows that vendor purchases are closely linked to availability," he wrote.

Bushey also pressed teachers to allow students to drink soda in the classroom, perhaps because the district's contract offered nearly $3 million in bonuses if the schools sold more than 70,000 cases of Coke products each year. The arrangement proved to be so successful that Coca-Cola and its competitor, Pepsi, began vying to sign similar deals with school districts around the country. It was a valuable investment for these corporations: in 1997, children aged four to twelve spent more than $24 billion, while twelve- to nineteen-year-olds accounted for another $141 billion in total spending.

Dan DeRose, a middle-aged former professional football player who helped broker corporate advertising deals for the school district in Colorado Springs, sensed that this was a profitable niche market waiting to be cornered. DeRose started his own company, DD Marketing, and began brokering million-dollar deals between soda companies and public schools and universities all over the country.

"Our philosophy," he said, "is if you're going to allow corporate America into your schools, maximize your return."

One day in May of 1999, DeRose was giving a presentation on the question of how to maximize returns for his latest client, Newark Public Schools, which had become so underfunded and mismanaged that the state of New Jersey had taken control of them a year earlier.

"Let's just say everyone drinks one product a day, and let's just count the students," he said. "At 45,000 [students] times 180 days of school, that's 8.1 million cans. At seventy-five cents apiece, that's six million dollars walking out the front door of your school every year in quarters and dollars."

His audience was a gathering of school principals, athletic directors, parent-teacher association officials, and a single student from Newark Public Schools, which was seeking bidders on a contract to supply the district's eighty-two school cafeterias and countless vending machines with soda, water, and other beverages. The buyer would need to be either Coke or Pepsi, DeRose advised, because these companies paid a premium for the opportunity to imprint brand loyalty on so many young minds. He used his own daughter, Anna, as an example, since he had negotiated the Coca-Cola contract with the Pueblo, Colorado, school where she attended first grade.

"From now until she's graduated, all she'll drink is Coke," DeRose said. "She goes out for pizza and we ask, 'What do you want to drink, honey?' 'Coke'; she doesn't even know how to spell Pepsi."

Between Colorado and Newark, DeRose negotiated a $5.3 million deal in Kansas City, earning himself a commission of between 25 and 35 percent, just like the other sixty-two deals he'd negotiated.

When he landed his sixty-third deal with Coke in Newark, the first thing he did was draw up a plan to install eight of the soda company's vending machines in each of the district's thirteen high schools, and four at each of its sixty-nine elementary and middle schools.

For the schools, the appetite for corporate sponsorship was simple: most states were following Oregon's lead with cuts to higher-education funding that forced public elementary schools, middle schools, and high schools to compete with state universities for access to dwindling money from a state general fund. Corporate contracts worth millions of dollars were an attractive alternative to the traditional methods of raising funds for public schools.

"The thought of generating that kind of revenue stream, where you didn't have to raise property taxes, you didn't have to increase the sales tax, and you didn't have to do battle with the county commissioners, was very attractive," said Barry Gaskins, a school district official in Greenville, North Carolina.

By the late 1990s, Coca-Cola had signed deals affecting more than a thousand schools across the country, including those in Washington, D.C., where a school official called the contract "a godsend." In exchange for the exclusive right to sell Coke products in D.C. public schools, the district received 65 percent of the sales from Coca-Cola, incentivizing the school to sell more soda to its students. This sometimes totaled as much as $50,000 per month for the school district.

Penny McConnell, a former president of the American School Food Service Association, opposed these kinds of contracts vehemently.

"I think it would be a real negative, a bad situation, for a district like ours that's working so hard to promote nutrition to then profit from ripping off kids with nonnutritious foods," McConnell said. "If I'm going to teach nutrition, I'm going to serve nutrition."

The National Soft Drink Association called her argument "an insult to consumer intelligence," which suggests that corporations thought of children in precisely the same terms as any adult demographic market.

Oxon Hill High School, in nearby Prince George's County, Maryland, signed a three-year contract with Pepsi, which principal David S. Stofa said paid for everything from landscaping to a scoreboard for athletic events.

"The kids know all that Pepsi has done for the school," he said. "And they really appreciate it."

At Greenbrier High School in Evans, Georgia, two students were suspended for wearing Pepsi T-shirts on the school's official Coke Day, which was established after the school won a district-wide contest called Team Up with Coca-Cola. In exchange for Coca-Cola's modest $500 prize, principal Gloria Hamilton induced her students to distribute Coke coupons near the school, posed them for an aerial photograph wearing color-coordinated shirts that spelled out "Coke," and, during class time, made them listen to speeches from Coca-Cola executives. When two students stripped off their sweaters to reveal Pepsi T-shirts underneath them, she suspended the students and accused them of "trying to destroy the school picture."

"It really would have been acceptable if it had just been in-house," she said. "But we had the regional president [of Coca-Cola] here and people flew in from Atlanta to do us the honor of being resource speakers."

In time, lack of state funds for public schools made K–12 education so dependent on contracts with soda corporations that a school in Ohio defied a state order that it comply with federal laws against selling soda and candy during the lunch break. And in Maryland, school districts became open allies with beverage-industry lobbyists and vending machine companies as they banded together to defeat legislation introduced by Senator Paul G. Pinsky, which sought to limit commercialism in public schools.

"The lobbyists kicked my ass," Pinsky said.

Most industry partnerships with university research began much later, and far less malevolently, than those undertaken by the big tobacco companies. For many industries, it began simply enough, in the 1970s, as corporations outsourced certain research to universities desperate to bring in cash during the waning years of the Cold War, when the military slowed its seeding of college research projects. The shift in funding was dramatic: in 1965, the federal government was responsible for financing more than 60 percent of all the research and development taking place in the United States, while four decades later the reverse would be true, with 65 percent of this same work being funded by various private interests. Initially, serious researchers, especially in medicine, sought to maintain "arm's-length relationships with their corporate sponsors," according to Marcia Angell, a former editor of the *New England Journal of Medicine*. But in 1980, a landmark piece of legislation called the Bayh–Dole Act changed the nature of research-based scientific inquiry at American universities.

The Bayh–Dole Act gave universities and professors automatic ownership of the federally funded research they produced, as well as the right to sell and market that research. More than anything else, the Bayh–Dole Act changed the avenues that academic research took on its way to industry. Prior to 1980, academic knowledge was monetized openly, through publications, conferences, and consulting that was more or less transparent. Since Bayh–Dole, university research has been quietly patented and licensed, creating more direct, less transparent financial ties between universities, professors, and the corporations to which they license their patented discoveries. And when it comes to trials and studies, there is evidence that researchers tend to reach the conclusions most desired by the interest groups funding their work. Research comparing different cholesterol medications, for instance, are twenty times more likely to favor the drug owned by the company that has funded the study, rather than its competitor. And one analysis in the *British Medical Journal* found that a drug was four times more likely to be looked on favorably in trials if the research had been funded by the pharmaceutical company that owned the patent to that drug.

Two decades after Bayh–Dole's passage, universities were generating ten times the number of patents they had prior to the landmark legislation, and corporate funding of university research surpassed $2 billion annually. Relationships between pharmaceutical corporations and medical researchers, meanwhile, became so cozy that the editors of the *New England Journal of Medicine*, the *Lancet*, and other leading medical journals were forced to come up with policies to determine whether an author could vouch completely for the claims they were advancing, and whether they even had full access to their own trial data. Drummond Rennie, an editor at the *Journal of the American Medical Association*, said that past a certain point, all they could really do was print a correction or notice when they found that they'd printed some falsehood advanced by a researcher on behalf of their corporate benefactor. "Usually they're lying on their way to the bank," she said of such characters. Over time, the bank opened up more branches, until conflicts of interests spread from university researchers up to administrators. One startling example of this could be found at Stanford University's medical school, where, by 2006, one-third of all the school's administrators and department heads had reported financial conflicts of interest related to their own research. Seven out of ten members of the committee tasked with policing conflicts of interest at the school also reported conflicts, which included consulting fees, stock options, and shared or licensed patents.

This kind of anything-goes attitude toward research funding eventually found its way into government agencies, and it didn't need to use the back door to get in—it was, in fact, an invited guest. During the presidential administration of George W. Bush, the Environmental Protection Agency, which is tasked with enforcing the laws meant to protect our environment, responded to budget pressures by outsourcing certain studies to the very groups meant to be subject to those laws and accountable to the agency. Consequently, the American Chemistry Council paid $2 million toward studying the effects of pesticides and household chemicals on young children in 2004; and in 2007, it was America's livestock producers, not its government or taxpayers, who paid for the first nationwide study to determine whether large-scale animal production had any detrimental effects on air quality.

Today, America's public universities are a veritable banquet on which corporate interests dine at their discretion. At the University of California, Davis, which grew out of the Morrill Act, Turner's idea of "industrial education" has taken on new meaning. Pharmaceutical representatives visit the campus regularly for roundtables, meet-and-greets, and coffee hours with professors, who must often sign nondisclosure agreements once introductions have been made and business cards have been exchanged. This is not particularly unusual. In fact, only America's original agricultural college, the University of Michigan, maintains a public database showing how its research is funded. Virtually all other public universities go to extraordinary lengths to avoid disclosing which corporations are funding them and how much money they've been given, often by receiving tax-deductible donations through university foundations, which are exempted from public records laws in many states. The corporations themselves are usually more forthcoming about the universities they fund—the Dow Chemical Company lists on its Web site thirty-four universities it considers "academic partners," including Stanford, MIT, Cornell, and state schools like the University of Minnesota and Texas A&M. The corporations have philanthropic credit to gain by broadcasting these relationships. The universities, however, stand to lose academic credit.

At Purdue University, it's food and chemical companies who send representatives to visit the campus, at a rate of nearly one company per day, in search of partnerships in the school's department of food science. Companies like Conagra, Pepsi, and Nestlé pay Purdue $5,000 a year for a vast array of privileges that include prepublication review of relevant research, influence over the department's curriculum, and access to students. Some of the school's professors even take periods of academic leave to collaborate directly with Purdue's corporate partners. Such partnerships typically have little to do with developing the next big snack cake.

In 2014, as it struggled to combat a slump in sales of sugary drinks, Coca-Cola helped put together a nonprofit group called the Global Energy Balance Network (GEBN), staffed with industry-friendly professors from the University of Colorado School of Medicine and the University of South Carolina (USC), and armed with $1.5 million from the soda company. The goal, according to a leaked email from a professor to a top Coke executive, was to "help your company avoid the image of being a problem in peoples' lives and back to being a company that brings important and fun things to them." When *The New York Times* revealed that Coke was funding the group's research, which emphasized exercise over diet in combating obesity, the University of Colorado said it would return the $1 million it received from the soda company, not because of ethical concerns but because it was creating a distraction. The University of South Carolina kept the $500,000 it received from Coke, saying that there was really no way to distance itself from the controversy since USC professor Steven N. Blair, who has received millions of dollars from Coke over the years, remains one of the leaders of the GEBN.

A year later, the International Life Sciences Institute (ILSI), which is funded by Coca-Cola, Hershey, and Red Bull, released a research paper suggesting that there is weak evidence behind dietary recommendations on limiting sugar intake—a claim so outrageous that the candy company Mars, Inc., which also funds the ILSI, disavowed the paper. *Annals of Internal Medicine*, which published the study, eventually issued a correction noting that one of the study's designers, Joanne Slavin, failed to disclose a $25,000 grant she'd received from Coca-Cola for research she'd done at the University of Minnesota in 2014. She called it an oversight, something that is bound to happen from time to time, and promised to include the Coca-Cola grant in a new disclosure she needed to file for an oatmeal study funded by Quaker Oats, which is owned by Coke's chief competitor, Pepsi.

It's easy to understand how a professor could forget one or two of their corporate benefactors these days: Iowa State University's athletics department is now brought to you by Dow and Monsanto; the University of Michigan receives financial consideration from various automobile and telecommunications companies; and the University of Washington has Amazon Catalyst, which provides grants across all disciplines and departments for any idea that grapples with a pressing societal issue.

It's been a long time coming: at a 2005 panel that included the National Academy of Sciences, the National Academy of Engineering, and the Institute of Medicine, former Food and Drug Administration (FDA) commissioner Jane E. Henney said of university-level researchers: "It's getting more difficult to get that pure person with no conflicts at all."

There are arguments to be made for the absolute efficiency of markets, but it's worth remembering that the atom bomb, the Internet, and a great number of lifesaving medicines were created by government-funded research, long before the passage of the Bayh–Dole Act. It's also worth considering some of the ways in which markets fail to be efficient. One example is a drug called sofosbuvir, which was discovered in 2007 by medical researchers who then sold the patent to Gilead, a U.S. pharmaceutical company, giving them the exclusive rights to market it for twenty years.

Under the trade name Sovaldi, the drug was approved for sale in the United States as a hepatitis C treatment in 2013, and the profit potential was immediately clear to Gilead, which earned $10.3 billion from the drug in its first full year on the market. These massive revenues were due in part to the fact that a full twelve-week treatment with Sovaldi costs an American patient $84,000—a price so steep that in states like Louisiana, Medicaid would not help cover the drug except in cases where the patient's liver had become severely damaged by the disease. Then, in 2015, the company hit a potentially disastrous snag with its international sales when India's patent office rejected Gilead's application to recognize its patent on sofosbuvir. This decision was eventually overturned, and an Indian patent was granted, but not before dozens of Indian firms began producing generic versions of the drug. In the face of crippling losses to counterfeiters, Gilead chose to license the drug to thirteen Indian drug manufacturers, allowing them to sell generic versions to Indian consumers at a dramatic discount—Cipla's licensed, legitimate generic brand of sofosbuvir costs $14 per pill, compared with Gilead's Sovaldi, which costs Americans $1,000 per pill; the full course of treatment recommended for hepatitis C sufferers, which costs $84,000 in the United States, can be had for $1,200 in India, a discount significant enough to boost India's thriving medical tourism industry.

The Bayh–Dole Act has, in other words, created a market system so inefficient that U.S. consumers are better off seeking this lifesaving treatment in a foreign country, where criminal counterfeiting syndicates and government bureaucrats collaborate in order to strong-arm the patent holder into licensing generic versions of the drug for sale at humane prices. It has also made possible a market in which there may be low-cost, equally effective alternatives to drugs like sofosbuvir that consumers will never hear about due to contracts between researchers and their corporate benefactors.

In the 1990s, a British pharmaceutical corporation called Boots UK gave clinical pharmacist Betty Dong $250,000 to conduct a study at the University of California, San Francisco, comparing its own hyperthyroid medication with lower-cost alternatives made by its competitors. But instead of demonstrating its drug's superiority, the study showed that hyperthyroid patients could save $356 million annually if they used alternatives to Boots UK's Synthroid, which dominated the $600-million market for synthetic hormones. Boots barred Dong from publishing her blind-reviewed study in the *Journal of the American Medical Association*, citing fine print in her contract stating the results "were not to be published or otherwise released without written consent" from Boots UK. When word of the study's results leaked and ended up in the pages of the *Wall Street Journal*, the pharmaceutical company attacked the very research it had funded. Dong, who was still contractually bound to the agreement she'd signed, was unable to defend herself from the company's attacks on her work.

There's reason to believe that this kind of suppression continues unabated. In 2006, a Cleveland cardiologist named Steven Nissen was searching the Internet when he stumbled across forty-two clinical trials for GlaxoSmithKline's top-selling diabetes drug, Avandia, which caught his attention because he knew only fifteen of the clinical trials had ever been published. Nissen had been concerned for some time about possible health risks associated with Avandia, but had been unable to convince the pharmaceutical giant to release any research on the drug. The clinical trials he found online were there, it turned out, due to the outcome of a 2004 lawsuit alleging that GlaxoSmithKline had concealed negative trial data associated with another one of its drugs, the antidepressant Paxil. An independent analysis of the Paxil trial data showed that children who took the drug were twice as likely to experience suicidal ideation than those given a placebo, and the ensuing settlement forced the pharmaceutical company to post the results of all of its clinical trials online, where Nissen found the data necessary to satisfy his curiosity about Avandia. He published what he found in the *New England Journal of Medicine*, reporting that Avandia raised the risk of heart attack by 43 percent, prompting the FDA to place its most severe warning on the diabetes medication's label. An independent analysis carried out by the FDA came to a remarkably similar conclusion, and yet Nissen soon found himself the subject of attacks from colleagues, including Valentin Fuster, who wrote a critique of his work in *Nature Clinical Practice Cardiovascular Medicine*. Fuster, it turned out, served as the chairman for GlaxoSmithKline's Research and Education Foundation, and received funding from the pharmaceutical giant.

In 2007, the University of California, Berkeley, entered into a historic and highly unusual partnership with the British oil company BP: the petroleum giant would spend $350 million building an Energy Biosciences Institute (EBI) at the Berkeley campus, and in exchange it would reap the benefits of the school's research into biofuels. More controversially, BP would be allowed to lease commercial research space on campus, where its employees could work side by side with students and professors. And while the school's own research would be publishable, anything done specifically for BP would be proprietary, meaning that research funded in part by taxpayers, and carried out in publicly owned research facilities, could be kept secret forever under the arrangement. It was a controversy of the sort UC Berkeley had seen before.

In *The Uses of the University*, UC Berkeley's first chancellor, Clark Kerr, described a postwar "multiversity" faced with balancing the interests of the government, the military, and private industry, as well as the interests of students and professors. A year after its 1963 publication, Kerr's book came to represent, for student protestors, a tacit endorsement of military and corporate incursions into university life and the university mission. Nearly four decades later, it was difficult to see these concerns as anything but prescient; Kerr himself was forced to admit that his notion of a "multiversity" was increasingly vulnerable to corruption by private interests.

"The university ought to remain a neutral agency," Kerr said. "Devoted to the public welfare, not private welfare."

Kerr's concern over the university's waning dedication to the public welfare was prompted by UC Berkeley's 1998 partnership with the Swiss pharmaceutical giant Novartis. Over the course of five years, Novartis, which also produced genetically engineered crops, would fund $25 million worth of research at UC Berkeley's Department of Plant and Microbial Biology. In exchange, the school granted Novartis the right to negotiate licenses on about one-third of the department's discoveries, including those which were funded by state and federal taxpayers. Most controversially, the agreement gave Novartis two of five seats on the department's research committee, which was tasked with making crucial decisions about how the department would spend its money; the other three committee seats were held by professors who had received, in total, more than half a million dollars in research funding from Novartis.

The backlash was immediate: students protested, the media descended, and faculty in the Department of Plant and Microbial Biology were isolated from their colleagues, who avoided discussing interdisciplinary research with them for fear that it would end up in the hands of Novartis. One UC Berkeley professor, Ignacio Chapela, criticized the partnership despite the fact that he had previously worked for Novartis.

"I'm not opposed to individual professors serving as consultants to industry," Chapela said. "If something goes wrong, it's their reputation that's at stake. But this is different. This deal institutionalizes the university's relationship with one company, whose interest is profit. Our role should be to serve the public good."

In the spring of 2000, the controversial partnership became the subject of tense hearings in California's state senate, where some Berkeley faculty learned for the first time that their contract with Novartis was not in every way what it had seemed. Access to genomics data owned by Novartis, which had been a key selling point for many UC Berkeley researchers, was contingent on signing a confidentiality provision with the Swiss company. This provision, Senator Steve Peace noted, would shrink the amount of agricultural knowledge available to the public while accelerating the monopolization of basic biological research tools necessary for certain kinds of plant breeding—important aspects of the global food system, increasingly under the control of a few large corporations. Four years later, after considerable rancor, an independent review conducted by a team from Michigan State University concluded what had long been obvious to critics of the deal: the Berkeley–Novartis partnership was a failed venture that should not be repeated.

And yet it was repeated, just a few years later, when Berkeley announced its partnership with BP. Many of the details were familiar: Berkeley's corporate partner would help choose the institute's director, while other high-level positions would be filled by appointees or employees of the oil giant; BP could end up co-owning some of the institute's intellectual property; and despite the fact that Berkeley banned classified military research on its campus, on the basis that scientific breakthroughs are meant to be published and shared, the school's agreement with BP allowed for a "no obligation to publish" clause. These ethically cloudy waters grew murkier still after BP's offshore drilling rig, Deepwater Horizon, began leaking oil into the Gulf of Mexico in April of 2010, sparking fresh concerns about the seventy projects Berkeley researchers were working on with the oil company.

Five years later, with oil prices plummeting and $100 million of BP's promised funds unspent, the oil company exercised its option to pull a third of its funding for 2015, and in each of the following two years. The school, meanwhile, remained on the hook for everything it had spent on the endeavor, including tuition increases, even though the thirst for biofuel research had been sated.

"All renewables are going to have to weather the storm," institute director Chris R. Somerville said. "We may have to wait it out until oil becomes expensive again."

Market conditions, in other words, forced the Berkeley institute to stop its research work on converting plants to fuel as it considered what other industries might benefit most from its laboratories and the expertise of its researchers—renewable lubricants, for instance, or perhaps converting sugarcane into jet fuel.

"All the big companies in renewable liquid fuels and chemicals" were on the table as potential replacements for BP, Somerville said, as though Berkeley were a NASCAR team in need of a new title sponsor.

The Bayh–Dole Act, which was meant to incentivize universities and professors to do significant, groundbreaking work, has instead forced one of America's most impressive universities into a kind of mercenary science; like the tail that wags the dog, the laboratory will let its patron lead the way—toward the next important breakthrough in science, technology, or medicine, perhaps, or maybe toward whatever will get the company's executives through their next shareholder meeting unscathed. Berkeley's disastrous partnerships with Novartis and BP were cautionary examples of all that could go wrong when public universities allowed private interests to lease vast swaths of their campus for years at a time. Phil Knight and the University of Oregon, meanwhile, moved toward a venture that seemed to be premised on a different takeaway from Berkeley's woes: don't lease what you can buy.

Six

A Different Way of Doing Things

Arthur Golden told just a few people how far Phil Knight had gone to teach Dave Frohnmayer a lesson, and those few people kept the secret mostly to themselves. Nathan Tublitz was among them.

"Those of us who heard about it thought it was outright extortion," Tublitz said. "But we kept our mouths shut because we felt terrible for Dave Frohnmayer and understood what he was going through. It was like there was a loaded gun pointed at his child's head."

When Knight returned to the fold at the University of Oregon, he was welcomed as a returning hero, not a villain. There was, however, a strange, almost superstitious lack of fanfare; the strings were now visible for all to see, even if Knight and Frohnmayer were the only ones who knew exactly how the puppet show worked.

The spring semester passed quietly, but by summer break it was clear that the old lines of communication between Nike executives and university administrators were crackling back to life. In early August of 2001, the school displayed renewed financial confidence as it broke ground on the expansion of Autzen Stadium, which had been stalled for a year after Knight withdrew his promised contribution of $30 million. Then, in September, the Nike CEO announced publicly what Frohnmayer had known for months: his commitments to the University of Oregon, financial and otherwise, had been renewed.

Knight's money quickly breathed new life into the stadium expansion, which had become saddled with ballooning costs necessary to make up for lost time and finish the job before the 2002 college football season. Instead of a projected $80-million price tag, the expansion would cost $89 million, plus unforeseen extras, like $1.3 million worth of brand-new artificial turf that had to be replaced after it proved to be too slick in the rain. Instead of the original $30-million pledge, Knight would pay nearly twice that sum toward the stadium expansion, while the remaining $29 million was funded by issuing state bonds that came with hefty interest payments. What wasn't covered by state bonds or Knight's money were the various operating costs—like the $2 million that Oregon's athletic department siphoned from the school's general fund each year—that got passed on to students whose tuition dollars replenished the fund whether they liked athletics or not. While the University of Oregon's top administrators scrambled to cobble together $90 million to improve the school's football stadium, its faculty was earning less than their contemporaries at each of the sixty-one universities in its cohort of similarly prestigious public research institutions.

"Coughing up ninety million dollars to build luxury skyboxes when you can't pay faculty is a form of insanity," said Jim Earl, who had become one of Knight's most vocal critics on campus.

It was not the first time the faculty was at loggerheads over Autzen Stadium, which owed both its conception and its construction to treachery and retribution within the school's administrative ranks. A decade and a half before its 1967 unveiling, the Ducks were playing up to three home games per season at Portland's Multnomah Stadium, after all but two other teams in the Pac-10 conference said they would no longer play at Hayward Field, which suffered from crumbling facilities and a seating capacity of just 21,000. So, without consulting university president Arthur S. Fleming, Oregon's athletics director, Leo Harris, began his own private campaign to raise funds for a dedicated football stadium. For fifteen years, Harris solicited donations and hid the money in secret accounts located throughout the state of Oregon, convinced that Fleming, who opposed the building of a football stadium, would spend the money on other university programs if he ever found it. By the time Harris resigned over his differences with Fleming, in 1966, he'd squirreled away $1 million in donations, all but obligating the university to go forward with construction of the stadium that year, lest it enrage Harris's legion of financial backers. President Fleming raised an additional $1 million by selling twenty-five-year leases on two thousand covered seats, which went for $500 each. Only $500,000 was raised privately, half of which came from Portland timber baron Thomas J. Autzen, whose gift gave Fleming a chance to get back at Harris.

"Fleming said Autzen had committed to the donation we needed to complete the financing, then he dropped the bomb on us," said assistant athletic director Norv Ritchey. "He said it was going to be named after Tom Autzen. We were speechless—everybody thought it was going to be Leo Harris stadium."

In the decades after its 1967 completion, Autzen had undergone only minor upgrades, like the installation of AstroTurf in 1969, and the addition of 381 club seats and 12 luxury seats in 1989. The $90-million makeover that began in August 2001 sparked both great hope for the football program's future and great anxiety over the school's priorities. There was a growing mistrust, throughout the nation, of the motives behind universities that had ostensibly sought to use college athletics as a tool for recruiting students and attracting donors in order to support its academic and research programs. Nathan Tublitz, another Knight critic among Oregon faculty, called the exponential growth of college football programs "a time bomb," built on an unsustainable model, which, he added, was "spiraling out of control financially and morally."

The University of Oregon, Frohnmayer claimed, had no intention of plunging its athletics department into "an arms race that's not sustainable except for the five or six more successful, richest institutions." In reality, the school was not only engaged in such an arms race, but leading it. Evidence of this could be found as close as Autzen Stadium and as far away as Manhattan, where the school had spent $250,000 on a massive 80-by-100-foot billboard to promote

Oregon's star quarterback, Joey Harrington, as a candidate for the 2001 Heisman Trophy. Then there was Oregon Ducks head coach Mike Bellotti, who led the team to a record ten victories in 2000, earning him a $750,000 salary with escalator clauses that made it possible for him to bring in $1 million per season. Just as Nike had become the national face of concerns over sweatshop labor, Oregon's football program suddenly became the focus of those concerned that academics had become secondary to athletics at a number of American universities.

"It frustrated me," Coach Bellotti said. "This perception that we sold out to something."

Tublitz was cautiously optimistic that the athletic department would make good on its promise to become financially self-sufficient by 2004, but many of his colleagues held the more pessimistic view that Oregon's football program, which had been a punch line only a decade earlier, had grown into a juggernaut that would consume more resources, not fewer, as it grew. As these concerns over out-of-control spending became more urgent, Frohnmayer summoned increasingly grandiose defenses to quell faculty protests.

"We don't want to become a pseudo-professional team," he said.

Pseudo-professional was, however, an apt description for what Oregon football was becoming: ticket revenues increased by $2 million annually after Autzen's expansion and face-lift; conference payouts for the right to broadcast Oregon football and basketball games brought in another $10 million each year; and with Knight's return came a cavalcade of Nike marketing executives, designers, and branding specialists who descended on the University of Oregon campus to discuss new deals, projects, and partnerships.

The key partnership remained, as ever, between Frohnmayer and Knight, who quietly finalized a deal one year in the making, recorded in the Fanconi Anemia Research Fund's 2001 tax filings as an "unusual grant" of $2 million, which, filings state, came from the same individual who donated $2 million to the organization in 1999—a donor who, conspicuously, had not offered a donation in 2000. And that donor, according to Lynn Frohnmayer, had been Phil Knight.

There was nothing remarkable about Nike's early football uniforms for Oregon. They looked much like the old ones, aside from Nike's signature swoosh. Feeling they could do better, Knight asked the company's creative director, Todd Van Horne, to work with designer Rick Bakas on a new brand identity for the Ducks.

It was radical, at the time, to think of a public university in terms of its brand identity. For centuries, universities had been defined by mottos that clearly spelled out the school's academic or civic mission. Cornell University's motto was a quote from Ezra Cornell, who said, "I would found an institution where any person can find instruction in any study." The nation's original agricultural college, Michigan State University, has an appropriately straightforward motto: "Advancing knowledge. Transforming lives." The University of Oregon's motto was taken from a Latin text by the poet Virgil, which roughly translates to: "The mind moves the mass." Implicit in each of these mottos, and many others, was a sense of the university's purpose and its responsibility to better the individual, benefit the public, and enlighten mankind. A brand identity, on the other hand, expresses only some vague sense of the product that is being sold—in this case, that product was the University of Oregon, a brand built in Nike's image.

After Bakas joined Nike in 1995, he was tasked with creating a new brand identity for the Denver Broncos, who subsequently showcased his work on the advertising world's biggest stage by winning back-to-back Super Bowl championships in 1998 and 1999. Knight had been impressed with the work. In 1999, the Nike CEO gave Bakas the assignment of creating a new image for the Ducks, which he hoped would "raise Oregon's status as a national title contender by attracting better players, better coaches, and grow the Oregon fan base."

Bakas was spending a lot of time at the University of Oregon's campus, where he had studied architecture in the 1980s. He was sensitive to what he felt was the school's legacy—Bowerman, Pre, and the Oregon Duck, a mascot based, with Walt Disney's permission, on Donald Duck. The key branding problem for Bakas and Van Horne was that Ducks, unlike Broncos, are not particularly tough.

This assignment presented another peculiar challenge of designing an "O" logo that managed to look sporty and modern without infringing on any trademarks owned by Oakley sunglasses. Bakas spent hours at his drafting table, sketching different "O" logos, many of which ended up looking like some alien weapon from a bad science fiction movie. Finally, during one of many visits to Eugene, he looked down on Hayward Field from the tallest bleachers and noticed how closely its oblong shape resembled the letter "O."

"I took the shape of the track and the shape of Autzen Stadium's footprint and punched the track shape out of the stadium shape," Bakas said. "With that, the Oregon 'O' was born."

Ten years later, the logo had become iconic enough that LeBron James used his hands to throw up an "O" while attending an Oregon game against USC.

In the years since Frohnmayer hired him to be the University of Oregon's director of communications, Thomas Hager had rarely been surprised during the course of his workday. His job, after all, was to make sure that the media and the public knew what was going on at the state's oldest liberal arts university, which made Hager and his small staff arguably the most informed people on campus. This made it especially shocking when they were corralled into a conference room one day and introduced to a team of Nike designers who had been working in secret on a new brand identity and logo for the Oregon Ducks.

"I was surprised about the unveiling of the new logo as a sort of fait accompli," Hager said. "Supposedly I was in charge of external communications for the university and I had not been privy to any discussions about changing things."

Hager had been excluded from the process for the same reason that virtually every other university employee found themselves out of the loop: Nike was now calling the shots on campus. The mingling of public and private labor became a growing problem in the late nineties, when Nike employees began consulting on various projects alongside university employees, who were ostensibly employees of the state. With its rebranding project, Nike established a new precedent, which was to compartmentalize some aspects of its partnership with the university to such an extent that faculty, staff, and student involvement were almost eliminated. Nike's Gulfstream V corporate jet became a veritable fixture at the Eugene airport, while Nike "suits" became a regular presence on campus. When they showed up in your department, Hager said, you learned to stay out of their way. Whatever they came to do was subject to little or no scrutiny, since Nike is not subject to the same level of accountability as a public university; this lack of transparency, meanwhile, made it more difficult to discern which decisions were being made by Frohnmayer and which were being made by Knight.

For a decade or more, taxpayers had been disinvesting in state universities across America, and any number of top administrators had responded by adopting more businesslike management techniques to ensure that a liberal arts education was defined, increasingly, by fewer costs and greater dividends. But among America's public universities, Oregon alone could claim to have been fashioned into a product, a brand to be marketed not by public stakeholders but by private interests.

The university's deepening partnership with Nike also represented an abandonment of the independence that had characterized the school since its establishment in 1876, when the school's founders dared to challenge Oregon's parochial system of education by making it a secular institution. As land-grant colleges went, it was more public than most, brought to life not only by the Morrill Act but also by $30,000 worth of bonds issued by the county court and $20,000 in donations from Eugene locals, some of whom raised funds by selling their own land. Eugene's religious groups also contributed to the effort to pay for the construction of the secular university, with funds raised through church suppers and "strawberry festivals." Labor for the construction of the campus, which was still underway when the school's first five students enrolled, was paid for in part through the sale of $6,000 worth of donated wheat, valued at $0.90 per bushel. What benefits the community reaped from these donations was clear enough from the first graduating class of 1878, which consisted of four local men and one local woman, who went on to be authors and historians, and judges in both the county court and the state supreme court.

When the Oregon and California Railroad connected Eugene to the rest of the West Coast near the end of the century, the town's population grew, along with its sense of what was happening in the rest of America, thanks to the telegraph lines that came along with the railroad. One of the things the town learned was that public universities east of the Mississippi River, like Cornell and the University of Chicago, were growing their enrollment and distinguishing themselves as some of America's premier liberal arts colleges. In the spirit of competition and industriousness that characterized the times, the University of Oregon hired an Easterner, Dr. C.H. Chapman, as its new president. Chapman, who was thirty-three, was the son of a farmer and had graduated from Johns Hopkins before arriving in Eugene, where he immediately began shaping the University of Oregon into the model of a liberal arts "industrial" college. He eliminated preparatory classes from the curriculum and added commercial and engineering courses, while broadening and liberalizing the courses already in place at the school. He also met with high school principals throughout the state in an effort to ensure that more Oregonians, regardless of their beginnings, had an opportunity to attend college. Oregon's public universities, Chapman believed, should be more closely aligned with the rest of the state's public education system, for the benefit of the state's economy and its industries as much as for the individual. This model persisted for a century at the University of Oregon, with a periodic rebalancing of the tensions between Jonathan Baldwin Turner's founding idea of an "industrial education," focused on training the labor force, and the more utopian ideal of the liberal arts university as a place where young minds are prepared for unimagined challenges through broad exposure to the western canon of knowledge. By means of the former, the school offered Oregon's "sons of toil" better lives through prosperity and social mobility, and by means of the latter it offered Oregon a better society through the democratization of privilege.

A century after the age of industry prompted American universities to consider courting the labor force, the age of marketing convinced them to view higher education as a product to be packaged, commercialized, and sold. When Thomas Hager began his stint as the University of Oregon's communications director, his first act was to rechristen his new department, which had been known for decades as the News Bureau before his predecessor changed it to the Office of Communications and Marketing in 1993. Hager was an alumnus of the school, where he earned his journalism degree before working for ten years as the editor of the university magazine. His approach to media relations reflected his journalism background, as well as his strong belief that a public institution ought to be a good and open steward of the public records it produced. But the marketing approach he'd tried to stamp out in the News Bureau soon took root elsewhere in the university.

"At some point the decision was made to let athletics have their own media people," Hager said. "One or two of them at first, and more when the money started rolling in, all of them in the habit of handling their own requests their own way, with an emphasis on the marketing."

Hager fought to bring the university's office of communications back under one roof, but it went nowhere, leaving the school with parallel media relations operations beholden to different stakeholders. The athletics department's public relations staff, with its emphasis on marketing and obfuscation, grew increasingly powerful as it aligned itself with marketing executives and public relations specialists from Nike. It was the school's new logo and brand identity, however, that signaled a turning point for Hager.

"After that there was a different way of doing things," he said.

There was tremendous pressure on the Oregon Ducks ahead of the 2001 college football season, and the weight of those expectations fell almost entirely on the broad shoulders of starting quarterback Joey Harrington. Those expectations began building in November of 1978, when Oregon football coach Len Casanova wrote a letter congratulating his 1967 quarterback, John Harrington, on the birth of his son Joey.

"Hoping to hear from you in about seventeen years," he wrote to the two-week-old.

Harrington began his career with the Ducks as a freshman in 1999, but it was during his junior year that he distinguished himself as a starting quarterback with NFL potential, throwing 2,967 passing yards while leading his team to its best record ever, with ten wins and two losses. In the process, Harrington set himself up as one of the top contenders for the 2001 Heisman Trophy, awarded annually to college football's best player. And with Knight's money once again rolling in, Oregon was anxious to flex its financial muscles and show off its star quarterback with an ostentatious display that set Harrington up for a kind of stardom rarely known by college athletes.

"For the better part of six months I had over a million views a day," Harrington said. "A ten-story billboard in New York City at the top of Penn Station, across from Madison Square Garden, has a way of attracting eyeballs."

The billboard pictured Harrington alone, in full uniform, and it sold him as "Joey Heisman," which transformed him into an overnight media sensation, prompting op-eds in *The New York Times* and hours of punditry on sports television and radio programs.

"Some people were thrilled that a player from a West Coast school not named USC was receiving this kind of national attention," Harrington said. "Some people were furious that someone would have the audacity to promote themselves in a way that was so in-your-face and over the top—but most of all, people were just curious who I was and what I had done to deserve this larger-than-life attention."

What Harrington had done was simple, if not easy: he'd won a lot of college football games—fourteen out of the sixteen he'd started by the time the 2001 season began—and he'd won many of them in spectacular fashion, racking up more than one-third of his college football victories with dramatic fourth-quarter comebacks. He'd also had the good fortune to be a winner at a time when winning really mattered for the University of Oregon. Harrington and his teammates were the first generation of Oregon football players to benefit from Knight's largesse, especially when it came to improved facilities like the state-of-the-art training facility, the Moshofsky Center, which Knight had helped fund. They also benefitted from access to the latest Nike shoes, uniforms, and equipment, and they enjoyed the fringe benefits that came with playing football at a school increasingly reliant on athletic programs for funding: cheerleaders who were encouraged to "date" them; tutors who were paid to help them with homework; and enough professors, in enough departments, who were willing to help carry them academically so that they could focus their efforts on the field.

Harrington studied business and enjoyed practicing classical piano on his great-grandmother's restored 1911 Baldwin. When he had time for live concerts, he preferred the mellow, folksy sounds of James Taylor or the Dave Matthews Band—a far cry from the larger-than-life Joey Heisman image, which he bought into as a means of conquering his own nerves from August until January, when his teammates relied on him to be a fearless, faultless leader. In time, he won so many games, under such stressful conditions, that his false bravado turned into confidence real enough to cast a shadow longer than his billboard near Times Square. By the time the 2001 season got under way, some people were comparing Harrington to Tom Brady, noting how quickly the three-step passer moved in the pocket, and how agile he was at rolling out of the pocket when it collapsed; they remarked on his poise and how rarely he forced the ball into traffic. At six feet four inches and 215 pounds, he could gain ten pounds of bulk and remain just as quick on his feet after going professional, which he was sure to do if his senior year with the Ducks went as well as his junior year had.

The season began with a hard-won opener against Wisconsin, which seesawed dramatically right up until Harrington led a masterful drive late in the fourth quarter to claim a 31–28 victory over the Badgers, who had been one of two teams to beat the Ducks in the previous season. A week later, the Ducks steamrolled Utah 24–10, keeping the team scoreless in the second half. Then, on September 29, 2001, Oregon hosted the USC Trojans at Autzen Stadium, where both teams took to the field before the start for a moment of silence to honor the victims of the September 11 terrorist attacks, which took place just a few days after the Ducks had played Utah. The U.S. invasion of Afghanistan followed on October 2, 2001, and President George W. Bush's War on Terror pushed campus protest movements in a new direction.

On the evening of January 11, 2001, two hundred state police officers surrounded a massive apparel factory on the outskirts of Puebla City, Mexico, not far from the slopes of an active volcano called Popocatépetl. The police were dressed in riot gear and armed with guns, shields, and clubs, and they arrived with leaders from a government-backed union that represented the factory's 850 workers, who had been engaged in a general strike for three days. With the riot squad behind him, one of the union leaders entered the compound, where 300 of the striking workers had been occupying the factory. There were a number of grievances behind the strike, including low wages and abusive supervisors, but at its core the work stoppage was about the lack of confidence factory workers had in their government-backed union, which had sided with management often enough to make them wonder whether its allegiance was to them or the company. When the union leader arrived with the riot squad behind him, the workers knew that they'd been right to worry; and when he spoke, it was clear that they might have more to worry about than they'd ever imagined.

"Are you frightened yet?" he asked.

These troubles had been brewing for months at the factory, which was, in many ways, a monument to the glory and the ugliness of the new global economy: a sprawling compound of hangar-like buildings where Mexican workers sewed and knitted apparel for the American companies Nike and Reebok, under the supervision of the Korean manufacturing firm Kukdong International. Some of the workers said they were paid less than minimum wage, which meant they were bringing home under $25 for a 45-hour work week; those who were paid a legal wage didn't make much more than that, and while most of the factory's workers were women, Kukdong International did not offer its workers maternity pay. The company also failed to pay the workers a Christmas bonus that is required by law in Mexico, and that wasn't the only law it was breaking: children between the ages of 13 and 15 were illegally working as many as 10 hours per day at the factory; workers were sickened by rancid meat served in the employee cafeteria; and factory managers had occasionally beaten employees with hammers or screwdrivers.

Near the end of 2000, these simmering resentments led five factory supervisors to organize a movement aimed at ousting their existing government-backed union in favor of one more willing to stand up to Kukdong International. Organized labor was not something the company wanted to find itself up against when it came time to meet a demanding production schedule from Reebok or Nike, which was at times responsible for 85 percent of the factory's orders. Terrified over this prospect, Kukdong International decided to crush the nascent shadow union by firing the five supervisors who had organized the effort. But instead of frightening the workers, these firings emboldened them. The workers held their ground for as long as they could before the police began beating them, with help from their own union representatives. At least four of the strikers ended up in the hospital with concussions and internal bleeding, and two pregnant women suffered miscarriages. After nursing their wounds, the workers agreed to return to work as long as Kukdong International didn't fire any of the factory's workers in retaliation. The company signed a document agreeing to these terms, but soon broke it by firing 250 of the workers who had taken part in the strike. State police continued to play a role in Kukdong's intimidation tactics by visiting the homes of the workers most deeply tied to the independent union, issuing several arrest warrants related to the general strike. Thirty police officers soon took up posts inside the factory, where they scrutinized workers for any sign of dissent or labor-organizing efforts.

A decade earlier, all of this might have gone unnoticed to the world beyond the shadow of Popocatépetl. Prior to the founding of the WRC in 1998, the movement to end sweatshop labor had advanced in fits and bursts, but with the new campus group came the structure and organization necessary to propel the cause forward. In less than three years, the group had spread from a handful of elite Eastern colleges, like Harvard, Johns Hopkins, and Wesleyan, to more than one hundred chapters at institutions ranging from the Ivy League to public universities like Western Michigan and Georgia State. Each new campus the group reached led to a renewed sense of purpose through protest, as well as a refreshed well of recruits to conduct fact-finding missions to the overseas factories where Nike shoes and apparel were made. When things began to fall apart at Kukdong International's factory, the WRC sent a team of seven activists to Puebla City, where they interviewed more than forty workers who outlined their grievances with Kukdong International and with Nike. The resulting report that the WRC issued later that month proved troublesome for the Korean manufacturing company and for its biggest clients, Nike and Reebok. It was also an unwelcome surprise for administrators and athletic directors at eleven universities that were named in the report: Nike had hired Kukdong International to make licensed apparel for these schools, which included Georgetown, Purdue, the University of Michigan, and the University of Oregon.

Nike's initial reaction was to downplay its relationship with Kukdong International, and to dismiss the WRC's fact-finding methodology as an unfair attempt to politicize the company's business dealings. Without conducting its own investigation, the industry-governed FLA suggested the issue might be resolved by allowing the factory workers to choose a new representative from the ranks of the same government-backed union that had already failed to support their interests—a suggestion Nike publicized while working behind the scenes with a Mexican lawyer who made his own recommendations about how the company should proceed. In the end, the attorney recommended some of the same solutions proposed in the WRC report, but Nike continued to ignore calls for action until the media coverage of campus protests prompted universities implicated in the scandal to publicly insist on some kind of compromise that might bring an end to the standoff. Facing intense pressure from the eleven universities named in the WRC report, Nike allowed delegates from the anti-sweatshop group to interview managers from the Kukdong factory and officials from the government-backed union—two groups that seemed to be following commands from Nike. This was a major concession that would have been unimaginable just months earlier, and it was important for a number of reasons. One was that it allowed members of the WRC fact-finding mission to speak with Kukdong employees who were not disgruntled, and who could dispassionately describe the factory's working conditions from the perspective of middle managers who saw a bit of everything on a daily basis. It also gave them a chance to speak to less radical factory workers, who nonetheless supported their activist colleagues. And, perhaps most important, it showed that orders were coming from Nike, not from Kukdong or the government-backed union. Over the course of several months, the WRC group interviewed more than 150 workers and managers from the factory, which gave them enough ammunition to pressure Nike into allowing Kukdong's workers to withdraw from the government-backed union in favor of one that was independent, with leaders elected by the workers themselves. It was an unprecedented victory for the factory workers, the labor rights group, and the broader anti-sweatshop movement, which was beginning to reach the public in ways that transcended growing membership and visibility.

"People are drawn in by the horror stories," one WRC activist said at the time. "But then they start to see how the whole system works."

In early September, Kukdong International formally recognized its workers' independent union, gaining momentum for a movement that was preparing to tackle a broad range of corporate abuses. Later that month, police were expecting 50,000 activists from this movement to converge on Washington, D.C., in protest of meetings between the International Monetary Fund and the World Bank. Then, as with so many other things, the September 11 terrorist attacks altered the course of the anti-sweatshop movement. USAS, the group responsible for founding the WRC, said it was "neither the time nor the place to gather in opposition," almost certainly unaware that their momentum would be nearly impossible to regain after the nation's period of mourning.

In the months that followed, campus protests went from looking unseemly to unpatriotic as more and more Americans moved on from grief to anger. After the United States invaded Afghanistan and began moving closer toward war in Iraq, activists and student protesters became reenergized with a sense of urgency and purpose not seen since the Vietnam War. The anti-sweatshop movement, which had been the most successful campus protest campaign since college students raised their voices against apartheid in South Africa, proved to be a casualty of the protests against war in the Middle East—and, in many ways, a casualty of its own success. The shocking speed with which the anti-war protest movement came together was, in part, a result of the culture of dissent left behind by anti-sweatshop activists who had been organizing on college campuses for years, where they forged enduring leftist networks. By November of 2001, the anti-war movement had taken over at more than 400 college campuses around the country.

Those few students who remained committed to the deflated anti-sweatshop movement had been dealt a staggering blow by Frohnmayer, who had given other university administrators a playbook for resisting WRC membership when he maneuvered Oregon out of its agreement in early 2001. At the same time that the labor movement was weakening, Nike was strengthening its position after learning, through Frohnmayer's capitulation to Knight, that it could effectively use financial pressure to bend university policies to the will of the company. Knight's company had also learned a few other tricks during its tussles with anti-sweatshop and human rights groups. In May of 2001, Nike began working to improve its damaged reputation by changing its messaging on the issue of sweatshop labor. The company that had spent years defending itself with the claim that it didn't *make* shoes, just designed and marketed them, portrayed itself very differently in a statement issued that month by its corporate and social responsibility manager, Harsh Saini.

"We were a bunch of shoe geeks who expanded so much without thinking of being socially responsible that we went from being a very big sexy brand name to suddenly becoming the poster boy for everything bad in manufacturing," Saini said.

After the moment of silence had passed, and the somber mood along with it, Oregon's game against the USC Trojans followed a script that had come to seem familiar since Harrington took over as starting quarterback for the Ducks: an early lead, a reversal of fortune, and a dramatic comeback to secure victory in the closing seconds of the game. In the final push, Harrington moved his team downfield in just forty seconds before throwing the touchdown pass that gave the Ducks their third win of the 2001 season. In the weeks that followed, Oregon took its dream season on the road, beating Utah State, Arizona, and California in away games that left them with an undefeated record as the season neared its halfway point. It was the first time since 1964 that the Ducks had held a 6–0 record, and with each thrilling victory came even greater hopes that Harrington's talent might cover the $250,000 check Oregon had written for his Joey Heisman billboard.

On October 20, 2001, Knight's two alma maters collided when Oregon hosted Stanford at Autzen Stadium, where the Ducks had won twenty-three consecutive home games—a streak longer than any other team in the nation could claim. In the spirit of magnanimity, Oregon allowed the Stanford marching band inside Autzen Stadium for the first time in eleven years, ending a ban that resulted from a 1990 halftime show when they'd poked fun at the standoff between Oregon's loggers and its spotted owl, a newly protected species with a habitat large enough to send the state's timber industry into a decline. Once the game started, the Cardinal proceeded to hurt Oregon's feelings all over again. Stanford took the lead early before ceding three touchdowns to the Ducks, but neither team could pull far enough ahead to get comfortable as the game seesawed relentlessly. Halfway through the fourth quarter, the Ducks had failed to move the ball beyond the fifty-yard line, while the Cardinal chipped away at Oregon's fourteen-point lead by blocking punts, intercepting passes, and capitalizing on every opportunity to score touchdowns. For only the third time since he became Oregon's quarterback, Harrington lost a football game.

After years of ignoring or denying accusations that it had relied on sweatshop labor, Nike began marketing itself as a company trapped by its own humble beginnings, unaware of the immense power it had accrued. But one jogger from San Francisco wasn't buying Nike's denials or its new image, and he set out to make his case in the Supreme Court of California.

As a fifty-four-year-old former marathoner with a history of environmental activism stretching back to his days at Yale, Marc Kasky had learned to recognize an injustice that needed action. The solution, he decided, was a lawsuit against the company that had sold him many of the old running shoes he had piled in his closet. But it wasn't really about the shoes.

In April of 1998, when Kasky filed his lawsuit in California Superior Court, he hadn't bought a pair of Nike shoes since reading about the deplorable conditions of its factories in Indonesia, seven years earlier. And for years, this modest personal boycott was enough to give Kasky peace of mind. But the sweatshop scandals kept erupting, each time bringing new denials and a fresh spin from Knight's company, which perversely sought to paint itself as a crusader for labor rights.

"Nike makes a very good product," he said. "But we all need to be accountable for our words and actions. Nike has been representing itself as a model corporate citizen, and it was disappointing and discouraging when I began to suspect otherwise."

Kasky's lawsuit accused Nike of violating California's state consumer laws by willfully misleading the public about the working conditions endured by hundreds of thousands of Chinese, Vietnamese, and Indonesian factory workers who made the company's shoes. California's unfair competition law, which bans false claims and advertising, allowed Kasky to file the suit as a representative of the state's public, alleging that the workers making Nike shoes throughout Asia were, in fact, subjected to physical punishment and sexual abuse, and that they were exposed to dangerous chemicals for prolonged periods of time, contrary to the company's claims. As evidence of this, Kasky's lawyers pointed to the leaked Ernst & Young audit, commissioned by Nike itself, which documented serious problems and recommended specific improvements that the company did not implement.

Nike's lawyers persuaded a superior court judge to toss the lawsuit by claiming it would violate the corporation's first amendment right to free speech, but the Supreme Court of California disagreed with the company's novel argument.

"When a business makes factual representations about its own products or its own operations, it must speak truthfully," the court said.

Nike then appealed to the U.S. Supreme Court, which agreed to take the case in January of 2003, but balked later that same year by deciding it had "improvidently granted" the scheduled hearing, which had been widely expected to produce a landmark ruling on the free speech rights of corporations. As a result, Nike was forced to return to California and defend itself in a court that had already denied its First Amendment argument. Faced with the strong possibility that a California judge would find that Nike had violated the state's laws against false advertising when it claimed not to use sweatshop labor, Knight's company chose to settle the case out of court. The settlement, which left intact the Supreme Court of California ruling that makes companies vulnerable to lawsuits over false advertising claims, cost Nike $1.5 million.

It was the kind of mixed result America's anti-sweatshop activists were learning to live with: in court, Nike suffered a black eye and lost $1.5 million to the movement, but insisted on paying its settlement to the industry-friendly FLA, rather than support a truly independent factory monitoring organization like the WRC. It was not unlike the settlement that forced tobacco companies to air anti-smoking television commercials, but allowed them to have enough creative control to produce ads that one tobacco industry critic called "as invisible and unwatchable as they possibly can be."

Victory was more clear in Mexico, where Kukdong International, and its clients Reebok and Nike, lost an eighteen-month battle with workers and signed a collective bargaining agreement resulting in the formation of Sitemex, one of the first independent unions in Mexico's maquiladora sector. And in American universities, where the WRC had reignited the fires of organized student protest, the movement was stronger than ever before, but reorganizing away from labor issues and toward keeping America out of wars in Afghanistan and Iraq.

The Ducks spent the rest of the college football season exacting revenge on other teams for the stinging loss they'd suffered to Stanford: the Washington State University Cougars fell in a game that saw the Ducks gain 565 yards of total offense; Harrington threw six touchdown passes, matching his own record from the previous season, in a rout of Arizona State; and the UCLA Bruins, considered Oregon's most capable challenger for the conference crown, lost by a single point in a nail-biter that earned Oregon its third conference title and burnished Harrington's chances at winning the Heisman. In December, the Pac-10 Conference champions took a victory lap around the Oregon State Beavers at the annual Civil War match, and on New Year's Day the number-two-ranked Ducks faced Colorado, ranked number three in the nation, at the Fiesta Bowl.

Harrington would rather have been playing in the Rose Bowl on January 1, 2002, but he didn't treat the Fiesta Bowl like a consolation prize. It was, in fact, some of the best football he and his team had ever played. Throughout the year, Oregon's offense had averaged thirty-four points per game, gaining the most yards per play while allowing the fewest sacks in their conference—strong numbers that the team handily surpassed while holding Colorado's potent offense to just forty-nine rushing yards. Harrington, in the final game of his college football career, threw for 350 yards and four touchdowns in the 38–16 victory over the Buffaloes. He was passed over for the Heisman, but Harrington was nevertheless elated over his team's performance throughout the season. He was picked third overall in the 2002 NFL draft.

"I was the kid that helped turn a local team into a national college football power," said Harrington, who won twenty-seven of the thirty games he played with the Ducks.

Years later, NBA broadcaster Ahmad Rashād, who had played football at the University of Oregon in the 1970s, recalled

Harrington's Fiesta Bowl performance, and his brilliant tenure with the Ducks, as a key reason for the team's ascension into the ranks of the perennial contenders in college football.

"For any kid in the country who wants to play for a big-time program, Oregon is a real option," he said. "In the past, it hasn't been."

Beyond Harrington's spectacular final season with the Ducks, Rashād offered two other reasons why the University of Oregon had become a college football powerhouse and a draw for the country's best young athletes: the newly renovated Autzen Stadium and its state-of-the-art locker rooms, which had both come courtesy of Knight's financial contributions to the program. These impressive facilities gave the Ducks an edge when it came to attracting the nation's top high-school football prospects, which was important in the increasingly competitive world of college football recruiting. Nike had transformed the University of Oregon into its own brand, but the value of that brand depended on bringing the best athletes to Eugene year after year. Anything less would slow the trickle-down economics of the University of Nike: good players ensured more lucrative television contracts for the conference, more donations and licensing revenue for the university, and higher performance bonuses for the coach. In pursuit of the best players, Oregon's athletic department sought to impress potential recruits by flying them to Eugene on one of Nike's corporate jets, or having an attractive cheerleader show them around campus. Sometimes, they resorted to even more extreme methods.

Seven

We'll Market You in Ways No One Ever Imagined

On an otherwise ordinary Saturday near the end of September in 1994, an important piece of college football lore began unfolding on the sidelines of Michigan Stadium, which is better known to college football fans as the Big House. For most of the afternoon, the fourth-ranked Michigan Wolverines obliged the oddsmakers as they laid the groundwork for a 26–14 rout of the visiting seventh-ranked Colorado Buffaloes. But with just over two minutes left to play in the fourth quarter, the Buffaloes scored a touchdown that put them back in the game.

The momentum shifted to the Colorado sideline as Rick Neuheisel rallied the team, exhorting them not to give up. Neuheisel was an assistant to the head coach of the Buffaloes. He earned a modest $60,000 each year to offer counsel, especially for Colorado's quarterbacks and wide receivers. It seemed, however, that his counsel proved especially worthwhile that day. After Colorado forced a three-and-out, their quarterback Kordell Stewart completed a twenty-one-yard pass that left his team on its own thirty-six-yard line with just six seconds remaining on the game clock. The Buffaloes were trailing Michigan 21–26 and had time for just one more play.

Earlier in the game, near the end of the first half, Neuheisel had called for a Hail Mary play in a desperate bid to bring the Buffaloes back into the game. The team ran with his play, which backfired horribly.

"Ty Law intercepted the pass at the goal line," Neuheisel said. "And never before in my life had I ever corrected a Hail Mary play, let alone drawn it up at halftime—but that's exactly what we did."

In the game's closing seconds, Neuheisel once again called for Stewart to throw a Hail Mary, this time for a chance at pulling off an upset victory. He told running back Rashaan Salaam to block the three-man rush that came for Stewart, giving the quarterback just enough time to choose from the three receivers who had made it to the Michigan goal line. The clock ran itself down while Stewart adjusted his footing and calmly looked far downfield to find his receivers. The ball left Stewart's hand just as the final second ticked away on the game clock, then hung in the air for three more seconds as it traveled nearly seventy yards downfield, where it bounced off the hands of Colorado wide receiver Blake Anderson before landing in the arms of wide receiver Michael Westbrook.

"So many things had to happen for that play to work," Westbrook said.

After the game, television camera crews streamed into the locker rooms and found a euphoric Neuheisel waxing poetic about Colorado's big win, which he said made him feel like "a little kid."

The so-called "Miracle at Michigan" proved to be a defining moment for the Colorado team. Westbrook would later say catching Stewart's Hail Mary pass that day was a bigger moment for him than winning the Heisman Trophy. It also proved to be a pivotal moment in Neuheisel's career. Soon he was earning $256,000 a year as the head coach of the Colorado Buffaloes, and when he threw his hat into the ring for the top coaching job with the University of Washington in 1998, he was still trading on the legend of that Hail Mary play. Pushing forty and without a conference championship win on his résumé, Neuheisel's contract with the University of Washington nevertheless made him one of just four college football coaches earning a seven-figure salary. When his $1-million contract with Washington was finalized in August of 1999, it amounted to $772,000 more than the university's president earned at the time.

The average University of Washington faculty member, meanwhile, earned just $60,000.

Neuheisel became a poster boy for college football's financial arms race: a relatively inexperienced and unaccomplished coach with just enough television celebrity to earn him the kind of paycheck previously reserved for coaches at football powerhouses like Tennessee and Florida State. He was also illustrative of the changes that were sweeping the Pac-10 conference, spurred by Nike's strategic spending on college football at Pac-10 schools like Oregon, Washington, and UCLA, the last of which raised its head football coach's salary to $578,000 the same weekend Neuheisel received his $1 million job offer at Washington.

Some of the broader consequences of Nike's spending on college football were unintended, if not unforeseeable: giving Oregon better facilities and world-class branding and marketing made the team better, which in turn forced other teams in the conference to spend more in an effort to compete. This increased competition made the conference itself more popular, and more valuable when it was time to renegotiate television contracts.

It was driven, in part, by the proliferation of Bowl money and increasingly lucrative television contracts. There were also more direct ways that Nike reshaped America's public universities. By subsidizing pay for top coaches at multiple schools, for instance, Nike helped inflate the market value of a college football or basketball coach well beyond what a university could afford to pay under the old system; eventually, schools where Nike did not subsidize coaching pay used more of their students' tuition dollars to hire competitive coaches, which then led the schools that did have Nike's backing to spend more tuition dollars on top of Nike's contribution. Before long, college football coaching contracts were layered with win bonuses and Bowl-appearance incentives that cost Nike, and the universities, more money.

The problems with these kinds of coaching contracts became obvious when Neuheisel's first University of Washington contract crossed the desk of an official at the state ethics commission.

Employees of the State of Washington are barred by law from receiving outside compensation for performing official duties, which meant that a public university should not be paying Neuheisel money to coach the school's college football team while Nike was also paying him to do the same thing, with the caveat that he did it exclusively outfitted in the company's shoes and apparel.

After Neuheisel signed with the University of Washington, Nike offered him $125,000 per year to exclusively wear the company's products while coaching the Huskies, and whenever appearing on television broadcasts. He would also receive an additional $25,000 from Nike if the Huskies played in a Bowl game. But unlike Colorado, where Nike had been paying Neuheisel $100,000 to advertise their products during widely televised college football games, the State of Washington took issue with the questionable ethics of selling corporate advertising space on the backs of state employees. In the end, it hardly mattered—Knight knew how to navigate around these little roadblocks. And in this case, Washington taxpayers footed the bill for the attorneys who helped Neuheisel find a shortcut around the legal barriers that separated him from his Nike paycheck.

Two different attorneys from the Washington attorney general's office argued the case—one representing the ethics commission and another representing the University of Washington, Neuheisel, and, effectively, Nike. The university first tried to make Neuheisel's contract acceptable by changing some of the language: instead of being required to exclusively use Nike products while participating in athletic activities, he would be contractually obligated to exclusively use Nike products while participating in all "non-official athletic or athletic-related activities." The assistant attorney general assigned to represent the ethics board didn't know what to make of the revised contract.

"We do not know what a 'non-official' game or football practice or telecast is," he wrote. What made even less sense, he added, was why Nike would pay Neuheisel $125,000 if not so that the University of Washington coach could help them sell shoes and apparel to college football fans.

The answer, according to the attorney general representing the school's interests, was that "the private market has established the value of Mr. Neuheisel's endorsement," adding that "Nike is in the best position to determine this value."

It took months to unravel and reassemble the contract so that Neuheisel could continue to receive his Nike paychecks while working for the state of Washington's largest public university. The solution, in the end, was to circumvent Washington State ethics rules through a multilayered payment structure: Nike paid the University of Washington, which in turn paid Neuheisel the additional funds as part of his contract, which was amended to require that he wear Nike products exclusively, as an employee of the state, rather than in his capacity as an individual.

Late on the morning of July 27, 2000, Neuheisel was enjoying a leisurely game of golf when someone drove up in a cart and handed him a phone. The voice on the other end of the line belonged to one of the communications staff in the University of Washington's athletics department: Jerramy Stevens, one of the school's best football players, had been arrested on suspicion of rape just hours earlier, they told him. A SWAT team had descended on the home that the player shared with some of his teammates, where detectives executed a search warrant and took Stevens into custody.

Neuheisel called the school's athletic director, Barbara Hedges, to see what kind of action the school would take. They acted quickly and decisively, and at 1:30 p.m. the lead detective in charge of the case received a fax from the law office of Mike Hunsinger, a University of Washington alumnus and longtime college football fan. He was going to be representing Jerramy Stevens, the fax said, and the detective in charge should contact his office immediately.

Hunsinger ran what could have amounted to a lucrative side business representing Neuheisel's football players. A *Seattle Times* investigation identified at least fourteen members of Washington's 2000 football squad who sought his counsel on a variety of criminal charges ranging from DUI and domestic violence to animal cruelty and sexual assault. The criminal charge he defended Stevens against related to an incident that had unfolded a month earlier, when a UW student called 911 to report a possible rape in progress shortly after three o'clock in the morning on June 4.

The 911 caller said he'd been walking back to his dorm, past rows of fraternities and sororities, when he saw a woman leaning against a wall, dressed only in a bra and maybe underwear, with her arms at her sides and a tall man facing her. It didn't look right, the caller said—the woman had obviously seen him, but her eyes seemed glazed over and she made no effort to cover herself from the passing stranger who had happened by the scene; the man eventually took the woman behind a bush, but the police who responded to the call couldn't find anyone in the area when they arrived.

Around noon the next day, a nineteen-year-old freshman awoke in her room at the Phi Beta Phi sorority, not far from where the incident had been reported. Her head throbbed, her stomach ached, and she had sore ribs and scratched legs. Her underwear was missing, and her bra was around her waist, covered in dirt. Her only clue as to what had happened to her was a fleece jacket that Jerramy Stevens had been wearing the night before, which had been left in her room, covered in dirt and smeared with blood. Later, when she recounted the evening's events to Seattle police, she would tell them she'd had three beers at dinner before going to a fraternity party, where she had seen Stevens. The last thing she remembered was taking a drink from a beer that someone had handed her—a beer that had already been opened. After that, everything was blank.

When she talked to Stevens about that night, he told her they'd only kissed, but the girl was worried about an unwanted pregnancy, so she went with her parents to Seattle's Harborview Medical Center, where staff found semen around her vagina and rectum, which doctors said had been lacerated. The semen was preserved for testing in a rape kit.

Detective Maryann Parker later told the *Seattle Times* that she immediately suspected the girl had been drugged without her knowledge, then raped. But by the time they were able to test her blood, too much time had passed for anything to show up in her system, and while Stevens had spent a night in jail, he didn't answer any of Detective Parker's questions. At his bail hearing, some of his teammates cheered in the courtroom when prosecutors asked the judge to release Stevens without charge, saying they'd need to take a closer look at the evidence. In the end, all that Parker managed to gain from the arrest was a sample of the suspect's blood drawn for comparison with the genetic material recovered from the girl's rape kit.

King County's elected prosecutor, Norm Maleng, was furious when he learned that Stevens had been arrested. His office called Detective Parker in for a meeting and asked her to explain why she'd arrested a star athlete. Her superiors, who accompanied her to the meeting, told the prosecutors that she didn't need their permission to make an arrest—just probable cause. And there was plenty of probable cause from the night in question, they said.

Hedges, meanwhile, assured members of the local media that the school would conduct a thorough investigation into what had happened that night. But that never happened. Instead, Hedges and Coach Neuheisel waited the scandal out while receiving regular updates from a prosecutor working in Maleng's office, which seemed to have wrested control of the case from the Seattle police department. On August 17, two weeks before the start of the 2000 college football season, they were told that the result of DNA testing revealed that Stevens's blood was a match with the sperm recovered from the girl's rape kit. Stevens maintained that the sex had been consensual.

When prosecutors met with top police officials to discuss the case, five weeks after DNA testing linked Stevens to the alleged rape, they insisted that the football player not be charged until after he had been interviewed for his side of the story. In arranging that interview, Maleng's office granted a number of unusual concessions: the interview would take place at Hunsinger's office, rather than the police department; Detective Parker, who led the investigation and knew the evidence best, would not be allowed to ask the suspect any questions; and most unusually, the district attorney's office agreed to hand over to Stevens and Hunsinger statements given to police by the accuser and witnesses. Typically, suspects are allowed to see the evidence against them only after they are charged, not before. Police balked at the terms, and the interview was canceled. It wasn't the first time Maleng had made things difficult for police who went after UW athletes.

Two years earlier, he had declined to prosecute three football players who had beaten a student on campus while a crowd of witnesses watched. A year later, Maleng declined to prosecute another set of three football players, this time for an assault at a fraternity house. His argument that there was a lack of evidence was proved to be without merit by the city prosecutor, who took up the frat-house assault case Maleng had passed on, leading to three guilty pleas. On October 24, 2000, Maleng gathered members of the local media for a press conference where he announced that his office would not bring any charges against Stevens. The reason, he said, was "insufficient evidence."

Detective Parker disagreed.

"I thought he should have been charged," she told the *Seattle Times*. "From the police perspective, I think there was overwhelming evidence that a crime had occurred."

The Stevens case, she said, had been "handled differently" than other rape cases Maleng's office prosecuted.

"And we felt it was because he was a University of Washington football star," she said.

Three days before Maleng's press conference, Stevens scored a key touchdown in a win over California, bringing Washington's record to 6–1. It was a pivotal moment on the team's road to the Rose Bowl, which they won on January 1, 2001, with a 34–24 victory over

Purdue. Stevens led the Huskies with five receptions that brought his season total to forty-three, making him perhaps the greatest tight end in the school's history.

The football program that helped shield Stevens from rape charges secured significant financial rewards from the team's 11–1 season and its Rose Bowl victory: contributions to the football program increased by $1.5 million, while ticket sales increased by another $1 million. Neuheisel's improved record, meanwhile, increased the value that Nike got out of its side deal with the coach.

In 2002, Stevens left the University of Washington a year early, without graduating, so that he could begin a professional football career with the Seattle Seahawks. His NFL contract promised him $6.2 million over the course of five seasons. The next year, he was reunited with two of his former Huskies teammates in the courtroom after four University of Washington students sued the football players over sexual assault allegations Maleng had declined to prosecute.

In depositions, Hedges was asked to explain why her promised investigation into the Stevens case had never materialized. She said she felt there were no grounds for punishing Stevens or the other football players accused of rape, and so there were no grounds for an investigation. It's hard to imagine Hedges making the same decisions, however, if it had been the rape victim, and not the rapist, who earned the school millions of dollars each year by wearing Nike shoes and apparel. Neuheisel, meanwhile, said that he only punished his players if they embarrassed themselves, their families, or the university—and while he admitted that the rape accusations had been an embarrassment for the school, the prosecutor's decision not to go forward with charges led the coach to believe that "Jerramy was not the reason for the embarrassment." For Neuheisel it was the victim, by implication, who had embarrassed the school.

For her, the intervening years had been tough. Abandoned by school administrators, depressed, and unable to face Stevens or his friends, she left UW and attended community college until the football player left the school. In her lawsuit, she was identified in court documents only by her initials, which Hunsinger seized on as a means of discrediting a girl who had already faced shame, scrutiny, or harassment from UW players, fans, or boosters. Rather than arguing the case on its merits, Hunsinger tried to stop the lawsuit by asking the judge to force the victim to use her full name in publicly available court filings. After the judge denied the motion, Hunsinger settled the case out of court in the spring of 2004. The woman who had accused Stevens of rape received a check from Hunsinger for $300,000, and signed an agreement barring her from talking about the case.

In the early days of "shoe money," when it was against the rules for a university to sell its loyalty, or the loyalty of its student-athletes, Nike learned that it could get these things for free if only it bought loyalty from the coach. Years later, Nike was still buying coaches, and for higher prices than ever before. But recession and deepening cuts to funding for higher education meant that buying a college football coach might also win the loyalty of university administrators desperate to keep the school afloat. Neuheisel's arrival at the University of Washington coincided with a sharp decline in state funding for the school, which subsequently raised its tuition and began recruiting more out-of-state students, just as the University of Oregon had done a decade earlier. To attract those students, the university bet on Nike and Neuheisel.

Two days before the biggest start of his college football career, in September 2003, sophomore Kellen Clemens was feeling overwhelmed in ways he had not anticipated—not by the pressure to perform against third-ranked Michigan, but by the sheer opulence of his surroundings in the Oregon Ducks' new locker room. Clemens had grown up in Burns, Oregon, a logging community with less than three thousand residents, and he couldn't quite wrap his head around the luxurious two-story locker room, which had cost $3.2 million.

"Things like this just blow me away," he said. "Sometimes it seems like a bit much."

As Clemens rummaged through his locker, which included a lockbox for valuables, three of his teammates lounged on a nearby sofa, where they played video games on a sixty-inch plasma-screen television. Dan Weaver, an offensive lineman, bristled at the assumption that posh facilities made for posh players.

"Just because we have a nice locker doesn't make us soft," he said.

In the afterglow of Harrington's sterling tenure with the Ducks, with money pouring into the promising football program as never before, a new nickname began to take hold: the University of Nike. It was, unquestionably, derisive. But the extent to which the Ducks and their fans minded this mockery would depend on whether or not the team would continue to backslide in 2003, as they had in the losing 2002 season following Harrington's graduation.

When Michigan arrived at Autzen Stadium on September 20, 2003, Knight left his private skybox in favor of a patch of artificial turf along the Oregon sideline. The Wolverines were coming off a decisive victory over Notre Dame and were scorching a path toward the team's first national championship since 1997, while the Ducks remained undefeated by virtue of three less impressive victories, which revealed a defense as weak as head coach Mike Bellotti's passing offense was strong.

As the tense match played out on the field, jeers from the visiting team's crowd proved that Knight's role in the drama of college football was not lost on Michigan's tradition-bound fans: "Hey, Knight!" fans shouted when the Wolverines neared Oregon's end zone. "How do you like that?"

At the end of the day, Knight liked it just fine; when the game clock ran out with the Ducks on top, Oregon improved its record to 4–0, and at the same time managed to stunt Michigan's run at another national title. For Clemens and his teammates, the win was an important statement aimed squarely at those who accused the team of using Knight's money to buy success. Bill Moos called it the most significant win in the history of the football program; in part because it was proof that bitter rivals had been right to think that money could give, and had given, the Ducks an edge that had previously eluded them.

USC and UCLA, as representatives of the old guard of the Pac-10 conference, had a much easier time talking potential recruits out of visiting Oregon before Knight built the Moshofsky Center, Moos said. And before the Joey Heisman billboard, they could tell recruits that no one would ever hear of them if they chose Oregon.

"Hey, guess what?" Moos said. "We'll put you on a billboard in Los Angeles or San Francisco or New York. We'll market you in ways no one ever imagined."

The locker room, like the billboards and the indoor practice facilities, was designed for recruitment as much as for luxury and comfort—a collection of unnecessary features, like thumbprint scanners for door locks and sliding doors that opened vertically, had no practical use beyond mesmerizing the teenage minds wandering through those doors as undeclared recruits.

Soon after Harrington's graduation, Frohnmayer realized that the necessity of winning college football's financial arms race outweighed the convenience of denying it. The University of Oregon's president knew it was an unsustainable system, but nevertheless he formed an intercollegiate athletics committee, stacked it with administrators and faculty who were friendly to athletics, and tasked it with helping "dispel some prevalent misinformation about the university's athletics program."

In reality, it was not misinformation but criticism that the committee sought to dampen.

"The 'arms race' and how to maintain competitiveness in athletics without compromising academics are issues of concern at the UO and nationally," administrator Dan Williams wrote in one committee memo. "Locally, the symbolism of the new arena project and the remodeled locker room will likely instigate discussions about the role of athletics in academics."

Many faculty members remained skeptical of a report issued by a university task force on intercollegiate athletics, which glossed over the deep-rooted problems unearthed by an earlier independent report which found that college athletics was increasingly commercialized, often to the detriment of an institution's academic excellence and its broader student body.

In one October 2003 meeting, the committee ignored legitimate grievances, such as graduation rates and conflicts of interest, in favor of discussing how better to win critical faculty members over. Chemistry professor Jim Hutchison expressed confusion as to why other departments did not emulate athletics.

"It's difficult to understand why some faculty members do not view the athletic department's innovation and success as positive for the university and something to aspire to by all departments on campus," Hutchison said.

The university's shift toward athletics had not diminished its academic reputation, the committee claimed, offering as evidence the fact that Moos had accepted the job in part because of Oregon's academic excellence. And because the athletics program was now its own self-sufficient entity, it could not possibly be a drain on other departments, Williams said. There was, however, a catch.

The department had exhausted the reserves it needed to continue building and renovating facilities, Williams said, and some donations for projects would be spread out over a few years, requiring the use of reserve funds to pay for projects during the building process. It would take years to build up the department's reserves.

On the field, Bellotti was making this more difficult. Following the victory over Michigan, the Ducks lost three consecutive games, including a home-game blowout loss to Washington State. Later in the season, Neuheisel's Huskies dealt the Ducks another loss before the team ended its season with a narrow defeat at the Sun Bowl.

"Hopefully," Clemens said, "we'll be known for our play pretty soon."

Near the end of 2004, as college football's regular season drew to a close, Jim McVay found himself explaining why new money was every bit as good as old money—something that was beneath the organizers of the Rose Bowl and the Sugar Bowl, but often necessary for the man in charge of a football game named after Outback Steakhouse.

"There are twenty-eight bowls, and people claw and scratch to distinguish themselves," McVay said. "We've worked hard, had good community involvement and positioned ourselves as one of the top six bowl games in the country in terms of the teams we select and what we pay."

The Outback Bowl, which pinned its fortunes on its title sponsor in 1995, would pay out $2.75 million each to Wisconsin and Georgia in 2004—significantly less than the $11–$14 million earned by teams competing in the four games comprising college football's Bowl Championship Series (BCS): the Rose Bowl, the Orange Bowl, the Fiesta Bowl, and the Sugar Bowl. But the bevy of smaller, corporate Bowl games still offered a big payday for the American universities that lacked the kind of college football firepower provided by billionaire boosters like Knight and T. Boone Pickens, who was trying to do for Oklahoma football what Knight had accomplished in Oregon.

Pickens began his career as a geologist for Phillips Petroleum in 1951, shortly after graduating from Oklahoma A&M University. The oil business was in his blood: his father had worked for Phillips before him, and had traveled the Texas panhandle as a roughneck, a fireman, and a refinery worker. Pickens had inherited his father's independent streak, and soon found himself chafing at the bureaucracy that surrounded him at Phillips, which was then one of the twenty largest corporations in America. In 1954, at the age of twenty-six, he quit the company and struck out on his own as an independent geologist. Two years later, he founded his first oil company, Petroleum Exploration Inc., along with two other investors. Ten years after he'd quit Phillips, Pickens brought his young company public under the new name Mesa Petroleum, and by 1968 it was bringing in more than $6 million annually. At forty years of age, Pickens was sitting on 62 billion cubic feet of natural gas reserves and millions of barrels of oil.

Pickens then acquired a bevy of companies like Hugoton, which controlled a significant portion of the largest natural gas field in the country, through corporate takeovers. Throughout the 1970s and '80s, his escapades as a corporate raider turned his millions into hundreds of millions, but his biggest score came in 2003. At the age of seventy-five, the oil millionaire turned corporate raider used his Dallas-based hedge fund to bet on energy futures. When the price of oil and natural gas rose precipitously, as Pickens had guessed, his fund skyrocketed in value, rising to as much as $4 billion.

In 2001, Pickens went quail hunting with Mike Holder, OSU's golf coach, who had raised tens of millions of dollars for the school's athletics over the years. Holder suggested that Pickens consider donating $20 million toward a stadium renovation. The idea appealed to Pickens, who had grown tired of showing up to OSU football games only to see the Cowboys lose time and again.

"I don't like that feeling," he said.

In March 2003, Pickens began spending his newfound billions on his alma mater, starting with a $20 million contribution toward the $293-million renovation of Oklahoma State's football stadium, which was renamed for the billionaire. In 2005, he hinted that he might be willing to give a considerably larger donation to the school if Holder would consider leaving his current job to take over for Harry Birdwell, who had announced he was retiring as the school's athletic director. Holder was the least qualified of eight applicants, and he didn't even really want the job. But Pickens made his wishes known to the hiring committee, and in the end, it was Holder who walked away with the position. A week after he took over as athletic director, he flew to Dallas and asked Pickens for $100 million for further football stadium renovations, including ninety-nine new luxury boxes. He also asked for another $265 million for various practice facilities and stadiums for sports other than football. Eventually, Pickens agreed to give the school's athletic department

$165 million—a gift that appreciated to more than $400 million after the university opted to reinvest the funds in BP Capital, the hedge-fund owned by Pickens.

A 2006 headline in *The Oklahoman* newspaper succinctly captured the dynamic at work: "Nike founder Phil Knight has helped build Oregon athletics to a level that Oklahoma hopes to surpass."

Pickens suffered big losses during the financial crisis, but that didn't keep him from pledging another $220 million to his alma mater, and before the economic downturn came to an end, the billionaire's money was leaving its mark on the Stillwater, Oklahoma, campus. In 2010, the Cowboys won eleven games in a season for the first time in the school's history. The next year, the team finished its season ranked third in the nation after winning twelve games and securing victory in the Big 12 Conference championship. The winning season Pickens had long dreamed of was capped with a win over Stanford in the Fiesta Bowl, and the once laughable football program was producing future NFL players by the dozen. Season ticket sales had risen to nearly 50,000, and student enrollment was up by 44 percent since the stadium renovation bankrolled by Pickens. But that didn't tell the whole story.

When the financial crisis wiped billions of dollars from the value of the hedge fund Pickens managed, the billionaire stalled an unfinished project to develop a massive athletics village for the university—a project for which the state had used its powers of eminent domain to secure eighty-seven properties, some of which were wrested from their owners using the force of the courts. The holdouts were forced to vacate less than a year before the financial crisis stopped the project in its tracks, leaving the land in limbo. There was suddenly a sense that the community was paying for the university's willingness to give Pickens whatever he wanted.

"The administration didn't seem to care about the overall good of the community," said OSU alumnus Garrett Hellman. "They pandered to whatever Boone wanted."

Knight's influence on the college football arms race seemed to grow exponentially, both by inspiring rival billionaires to take up the cause, and by elevating competition to the degree that it attracted increasingly lucrative television contracts and corporate Bowl sponsors. Twenty of twenty-eight Bowl games were picked up for broadcast by ESPN and ESPN2, which earned its biggest ratings of the year from the Bowl season and doled out broadcast fees accordingly. In 2003, ESPN paid $2.1 million for the rights to broadcast the Outback Bowl, while ABC paid a whopping $26 million for the rights to air the Rose Bowl.

The BCS system was created in 1998, when the six most powerful Division I conferences agreed on a structure that guaranteed the champion from each league would have an opportunity to play in one of the four most lucrative postseason Bowl games, leaving two at-large berths. Complex and unwieldy, with none of the simple elegance of a unified championship system like the one used in the NFL, the BCS instead relies on the overwhelming sense of history and tradition surrounding its four oldest bowl games—a sense that was soon undermined by a cash-grab culture that produced copious new Bowl games, with new corporate sponsors, backed by new money.

As chair of the Pac-10 conference CEO group, Frohnmayer was well aware of a growing backlash against the BCS system, which threatened to impede negotiations for a new television contract to replace the one that would expire after the 2006 Bowl games aired. The leader of the rebellion was Tulane president Scott Cowen, who represented a growing number of smaller colleges who argued that the BCS system benefitted big-money football powerhouses like Oregon, Nebraska, and Penn State, while shutting smaller schools out of contention for a national championship, which then put them at a disadvantage when it was time to recruit new athletes. In 1998, for example, Tulane had been shut out of the national championship Bowl games because of its low ranking in polls, despite its 11–0 record. The BCS contract also put smaller schools at a financial disadvantage, generating a total of $900 million to be divided among the big conferences, like Oregon's Pac-10, with just $42 million left over for the smaller conferences to share.

Backed by a coalition of forty-four university presidents, Cowen threatened to bring an antitrust lawsuit against the BCS system if smaller colleges weren't brought into the fold.

"Our preference," Cowen said, "is that the BCS would go away completely."

Harvey Perlman, who served as chancellor of the University of Nebraska, wrote to Frohnmayer on February 16, 2004, warning him of the dire situation developing as Cowen's coalition gained strength.

Unless they were prepared to do whatever was necessary to significantly increase the BCS income and give a larger share to the coalition, Perlman wrote, then they might as well "face up to the reality that no agreement is possible."

When Phil Knight stepped down from his role as Nike's CEO in November 2004, a spokesman for the company joked with reporters about the possibility that he might spend his retirement coaching the University of Oregon football team. Knight retained his post as chairman of the board at Nike, which would keep him tethered to the company he'd cofounded and built. And while Frohnmayer hoped Knight would remain tethered to his alma mater as well, the university president's statement at the time was tinged with a sense of desperate uncertainty.

"Phil has been intensively involved with the school for years," Frohnmayer said. "We hope and expect to enjoy a continuing good relationship with Nike and Phil and Penny Knight."

The source of Frohnmayer's uncertainty was simple: Knight wasn't getting what he wanted. For one thing, Oregon's football team was in the midst of a disappointing backslide that would leave it with a dismal 5–6 record by the end of the season. More worrying still was the fact that Knight was ready to help build a new basketball arena for the school, and Frohnmayer hadn't been able to secure the piece of real estate where the billionaire wanted to put it. On November 22, less than a week after Knight stepped down as Nike's CEO, the two men talked about it on the phone.

The problem, Frohnmayer explained, was that the land was unattainable: Williams Bakery had been in operation at the edge of campus, a stone's throw away from the Willamette River, since 1908; the owners had no interest in selling. Knight was unmoved, and uninterested in compromise. He told Frohnmayer to pursue the bakery site anyhow.

Later that day, Frohnmayer sent Knight a fax to make sure the Nike billionaire knew he'd gotten the message. He would pursue the site, he wrote, regardless of the obstacles standing in the way.

While Frohnmayer was busy doing his best to please Knight and to negotiate a lucrative new BCS contract, Bellotti was barely hanging on. Oregon's head coach had decided in 2005 to shake things up by changing to a no-huddle "spread offense," using three-, four-, or five-receiver sets to force the opposing defense to spread out. He'd had only sporadic success, however, and his team struggled to adapt to the faster pace of the new playbook. Desperate for a fix, Bellotti turned to a new offensive coordinator named Chip Kelly, who was building a reputation as a man religiously devoted to the kind of up-tempo offense Oregon was after.

"When we started this offense, we could figure out after the game what we should have done," Bellotti said. "We progressed to the point where we could figure it out during the game. When I interviewed Chip, I realized he was the guy who would know, going into the game, what we should do."

Kelly, who was in his forties, had grown up in New England, where he spent winters playing hockey and summers surfing off the coast of Maine. He'd graduated from the University of New Hampshire, where he was working as an assistant coach when Bellotti tapped him for the offensive coordinator job in Oregon. His résumé also included stints at Columbia and Johns Hopkins—the kind of schools where administrators were pleased if the football team won any games at all. And yet he'd managed to cultivate offenses that would lead football fans to call him a guru and a genius, often enough that he had a reflexive, self-deprecating reply: "Jonas Salk was a genius."

Oregon's offense clicked as soon as Kelly arrived in Eugene, and in his first year as offensive coordinator, in 2007, the Ducks improved to a 9–4 record. Bellotti credited Kelly's spread offense with elevating Oregon "to the level where we were not the ones having to make adjustments; we were dictating to other teams."

The following year, Syracuse wanted to hire Kelly as its new head coach, and Bellotti could see that his offensive coordinator was eager to step up. So he and Frohnmayer decided to make Kelly the coach-in-waiting. In 2008, Bellotti ended his college football coaching career with a respectable 10–3 season that owed as much to freshman quarterback Jeremiah Masoli as it did to Kelly. In 2009, when Kelly took over as head coach, Bellotti became the school's new athletic director. He knew Frohnmayer would be retiring soon, and he was worried about what the new president's attitude toward athletics might be.

"I could do the best job protecting the football program by going into the athletic director's chair," he said.

On paper, most of Kelly's first season looked very much like Bellotti's final season, with a 10–3 record, but there was more happening on the field than these numbers reflect. Oregon's defensive line, which had been stocked with richer talent in 2008, managed to do more with less under Kelly's leadership. Behind this was a heightened emphasis on Kelly's favorite weapon: speed.

During practice, Kelly had his team "hitting the sled until they're blue in the face," according to defensive coordinator Nick Aliotti.

Under Kelly's tutelage, his team sometimes ran thirty plays during just twelve minutes of practice drilling—fast enough that Aliotti sometimes had trouble getting the call out of his mouth before the ball was in play. The new system worked: with help from Masoli's arm, Kelly led the Ducks to the Rose Bowl during his first season as head coach.

Just weeks into the 2010 football season, a peculiar new ritual had sprung from the fruits of Kelly's relentless drilling and his intense emphasis on speed: the crowds at Autzen Stadium, long known for the cacophony of sound they created, could often be heard booing after the Ducks moved the ball downfield for a first down. The focus of their ire were the officials, who never quite managed to move the line of scrimmage quickly enough for Oregon fans, who would accuse them of slowing the tempo of the game in order to give the opposing team enough time to catch its breath.

"Some people call it a no-huddle offense," said offensive lineman Mark Asper. "But I call it a no-breathing offense."

On the sidelines, Kelly would wait out these pauses in a crouch, with his hands on his knees, like a baseball catcher rising to block a wild pitch. He had more patience than most college football coaches, and never seemed to panic when his team took time to find its rhythm. Under Kelly, the Ducks often failed to take the lead early, but week after week, teams great and small fell to Oregon after succumbing to the lung-bursting workout Kelly's team forced on them.

"It's still football," Asper said of his team's game. "We hit people. But after a while, the guys on the other side of the line are so gassed that you don't have to hit them very hard to make them fall over."

Once, Asper said, a player from Tennessee told him he was going to throw up if the pace of the game didn't come down. Sometimes he explained that he had no choice but to keep following his coach's instructions. Other times, he got inside his opponent's head by warning them that the tempo was only going to get more difficult as the game went on.

During practice, Kelly put his team through the paces in the cavernous indoor training facility his predecessor had convinced

Knight to build. With the 2010 season nearing its end, the Ducks remained undefeated, with ten wins, making it easy to imagine that the Moshofsky Center had been built for just such a moment in Oregon football history.

With loud rap music draining into the massive indoor practice space from two giant speakers attached to the ceiling, Kelly shouted at players who fell behind the tempo.

Kelly liked using music to energize his players, and to distract them from the blistering speed of his practices, where plays were executed even more quickly than they could be during a real game, when officials helped temper the brutal pace. It was an unreal scene for most football players, and for most athletes, who are used to being slowed down in practice—from Little League to ballet, practice is a time for taps on the shoulder and brief chats about posture, technique, and patience. But for Kelly, practice was a chance to go faster than one can manage in competition, and to drill into his athletes the ability to read his signals and execute his plays more quickly than any other team executing a spread offense. His players, young and eager, adapted to Kelly's rituals easily, but it was mentally taxing for veterans like Aliotti, who had far more coaching experience than his boss, including a stint in the NFL.

Off the field, Kelly was much the same as he was on the field: all about football. Few people at Oregon would claim to have really known Chip Kelly, and those who did would tell you that he rarely talked about anything other than the game. Which was just fine with everyone in Eugene, so long as he kept on winning. Earlier in the season, he signed a contract extension that would pay him as much as $20.5 million through 2015, but he preferred not to justify his massive salary with the kind of bluster most college football coaches relied on. Most of his job, he would say, boiled down to watching his players on film, coming up with game plans, and pushing his team as far as he could in training. The goal, Kelly said, was "to bombard our kids."

Off the field, Kelly's kids were being bombarded with unwanted media attention. Masoli, who led the Ducks to the Rose Bowl in

2009, seemed set to compete for the Heisman Trophy in 2010, but instead left the team in disgrace after pleading guilty to burglary for stealing a laptop. Off the field, Oregon's attorney general, John Kroger, investigated procedural irregularities in the $2.3-million buyout awarded to Bellotti when he left his coaching job to become the school's athletic director. Bellotti's replacement would need to find a way to make the bond payments that would soon come due for the school's new basketball arena, which was going to cost the school $227 million. Nathan Tublitz was flabbergasted as to why the school continued to build expensive athletic facilities even without Knight's backing; the athletic department, which had prided itself on being self-sufficient, seemed unable to stop itself from creating more buildings, each of them resting on foundations thick with debt.

"It's time for the athletic department to do a little soul searching on how they can serve the university," Tublitz said. "The athletic department is out of control here."

Well before the start of the 2010 season, Kelly gathered his players to address a spate of arrests related to the program. He laid out the kind of behavior he expected from his team, and asked them to do better. The very next day, he learned that linebacker Kiko Alonso had been arrested for driving under the influence. Kelly dismissed Alonso and Masoli, as well as Jamere Holland, who had lashed out at his coach on Facebook.

"It happens everywhere, it happens in every sport," Kelly said. "The problem is we're a high-profile sport and we live in a fish bowl, so people know about it."

Near the end of that same year, Kelly's team was unbeaten and ranked number one in the nation, with an average of 50.7 points scored over the course of ten games. Many of the teams they bested lost to Oregon by nearly five touchdowns. New Mexico lost to the Ducks 72–0, and UCLA scored just thirteen points to Oregon's sixty. Oregon's offense, some argued, would do more than earn the team a championship—under Kelly's leadership, this team would change how the game of football was played for years to come.

"Nobody in the whole history of football can snap off plays as quickly as this team does," said former NFL pro Brian Baldinger. "Other teams can't condition for it. It's a great equalizer—if you've got a 350-pound guy, I don't care how good he is, you've got to get him off the field. He can't keep up."

Oregon's focus on conditioning, and its studious devotion to a secretive, opaque system of communicating plays using flash cards, put it on another level. In the final weeks of the regular season, Kelly's team maintained its number-one ranking by toppling Arizona at Autzen Stadium, then plowing through cross-state rivals Oregon State at the annual Civil War game. A month later, on January 10, Kelly's team did the one thing they hadn't done all season: in the BCS national championship game, up against number-two-ranked Auburn, Oregon lost.

In early 2005, the property Knight wanted for the university's new basketball arena finally became available. It was going to cost the school $22.2 million, which was not an ideal starting point for a project that was supposed to cost $100 million in total. This, too, became a point of contention for Knight, who wanted a much more expensive arena and didn't want to pay for it himself—especially after he began butting heads with Moos that same year. Frustrated, he did the one thing that had always gotten him a free lunch in the past: he left his wallet at home.

While trying to appease Knight, Frohnmayer once again turned to a state bond initiative to fund a University of Oregon building project. This time the school was asking for $227 million worth of bonds, which the legislature approved on the condition that the project would eventually be paid for by private donors and the athletic department, rather than taxpayer funds or tuition dollars. And to make sure that happened, Frohnmayer would need to make Knight happy enough to pay his share.

Eight

The World Thinks of Us as a Sports Franchise

One morning in 1995, before he had met most of his new colleagues at the University of Oregon, the school's new athletic director, Bill Moos, traveled to Nike's Beaverton headquarters for a meeting with Phil Knight. Moos, who had been on the job just two days, figured there was nothing he could say about the program that Knight didn't already know, especially in the brief fifteen-minute slot he'd been promised. So he told the Nike cofounder a story instead.

In 1972, while Moos was a senior offensive tackle for Washington State, a pair of shoe promoters approached him and a teammate with a stack of orange shoe boxes with check marks on the side.

"Will you wear our shoes?" they asked the players.

"We'd wear anybody's shoes," Moos told the men.

He was given two pairs of Nike shoes, one for practice and one for games, and he told Knight he'd kept them for twenty years.

"That was our very first shoe," Knight said.

The two men talked for ninety minutes that day, laying the foundation for twelve years of productive collaboration. The school's athletics budget swelled from $18 million to $41 million during Moos's tenure, which was characterized by audacious marketing campaigns, like the Joey Heisman billboard, and a building spree that left the campus stippled with new athletic centers and renovated stadiums. In his first year, the school's football team sold 14,000 season tickets; in 2006, which would be his last season, they sold 41,000.

In all those years, Moos had just one significant disagreement with Knight, who wanted him to fire the University of Oregon's track and field coach, Martin Smith. Moos refused, so Knight told Frohnmayer he would not contribute to the construction of the school's new basketball arena until both men were gone. Coach Smith was forced out late in 2005, and Moos retired a little more than a year later and moved to a cattle ranch in Valleyford, Washington.

"I guess I'm at a point in my life where I'd rather step in it than put up with it," Moos said.

Knight wanted his friend Pat Kilkenny to take over for Moos, who had been the most successful athletic director in Oregon history. Kilkenny was an unusual candidate for the job. While Moos had made a long career as an athletic director, Kilkenny was a former insurance executive whose only ties to college athletics were as a booster. Over the years, Kilkenny had given millions of dollars to the University of Oregon, and when Moos agreed to leave in early 2007, it was his prospective replacement, Kilkenny, who paid the $2-million severance package for the athletic director he was forcing out.

"I created the monster that ate me," Moos said.

When Knight helped build the Moshofsky Center, near the end of the 1990s, the goal had been to transform Oregon's football team into perennial contenders. Several years later, his renovation of Autzen Stadium gave the school's blossoming athletic department the tools to bring in more cash through ticket sales and alumni fundraising. Matthew Knight Arena, which was unveiled in 2008, gave the University of Oregon a chance to raise the level of its basketball squad by using the $227-million court to attract better talent; with Moos and Smith gone, Knight pledged $100 million to help repay the bonds that secured construction costs for the world-class arena, which memorialized his late son, who had died at the age of thirty-four while scuba diving in El Salvador.

In 2009, with the arena project behind him, Dave Frohnmayer retired as president of the University of Oregon, after learning—but not revealing—that he was seriously ill. Dr. Richard Lariviere took over for Frohnmayer amid the political fallout of the contentious arena project and faced additional distractions from the controversy surrounding Kelly's troubled football players. Early in his tenure, he was forced to shift his focus from raising the salaries of Oregon's professors, which still lagged behind the national average, to managing one "unacceptable" sports scandal after another.

He began by cleaning house: Bellotti, who was tarnished by Kroger's investigation over his golden parachute, was out. He also got rid of Melinda Grier, who had come to symbolize the veil of secrecy that surrounded so much of what went on at the university. It was Grier, for example, who had helped Frohnmayer maneuver the school out of its agreement with the WRC. During her years as general counsel, she had earned a reputation as a fixer for the fiefdom jointly operated by Nike and Oregon's athletic department, according to Nathan Tublitz; the school's office of public records was founded, in fact, because of Grier's habit of preventing the release of public records, which were previously under her control. And it was Grier who the *Oregonian* wrote was responsible for "enforcing the culture of secrecy around Mike Bellotti's $2.3 million compensation package." Her contract, Lariviere said, would not be renewed when it expired in 2011.

This personnel shake-up was especially consequential in the wake of Frohnmayer's retirement: over the years, Knight and Frohnmayer had developed a kind of shorthand—an unwritten contract between the two of them, forged through painful experience, that spelled out the rules that could be bent, the rules that could be broken, and, above all, what one man could expect from the other. With Frohnmayer and his general counsel gone, and Lariviere learning the ropes, there was a power vacuum that needed to be filled. The bureaucrats who stepped in to fill it were those people on campus who had the closest ties to Nike's day-to-day operations on campus: a handful of key administrators and athletic department personnel, the new general counsel, and the leaders of the school's public relations and marketing departments.

Lariviere, who was rarely seen without his signature brown fedora, had still bigger changes in mind for his tenure as the University of Oregon's president. After decades of stagnation, it was time for Oregon's flagship university to become independent from the state's broader university system.

"The demand for fresh thinking and new models has never been more urgent," he said.

Lariviere's model for the semiprivate university of the future was one of independence—not from the corrupting influence of industry, but from the constraints of its ties to the state government from which it had emerged and under which it had flourished for so many years.

While Oregon athletics was in the throes of the Chip Kelly years, Knight chose Eugene as the battlefield on which to win the arms race Nike had helped ignite in college athletics. His closing volley began with an elegant three-story cube of glass and steel called the John E. Jaqua Academic Center for Student Athletes, which was unveiled in 2009 after Knight paid $42 million for its construction. Like all of his building projects, the 37,000-square-foot structure was built on land that Knight leased from the university until construction was completed. The academic center is perched in the middle of a shallow moat, with stone walkways leading to its glass façade, which makes it look like an Apple Store from which the tech company's logo has ripened and fallen away. Inside, student-athletes can relax behind glass windows, made opaque by thin strips of brushed steel that hang across them like strands of tin spaghetti; they lounge on chairs and couches made from soft Italian leather that rest on white oak floors; glass elevators transport them to appointments with their own private tutors; and a café serves food and coffee to weary football and basketball players.

Situated amid a cluster of hundred-year-old dormitories and offices made from faded red brick, it's easy to imagine that the incongruous Jaqua Center fell gently to earth after being made on some other planet. And for the ordinary students whose tuition dollars help sustain the academic center, it might as well be just that—the building, known around campus as "the jock box," is off-limits to students who are not involved in Oregon athletics. The secrecy surrounding the jewel-like building has made it a monument to two different ways of thinking about the balance between athletic excellence and academic achievement: for boosters, it symbolizes Oregon's commitment to educating its star athletes, whose burdens are eased by tutoring and support tailored to fit their unique needs; for skeptics, it is a feeble attempt to pretend its tutors are helping student-athletes, rather than cheating for them. It is also proof that the University of Oregon's athletics department is not the independent machine it claims to be.

Like each of Knight's gifts to the university, the Jaqua Center came with strings attached—staffing requirements calling for sixteen employees, and building maintenance costs amounting to $480,000 annually, much of which was drawn from the University of Oregon's general fund. In the nine years before the luxurious academic center opened, Oregon's athletic department quietly drew $8.5 million from the school's general fund, which it used to pay tutoring and counseling costs for student-athletes. This served a dual purpose: it allowed administrators like Dan Williams to obscure the fact that Oregon's athletic department was not, in reality, self-sufficient; and it forced ordinary students to subsidize athletic activities, even as tuition doubled and state support for higher education fell to just 7 percent of the school's overall budget. By the time the Jaqua Center opened its doors, the annual cost of tutoring and counseling for Oregon's student-athletes had swelled to $1.8 million.

This kind of creative accounting covered up a larger truth about college athletics, which was that it was rarely a profitable venture. On average, athletic departments in the NCAA's top division received a subsidy of about $10 million from other corners of the university—only 14 out of 120 Division I athletic departments actually generated a profit. Like Williams before him, Kilkenny, who was then athletic director for the Ducks, falsely claimed that Oregon was among these profitable schools in a 2007 newspaper editorial.

"We receive no funding from the state or the university general funds," Kilkenny wrote in Eugene's *Register-Guard.*

In the summer of 2013, the ultimate expression of Nike's alliance with the University of Oregon emerged with the opening of the $68-million Football Performance Center. The 145,000-square-foot facility was dizzyingly luxurious, even for Knight, who paid for its construction; no other college football program in the nation could dare to imagine such a facility, which was elegant beyond what most NFL teams could claim.

It was easy, strolling through the facility, to mistake it for many things that it was not: an art installation on the sixth-floor sky bridge gave the impression of a museum; a private barbershop, stocked with utensils from Milan and staffed with a private hairdresser for shaggy Ducks, seemed as though it belonged in a European spa; lockers outfitted with biometric scanners added a touch of Silicon Valley to the shower room. When the school first gave reporters a glimpse of the facility, late in July of 2013, the tour lasted three hours. And for the first time, athletic department staff like Jeff Hawkins embraced a nickname that had once been considered derisive.

"We are the University of Nike," Hawkins said. "We embrace it. We tell that to our recruits."

With Knight's help, the University of Oregon was finally able to sell its recruits, and its fans, the one thing that could compete with the lure of tradition that had long sustained football programs at schools like Alabama and Notre Dame: what the Ducks were selling, better than any other team in football, was the future.

And, like the Jaqua Center, the Football Performance Center looked like it came from the future: granite, corrugated metal, and fritted glass, arranged into massive structures that suggested an angular conceptual rendering of the Death Star. Its form suggested both the boundless imagination of its architects and the limitless resources of the man footing the bill; one of the architects traveled to China in search of the rock quarry that produced the stones used in the ground-floor plaza. Such understated flourishes were accentuated by flashy toys that served as reminders of the building's chief function, which was to lure young minds: Sony PlayStation consoles, custom-made in Oregon green, and pool tables made by a Portland company that had designed a pair for Michael Jackson's Neverland Ranch. Other small touches were less ostentatious—elevators decorated with famous plays from Oregon's history; extra-sturdy furniture made to withstand five hundred pounds; and shelves that charge any phone or tablet that is placed on them, without any outlets or cords.

Standard amenities, like the cafeteria, were taken to the next level with deluxe espresso machines and farm-to-table meals; training facilities were taken to outlandish extremes, with a forty-yard track surrounding the weight room, where video cameras recorded and measured the efficiency of each step that fell upon the Brazilian ipe-wood floors.

"It's the densest wood known to mankind," said Craig Pintens, an associate athletic director for the Ducks. "It doesn't float, doesn't burn—that makes it ideal for a weight room."

For recovery, there were hydrotherapy pools and steam showers, and for hygiene there were deep sinks sitting in front of mirrors fitted with built-in televisions. Oregon athletic director Rob Mullens, in a feat of understatement, called it "probably the most complete space in college sports." More than that, it was the most complete weapon the college football arms race had ever seen—a game-changer.

On September 3, 2011, the head of Oregon's State Board of Higher Education, Matt Donegan, was packing his suitcase for a flight when he received a distressing phone call. University of Oregon president Richard Lariviere, who he was about to meet at a Ducks game against LSU, had escalated his rebellion against the rest of the OUS, and it was going to cost the state's six other schools money—unless he was stopped.

Since taking over for Frohnmayer two years earlier, Lariviere had become a beloved figure on campus. He was plainspoken, despite holding a doctorate in Sanskrit, and remained a fierce advocate of the brand of affordable public education that had allowed him to become the first member of his Iowa family to attend college.

"I owe everything I have to the remarkable power of education," he said.

In Eugene, Lariviere had shown his willingness to embrace change by throwing out Frohnmayer's fixer, Melinda Grier, but he also made clear his willingness to accept those things he could not change. He met with Knight soon after arriving on campus, and traveled occasionally to meet the billionaire at Nike's Beaverton headquarters. The two men spoke on the phone regularly, and Lariviere put great stock in Knight's opinions, which he found to be "realistic and hard-eyed." He was no pushover, though, as his treatment of Grier had shown—he knew that athletics paid the bills at Oregon, but he was unwilling to let the tail wag the dog.

"I'm very grateful that we have that vehicle to get our name and our mission out," he said. "But it's entertainment, it's not education. It's not research. It's not pedagogy. It's entertainment."

When Oregon's attorney general asked why Mike Bellotti had received a $2.3-million buyout that was not written into his coaching contract, Lariviere did not hesitate before firing the beloved athletic director. And while he was prone to explaining away the athletic department's follies and misdemeanors, he was refreshingly curt when discussing his criticisms.

The University of Oregon's athletic department "ha[s] had sloppy business practices—an immature, amateurish way of running this business," Lariviere said. "I understand why that happened, because they got out of bed one morning and they were a $70-million-a-year business."

Above all, Lariviere was beloved around Eugene for his bold

vision, which took Frohnmayer's ideas about outside funding a step further. A year into his tenure as the University of Oregon's president, Lariviere approached Oregon's legislature with a bold new plan for funding higher education at the state's flagship university: if Oregon would agree to issue $800 million worth of thirty-year bonds for the university, while furnishing the school with the $64.5 million necessary for servicing the annual debt on those bonds, the school would invest the full $800 million, along with privately raised funds, and use the cash to operate independently. The university would have greater independence from the OUS, while the state would contribute less money, overall, to the annual operating budget of the school. Timing was key, Lariviere felt, because the financial crisis had created some of the most favorable rates they were likely to see for some time.

Lariviere's plan earned the ire of the Oregon State Board of Higher Education, which would have to cede its influence over the University of Oregon to an independent governing board in order for the plan to succeed. George Pernsteiner, who oversaw the OUS, asked Lariviere to wait on his plan until the board finished its lengthy, contentious negotiations with the unions representing clerical and support staff at Oregon's seven universities. Governor Kitzhaber echoed Persteiner's request, and asked Lariviere not to increase any wages at the University of Oregon until the contract negotiations were settled with the unions. The University of Oregon president ignored both men.

In the midst of the contentious union negotiations, Lariviere spent nearly $5 million on long-overdue raises for more than 1,100 faculty and administrators at his school. This enraged Governor Kitzhaber, who complained that the University of Oregon president had "disregarded my specific direction on holding tight and delaying discussion about retention and equity pay increases until the next biennium to allow for a consistent, system-side policy on salaries." With its bargaining position weakened, the OUS conceded $10 million more than it hoped to in annual raises and benefits for union clerical and support staff at the state's other six universities.

In September of 2011, when Donegan picked up the phone and

learned about Lariviere's pay increases, he confronted the University of Oregon president, who surprised him with his reply: he was going to do what was best for the University of Oregon, which he felt had been held back for the past thirty years.

"At that point, I realized this is a gravely serious matter," Donegan said, calling Lariviere's actions "insubordination that would never be tolerated in the private sector."

A few months later, on a Monday afternoon in late November, the OUS board voted to terminate Lariviere's contract. Pernsteiner, who was booed loudly when he recommended the motion, returned home to find his house had been pelted with eggs and spray-painted with graffiti that spelled out the reason behind the vandalism with a reference to Lariviere's signature accessory: "The Hat."

Knight had been a supporter of Lariviere's vision for a more private kind of public university—the kind of school that could operate more or less as it wished, with minimal oversight from state institutions, and minimal friction to slow the gears of industry as they chewed through the valuable infrastructure of a once-public institution. Freed from the bureaucracy of the state's broader university system, Oregon might have transformed its nickname into its reality: the University of Nike. Instead, Michael Gottfredson took over as president of the school, and Knight retained his position as the most powerful man behind the scenes. On the other side of the country, at the University of Connecticut, a different kind of booster was straying from the template of quiet, calm control that Knight had come to exemplify in Oregon.

Robert Burton grew up in Kentucky's coal country, where he escaped a life in the mines because of a football scholarship that allowed him to go to college at Murray State University. After earning a degree in business administration in 1962, he was drafted into the NFL by the San Francisco 49ers, and later played for the Buffalo Bills. When his modest professional football career ended, Burton made a fortune as an executive in the printing and publishing industries. In 2011, the seventy-two-year-old was managing his own private equity firm while donating small chunks of his wealth to the University of Connecticut's football program—$7 million, in total, by the time his relationship with the school began to sour.

In a letter to the school's athletic director, Jeff Hathaway, Burton demanded that the school return a $3-million donation and remove his name from a football complex built with his money. The reason, Burton said, was that he was not consulted about the hiring of the school's new head coach, Paul Pasqualoni, who the millionaire had disliked since he'd coached his son at Syracuse years earlier.

"You are not qualified to be a Division I A.D. and I would have fired you a long time ago," Burton wrote. "You do not have the skills to cultivate new donors."

The school's interim president, Philip Austin, struggled to mend fences with Burton, who had been the biggest financial supporter of its sports programs. Seeking insights, *The New York Times* turned to Jim Earl, who warned about what might happen in Connecticut if the school's president acquiesced to Burton's wishes, as Frohnmayer had done over the WRC.

"In the university," Earl said, "a general rule is that your money does not win you influence. When word gets out that the donor is pulling this string, it's a scandal."

It was too late for Oregon, he felt, but other schools had the opportunity to look at the University of Nike as a cautionary tale rather than a road map for funding higher education.

"We're so deep in this that we can never go back," Earl said. "A professor can only do so much, and money talks. Phil Knight is a major donor. You really don't want to get in his way or cross him. It does not take much to get him to walk away."

The only way to stop America's public universities from becoming mere instruments of corporate raiders, he said, was to eliminate tax breaks for contributions to intercollegiate athletics. Earl had seen the fruits of the devil's bargain firsthand, and he'd learned that they were not worth the costs.

"Do you think our university is getting better?" Earl asked. "The world thinks of us as a sports franchise. They don't care what we do on the other side of campus. The team is owned by an institution that is flat broke," he said, referring to the University of Oregon Foundation. "And a football game isn't helping at all."

After leaving Eugene, Bill Moos spent three years raising angus cattle on his ranch in Valleyford, Washington, earning $200,000 a year from the ten-year non-compete clause he'd signed with Oregon. It was a quiet, restful existence that came to an end in late February of 2010, when the president of Washington State University called Moos and asked him to leave his non-compete payments behind and take over as athletic director at his alma mater—an irresistible challenge for the man who had helped bring Oregon to the upper echelon of the Pac-10 conference, in which Washington State athletics ranked lowest in terms of its operating budget.

The timing proved to be fortuitous. A year after Moos took over at Washington State, the conference had added Colorado and Utah to become the Pac-12, and its coffers were swollen with cash after signing a twelve-year $3-billion broadcast agreement with ESPN and Fox. Washington State's share of the conference television rights soared from $3.7 million to $14.7 million, bringing its total conference revenue to $17.8 million—more than double what it had been before Moos arrived.

Soon Moos was overseeing $130 million worth of building projects, including a renovation of Martin Stadium, which grew by 89,000 square feet, gaining 42 luxury boxes and 23 luxury suites reserved for boosters. In the spring of 2013, he unveiled a new 84,000-square-foot building that acted as the nerve center for Washington State's football operations, which were led by head coach Mike Leach, who Moos had lured with a $2.25 million annual contract—four times what his predecessor had earned for coaching the Cougars.

Washington State was not alone—schools throughout the Pac-12 conference had embarked on a $1-billion building spree in the wake of the new television contract, which guaranteed massive yearly payouts and increased national exposure, with the number of televised conference events rising from 550 to 750 per year.

Stanford expanded its football complex and its field hockey venue, and poured money into infrastructure upgrades that would give television broadcasters easier access to more parts of the school's sports venues. Utah saw its television revenue grow from $2 million to $8 million in its first year as part of the Pac-12 conference, and immediately put the money toward paying off a new $32-million football center. Colorado's athletic department, while saddled with $22 million in debt, sought to finance a new indoor practice facility to replace its flood-damaged athletic center. At the University of Washington, athletic director Scott Woodward thought of just one thing when he first learned how much money the Pac-12 television deal would bring his school: the arms race against Oregon, in which th Ducks had gained the upper hand thanks to Phil Knight.

"It's obvious the resources have helped them," Woodward said. "Phil Knight's a brilliant guy, and he understood that money matters."

The new television contract, Woodward said, was a chance for the Pac-12 to catch up with the Big Ten and the Southeastern Conference (SEC). But it was also an opportunity for the Huskies, and other Pac-12 teams, to catch up with Oregon. Each year, Washington would go $3 million into debt on capital projects that included a $15-million baseball stadium, a new basketball operations facility, and upgraded facilities for Olympic sports. Athletic department staff got raises and teams got generous new travel budgets, while the football stadium, perched beside Lake Washington, underwent a $280-million renovation.

"We had to play catch-up," Woodward said. "We had to invest. It's going to take a good decade to do that."

In the summer of 2009, there were few college football prospects hotter than running back Lache Seastrunk, who had made a name for himself playing high school ball in Temple, Texas. He was fast and agile, with snappy acceleration and an ability to change direction without losing speed; his nimble footwork made him a chore to defend, and his exceptional balance helped him break tackles that other players couldn't—one scout reported seeing him recover and gain extra yards after a defender had him just about bent over backward. Lots of schools courted him, including California, USC, LSU, and Tennessee, the last of which flew Seastrunk and his mother to Knoxville for an unofficial visit less than a month after he'd graduated from high school. But none wanted him more than the University of Oregon, where Seastrunk's tools made him the perfect player for Chip Kelly's spread offense.

Seastrunk signed a letter of intent with the Ducks on February 3, 2010, and for years afterward the factors influencing that decision would be a matter of interest for NCAA investigators. At the center of the controversy was a Houston-based talent scout named Willie Lyles.

The month after Seastrunk and his mother flew to Knoxville, Tennessee's assistant coach, Mack Garza, wired Lyles $1,500 to reimburse him for the money he'd spent on their airfare—a violation of NCAA rules. If Lyles had influenced Seastrunk's decision to sign with Oregon, it would constitute another rule violation. Evidence suggested he may have done just that.

On March 24, 2010, the University of Oregon paid Lyles $25,000, which Chip Kelly said was for his scouting services. There was plenty for investigators to be suspicious about, however: talent scouts typically sent schools hours of highlight reels taken at games and practices, but the University of Oregon could produce no such video footage from Lyles. The payment, which came the month after Seastrunk signed, was much larger than the $16,500 Oregon had paid another Texas scouting company for two years of its services; and Seastrunk's mother was surprised to learn that Lyles was a talent scout.

"Willie said he was a trainer," Evelyn Seastrunk said. "Now Oregon says he's a scout? Is he on Oregon's payroll? If Willie collected $25,000 off my son, he needs to be held accountable. The NCAA must find out for me. I don't know how to digest someone cashing in on my son."

In the end, Seastrunk transferred to Baylor without ever playing a game for Oregon. But the Lyles controversy didn't go away when he did.

LaMichael James rushed for 1,731 yards in 2010, and ran third in votes for the Heisman Trophy, but his fondest memory from his sophomore season involved dumping flour on his Oregon teammates while they slept. He loved the game, but he loved his teammates even more, because they made football feel like comedy rather than drama. His junior year would not be as blessed with levity and hijinks; Oregon football in 2011 was a nonstop drama.

The Ducks started the season with some unexpected holes in the team's lineup, including one left by Cliff Harris, who had been suspended indefinitely for driving 118 miles per hour with a suspended driver's license. And James himself, who remained a strong contender for the Heisman Trophy, was unexpectedly ensnared in the NCAA investigation into talent scout Willie Lyles, who he considered a trainer and advisor.

These dark clouds seemed to be hanging over the Ducks as the team lost its season opener to fourth-ranked LSU in a game plagued by turnovers. The following Saturday, however, James found his old form, scoring one touchdown after another in a 69–20 blowout over Nevada. Week after week, more rivals fell, with the exception of USC, which narrowly beat the Ducks in a late-November match. A late-season loss to the Trojans wasn't enough to stop Oregon from winning the Pac-12 championship game against UCLA, giving the Ducks a third consecutive conference title. The pinnacle came later, on January 2, 2012, when the Ducks returned to the Rose Bowl.

The week before Oregon faced Wisconsin in Pasadena, Nike revealed the uniforms the Ducks would be wearing for the game. These ritual uniform unveilings had become a central part of the University of Nike experience, and the potential combinations of custom colors, designs, and helmets had led Nike to employ an algorithm to help decide what the Ducks would wear on any given Saturday; over the years, hundreds of sports columns had been dedicated to the head-turning looks, like the all-white Stormtrooper uniform, and a neon-yellow uniform that made the team look like highlighter pens. Once, the Ducks shocked college football fans by wearing non-team colors during a national championship game. Win or lose, the uniforms Nike made for the Ducks always got noticed. And that was precisely the point for Nike designer Tinker Hatfield, a trim, soft-spoken former pole-vaulter who did for Nike what Jony Ive would later do for Apple.

"What is a more visible way to turn up the heat and create a personality than through the football uniforms?" Hatfield said.

Some college football watchers went so far as to claim that the uniforms were a key part of Oregon's rise as a football power.

"It all starts with the uniforms," said *Oregonian* reporter Rachel Bachman.

For the 2012 Rose Bowl, the uniforms started with a reflective dark-silver-colored helmet that had been polished to a high sheen. Dark-green jerseys, accented with neon yellow, completed the look, which drew typically mixed reviews from football fans.

"I'm old school," said Oregon running instructor Joe Henderson. "I still like the old green and yellow uniforms."

One graphic designer called the look "a techy, cyborgy kind of thing." The Ducks Store, which sits at the edge of the University of Oregon's Eugene campus, was nevertheless deluged with phone calls from fans who wanted to buy the jerseys from the moment Nike announced them.

Wisconsin scored first, but Kelly was never bothered by playing from behind early in the game. He'd conditioned his team to win by attrition, and it only took a few minutes for the Ducks to storm their way downfield for a touchdown. The Badgers scored again to retake the lead near the end of the first quarter, but with just three seconds remaining on the clock, Oregon quarterback Darron Thomas handed the ball to De'Anthony Thomas, who ran it ninety-one yards for a touchdown. The man nicknamed the Black Mamba tore through Wisconsin's formidable defense, showing off his explosive speed in the process. But his run also showcased how Kelly's unique offense worked.

Most college football teams were using gap control, assigning each defender a space to fill between the opposing team's offensive linemen. When they do this well, the defenders "spill" the other team's offense to the outside, forcing runners to head for the edges of the field, where oncoming defenders are waiting for them. Wisconsin had all of Oregon's gaps covered as the Rose Bowl's first half wound to an end, but because Kelly had placed Thomas and Kenjon Barner in the backfield, the defense needed to account for the additional gaps these backs could create if a runner passed by either side of them. If Oregon had been running a traditional offense, they would have been well covered by the Badgers defense. But there was nothing traditional about Kelly's plays.

Kelly called for quarterback Darron Thomas to read the backside linebacker—if he stayed put, Thomas would hand the ball off to a running back; if he moved back, the quarterback himself would take the ball outside; and if another defender threatened Thomas, he would have a second running back waiting behind him to take the ball. The backfield action caused Wisconsin's defenders to head outside, leaving a massive gap for the Black Mamba to exploit when Thomas handed him the ball.

Throughout the first half, Wisconsin continued to retake the lead and Oregon continued to match them in dramatic fashion. In the second half, the relentless pace of Kelly's spread offense began to take its toll on the Badgers, and the Ducks took the lead. But the Badgers seemed to come up with an answer for everything the Ducks threw at them.

With just over four minutes remaining in the game, Wisconsin's Russell Wilson connected with Jared Abbrederis on a twenty-nine-yard play that brought the Badgers to Oregon's twenty-seven-yard line. But the Ducks' Terrance Mitchell punched the ball, which slipped loose and landed just inside the field of play, where Oregon's Michael Clay picked it up. Oregon had a seven-point lead and they had possession of the ball. Minutes later, with the game ticking away, Wilson managed to get the ball back to Oregon's twenty-five-yard line. But speed was not Wisconsin's specialty, and when Wilson tried to stop the game clock at two seconds by spiking the ball, the referees said he'd acted too late—the clock had run out, and the game was over. Oregon had ended its seven-game losing streak in the Rose Bowl, which it had won just once before, in a 1917 victory over the University of Pennsylvania. In front of 91,245 fans, with the light of fireworks reflecting off their highly polished helmets, the Ducks celebrated the 45–38 victory over Wisconsin, which set a record as the highest-scoring Rose Bowl in history.

LaMichael James had played a huge role in Oregon's win, with 25 carries and 159 yards, including a scintillating 15-yard drive to throw down a gauntlet, of sorts, after Wisconsin fans celebrated as Oregon guard Carson York was carried off the field with an injury. In 2011, James had rushed for a school-record 1,805 yards, and proved himself to be a perfect complement for Kelly's unique zone-blocking scheme. Amid the celebrations, however, were lingering questions about the season to come. In the locker room, reporters wanted to know whether James was going to finish school as a Duck or leave early for the NFL draft.

"I really don't know," James told them. "This is the happiest I've ever been in my life, and I can't put money in front of my happiness."

Soon, however, James decided that the NFL was a safer bet than sticking it out in college, where he risked injuries that could lower his value as a professional player. When the San Francisco 49ers drafted him with the sixty-first pick of the 2012 NFL draft, messages of congratulations flooded into his phone faster than he could respond to them. At his draft-day party, James celebrated the start of his professional career with his friend Willie Lyles, who was still under investigation by the NCAA for selling high school recruits to teams like Oregon and LSU.

The Ducks were hardly slowed down by the loss of LaMichael James. Under Kelly's leadership, the 2012 season unfolded much as the previous season had: for sixty thrilling minutes each Saturday, the Ducks used Kelly's signature fast-tempo, no-huddle spread offense to obliterate rivals in spectacular fashion. While remaining undefeated through its first ten games of the season, Oregon chalked up an impressive list of statistics: fourth in the nation for rushing yards, second in total yards, and first in scoring, with an average of more than fifty-four points per game.

"We don't run a gimmick deal," Kelly said. "We run the ball. We throw the ball. We're very balanced."

One of the cornerstones of that balance was a nineteen-year-old freshman quarterback from Honolulu, Hawaii. Marcus Mariota impressed Kelly by throwing for 202 yards in his team's spring training game to beat out veteran Bryan Bennett for the starting spot in summer camp. In his debut game, Mariota threw for 200 yards and three touchdowns. A week later, he racked up 260 yards and two more touchdowns against Arizona.

While Mariota executed Kelly's frenetic playbook, his poise and calm sometimes made him appear to be moving in slow motion, even as he orchestrated attacks that chewed up the opposing team's defense. He quickly became one of college football's most efficient passers, with quick feet and a sharp release that gave him the time to choose his moment carefully. And like most good magicians, he claimed not to know the secret to his own tricks.

"I don't know how it works," he said of Kelly's spread offense. "But it does."

It worked, in part, because the six-foot-four quarterback had De'Anthony Thomas and Kenjon Barner, who could be relied on to do something just about anytime Mariota put the ball in their hands. Barner had taken an unlikely path toward developing the speed and agility that made him a star running back for the Ducks in 2012; after Kelly's grueling practices, Barner would drive his Camaro across town for ballet lessons, which he credited for helping him achieve some of his more impressive statistics: five touchdowns in a single game; fourth in career kick returns at Oregon; and the first Duck since 1965 to score touchdowns while rushing, receiving, returning a punt, and returning a kickoff.

When his receivers couldn't get open, Mariota had enough speed to move the ball downfield on his own, often enough that he was Oregon's third-leading rusher after Barner and Thomas.

"When he gets in the open field, he just runs away from people," said USC coach Lane Kiffin.

During a spring clinic in 2011, Kelly explained why he loved a quarterback like Mariota, who could run fast but did so less often than he probably could.

"I look for a quarterback who can run and not a running back who can throw," he said. "We are not a Tim Tebow type of quarterback team. I am not going to run my quarterback 20 times on power runs."

Like the previous season, the Ducks lost just one game, this time against Stanford, which managed to pull off the upset victory over Oregon in overtime. And for the fifth-straight season, the Ducks swept the Pac-12 and retained the conference title. In the Fiesta Bowl, they trampled Kansas State 35–17, and once again the locker-room celebrations were bittersweet. But this time it wasn't a star player who was rumored to be leaving college football's best team in the west—it was Chip Kelly.

In the two days after the Ducks won the Fiesta Bowl, Kelly interviewed with the Philadelphia Eagles, the Cleveland Browns, and the Buffalo Bills before announcing that he'd be staying at Oregon. Ten days later, in mid-January, he reversed course and decided to leave college football for an NFL job coaching the Eagles. In his four years at Oregon, Kelly's Ducks had won forty-seven games and lost just seven times. Clouding his brilliant legacy, however, was the Willie Lyles scandal, which seemed to loom even over his decision to leave college football for the NFL. At Oregon, he was still subject to whatever penalties the NCAA might choose to impose on him if the investigation determined that he had violated the association's rules about recruiting; with the Eagles, he could be sure that his livelihood would remain intact, even if his reputation did not.

"We've cooperated fully with them," Kelly said of the NCAA investigators. "If they want to talk to us again, we'll continue to cooperate fully. I feel confident in the situation."

The week after Oregon fans learned that Kelly was leaving the Ducks for the Eagles, the NCAA finally meted out its punishment after a two-year investigation into the Lyles affair: Oregon would face a three-year reduction of one scholarship for its football program, and further reductions in scouting days and the number of paid visits the program was allowed to host—a slap on the wrist, considering that a Bowl ban had been on the table. The harshest punishment went to Chip Kelly, who faced an eighteen-month ban that would run its course while he was coaching in Philadelphia; many speculated that someone within the NCAA had forewarned Kelly about the sanction, leading him to suddenly reverse his decision to stay in Oregon.

Chip Kelly's maverick turn as Oregon's head football coach left an indelible mark on the team's identity and its bottom line. Nike had been selling Oregon's sizzle for so long that the steak sold itself once Kelly brought consistent, spectacular wins to the program. The results, in dollars and cents, couldn't have been clearer: in the afterglow of the Kelly years, the University of Oregon's licensing business exploded into the ranks of the top ten most popular college teams in terms of licensing royalties. Like Mickey Mouse or the Playboy bunny, the Oregon Ducks logo was capable of generating millions of dollars in revenue on its own.

One year after Kelly left the team, Oregon's licensing royalties brought in nearly $5 million, four times what it had generated before the coach arrived in Eugene. Behind the increase was an unprecedented rise in the number of college football fans cheering the team on from outside Oregon. Part of the audacity of the Joey Heisman billboards was that, in 2001, Oregon was a regional team with outsized ambitions; the subtext of *The New York Times* op-eds on the billboard was that a regional team from the West Coast didn't have any business advertising itself in New York City. A little more than a decade later, college sports fans in New York were buying more gear from the Ducks Store than people in almost every other state, with the exception of Oregon, California, Washington, and Texas.

"We're fast becoming people's second-favorite team," said Ducks Store manager Arlyn Schaufler.

In Northern California, the Ducks are more popular than Stanford, and throughout the United States no other college team has fans as geographically widespread as Oregon. According to Facebook data, Oregon supporters account for more than 10 percent of all college football fans in more zip codes than any other team in America. And while Florida State won college football's national championship in 2014, Oregon made $200,000 more than the Seminoles in merchandising royalties. Hatfield's uniforms have also reaped less tangible benefits when it comes to recruiting talent. Kenjon Barner, for one, chose Oregon over other schools because one of his brothers liked the flashy uniforms.

Miraculously, sales of Nike products accounted for only one-third of these royalties, meaning that two-thirds was accounted for, in large part, by independent and local retailers. One screen-printing company in Springfield, Oregon, doubled its number of employees, from twenty-five to fifty, during the years Kelly was coaching the Ducks. When the company was founded, shortly after Knight committed to building the Moshofsky Center, the owner expected to eke out a humble profit selling iron-on patches. During the Kelly years, he had standing purchase orders worth six-figure sums ready to go whenever Oregon competed in a Rose Bowl or a championship game.

The University of Oregon, like Nike, had built a multimillion-dollar brand. And like Nike, it would face tough decisions about how far it was willing to go to protect that brand.

Nine

Public Interest

Shortly after eleven on the morning of Saturday, April 5, 1986, a student at Lehigh University was walking the halls of the Stoughton House dormitory, on the third floor, when she noticed that the door to room number 301 was ajar. She peeked her head inside to check on the room's occupant, Jeanne Ann Clery, and found the nineteen-year-old freshman's lifeless body. When homicide detectives from the Bethlehem, Pennsylvania, police department arrived, they immediately suspected foul play.

Clery was found in her own bed, with suspicious marks on her body, and an autopsy would confirm she'd been strangled and raped. She'd fought her attacker, and was still alive when she was raped and sodomized, forensic pathologists confirmed; down her back, a series of small cuts seemed to indicate she'd been threatened and held at bay with a sharp object at some point during the assault; her neck had cuts made with pieces of a broken glass bottle; and there were teeth marks on her face and breasts. Her wallet was missing, along with a camera and a radio she'd kept in her dorm room.

With the school in a panic, campus police doubled patrols and ordered all of the private school's dormitories be locked around the clock, instead of just at night. But it soon became clear that the danger was from within the campus community: a day after the killing, two students told police that their friend, Josoph Henry, had made a shocking confession to them at a party the night before. Henry, a twenty-year-old Lehigh student from Newark, New Jersey, had burglarized Clery's room after finding the door ajar; he left with her wallet, radio, and camera, but returned after realizing his own wallet was missing and that he might have left it in her room. Clery woke up when he returned to her room, and he decided to kill the girl so she couldn't identify him. There were cuts still visible on Henry's hands when police arrested him, and Clery's missing wallet, camera, and radio were found in his room. He confessed to the crime, and later pleaded not guilty by reason of insanity, but was convicted and sentenced to die in the electric chair.

Clery had graduated from the exclusive Agnes Irwin School, a private, all-girls academy founded by Benjamin Franklin's great-great-granddaughter in 1869. At Lehigh, she had studied liberal arts and played on the women's tennis team, but had spent less time on the court in the weeks leading up to her death, so she could focus on her studies. Her parents, Connie and Howard, lived a little more than an hour from Lehigh's campus, and saw her far more often than her two older brothers, who had gone to college at Tulane in New Orleans; a week before the murder, Clery had attended mass with her parents.

"It was the happiest year of her life," her mother said.

Soon after Henry's conviction, the Clerys filed a $25-million lawsuit accusing the university of negligence, and lashed out at the school in the media. Their daughter, they claimed, had died because of "slipshod" security and the university's "rapidly escalating crime rate, which they didn't tell anybody about."

Among these security lapses, they argued, was the fact that Henry, who lived off campus, was able to gain entry to the Stoughton Hall dormitory after hours, when it was locked, because other students had used pizza boxes to keep its doors open so their friends could come and go throughout the weekend. The political dimension of the Clery family's crusade was amplified by the racial subtext of the media coverage: local newspapers repeatedly mentioned the fact that Henry, a black man, was upset after losing a recent bid to lead a student minority group on campus, and implied that he may have had a grudge against more privileged white students. The *Los Angeles Times* offered its own unnecessary racial commentary, writing: "Blonde, blue-eyed Jeanne Clery was Henry's random victim." Equally sinister racial implications seemed to sit beneath the surface of the Clerys' activism concerning crime on college campuses.

A felon, Connie Clery said, could be your roommate in college these days, and she argued for character references and criminal-background checks to keep criminals from gaining admission to college. The implication of such comments was, ultimately, that Henry didn't belong at any American university—an argument not supported by his past and not compatible with American notions of criminal justice, education, and human rights. Apart from these calls for wide-scale disenfranchisement, the Clerys did advocate for more reasonable and legitimate reforms on college campuses. They argued, for instance, that people should have easy access to information about the crime rate in their own campus communities, and on this issue they steadily gained traction until, in 1992, Congress passed the Jeanne Clery Disclosure of Campus Security Policy and Campus Crime Statistics Act. Among other things, the Clery Act mandated that colleges and universities maintain records, and file public reports, concerning violent crimes like murder and manslaughter, forcible and non-forcible sex offenses, robbery and burglary, and domestic violence and stalking. One of the great legacies of this law is still found in police departments and campus safety offices today, where a public Clery crime log is regularly updated and available for all to see.

Sundays were an ideal time for catching up on paperwork at the University of Oregon's campus police department. The last of the weekend house parties were over, and with them went the attendant misdemeanors: noise complaints, fistfights, and calls about underage drinking. Later in the day, when students began flooding Knight Library to cram for the week ahead, some officers might get bored enough to hustle homeless people out of the building for the night. When reporters from the university's student newspaper stopped by to peruse Sunday entries in the Clery crime log, they were lucky if they managed to find an amusing anecdote for the crime blotter.

On March 9, 2014, Oregon's Clery crime log recorded a Sunday as slow as any other, but these federal crime statistics are only as honest as the police who record them. In truth, a serious crime had been reported that day, but it had not been recorded in the Clery log: a distraught father told campus police that his daughter, a freshman, had been raped multiple times after attending a house party on Saturday night; the party had been held at a house in the 1200 block of East Twenty-Second Avenue, at University Street, just a few blocks from Hayward Field, and the three men accused of raping the girl were University of Oregon basketball players. Instead of recording the report in the public log, which is checked regularly by reporters, campus police chose to keep the crime quiet; and instead of launching a criminal investigation, they passed it up the chain of command, from the campus police chief to the vice president of student affairs, Robin Holmes.

This unusual series of events was by design. As the person responsible for renewing the campus police chief's one-year contract, Holmes held tremendous power over the school's top law-enforcement officer, Carolyn McDermed; her predecessor, former officers said, had been forced out of the job over a disagreement with Holmes, who deliberately kept the police chief on a yearly contract as a means of exercising leverage over the department. In March of 2014, what that leverage bought was a chance at containing what promised to be a major scandal; instead of a criminal investigation, there would be a public-relations strategy of the sort that the University of Oregon was uniquely qualified to handle, as it employed some eighty communications, public relations, and marketing staff, on top of the various Nike employees who quietly contributed these services to the school in an unofficial capacity—that's one communications professional for every 295 students enrolled at the school, which is more than the combined faculty in Oregon's departments of history, economics, and philosophy.

The crisis these public relations professionals needed to manage was twofold: it was a problem that three Oregon basketball players had been accused of rape while representing both the school's brand and the Nike brand; it was an even bigger problem because these accusations came just as the Ducks had advanced to the second round of the Division I national championship tournament. And so, less than thirty-six hours after the rape took place, a decision was made and a plan began to take shape: campus police would do nothing with the criminal report, school officials would delay an administrative investigation, and the matter would be kept as quiet as possible while a public-relations team developed a strategy for managing and containing the crisis.

The University of Oregon's communications director, Julie Brown, worked swiftly. By lunch time on Monday, March 10, she already had a draft of a public-relations plan, which she emailed to her colleague, Rita Radostitz. The document was titled "UO Sexual Violence Prevention Communications Plan March 2014," but it was not a plan for preventing sexual violence; if it had been, it might have recommended sending students an alert about the sexual assault that had taken place over the previous weekend. Instead, the report was focused on a number of "key messages" to advance in the event that the rape accusations became public. Among the key messages Brown wanted to push was the idea that the "University of Oregon provides a safe environment for its students, and leaders are committed to cultural change to focus on survivor support and shared responsibility of each member of our community to prevent and respond to misconduct." Another section, labeled "strategies/tactics," emphasized planting media "stories about sexual violence prevention, education and resources to inform campus audiences."

Put more simply, the school sought to promote positive media stories about its efforts to educate its students about sexual assault, even as it failed to comply with the Clery Act by alerting them to a rape that had been reported in the community, and which involved multiple students. While seeking to portray itself as an institution focused on "cultural change" and "survivor support," the focus was clearly on obfuscating the details of a violent crime until after the accused were finished competing in a basketball tournament.

Five days after campus police and university officials learned of the incident, detectives at the Eugene Police Department opened their own rape investigation into Brandon Austin, Damyean Dotson, and Dominic Artis, who maintain that the sex was consensual. In a police report, the victim said she'd gone to a house party hosted by another Oregon basketball player named Johnathan Lloyd. She was intoxicated, she said, and went to the bathroom, where Austin, Dotson, and Artis cornered her. When she tried to push the men away, they overwhelmed her with their size and strength, and when she reached for her cell phone, one of the men pushed it out of her reach.

"No one wants to talk to you," they said, and proceeded to take turns raping her, according to the police report.

Later, they put her in a taxi and traveled to a different apartment, where she said they raped her again, until she cried so much that the men lost interest. The next morning, she sent her father a series of text messages about what had happened, and he immediately contacted the campus police department.

The most aggressive instigator in the assaults, she said, was Austin, who had arrived in Eugene in January after transferring from Providence College. He'd been a prized recruit at his previous school, but in early November 2013, he and a teammate were quietly suspended before playing a single game for Providence. The following month, Austin's indefinite suspension became a season-long suspension after Providence officials found him responsible for misconduct—he and his teammate had allegedly gang-raped another Providence student. Rather than staying in Providence, he was given the option of quietly transferring to another school, where he would be eligible to play ball in the 2015 season. Oregon's head basketball coach, Dana Altman, immediately recruited him, despite his behavior, which Altman and his assistant coach discussed with Providence officials and with Austin's family.

Altman was hired for the men's basketball coaching job in April 2010, but his seven-year contract proved to be so complex that it took 310 days for University of Oregon athletic director Rob Mullens to sign off on it.

"We just had to wait on the legal language," Mullens said.

This was hardly unusual. College coaching contracts, which once consisted of nothing more than a base salary from the university, had been transformed by corporate sponsorships and media partnerships into a complex web of win bonuses, media incentives, and endorsement revenues. Some contracts even include guaranteed perks like noncommercial air travel.

Altman's fifteen-page contract, which guaranteed him $1.8 million per year, included a $450,000 base salary from the university, plus $1.35 million for "activities related to media broadcasts and other activities" arising out of the school's agreements with IMG Communications and Nike. Altman owed much more of his livelihood to Nike, and to the school's broadcast partner, than to the university itself, which meant that his greater responsibility, in a sense, was to the Ducks brand and the Nike brand.

Coach Altman's contract also included certain financial incentives for advancing through certain stages of NCAA tournament play, which might explain why he allowed Dotson and Artis to participate in Oregon's second-round NCAA tournament win over Brigham Young University. And when Oregon was eliminated by Wisconsin during the tournament's third round, both players saw time on the court, despite the rape accusations looming over them while Austin remained sidelined. In total, Altman received $50,000 in bonuses for his team's performance in the tournament. Nike, meanwhile, made it through a widely viewed NCAA tournament without a major scandal surrounding players who were, in effect, walking billboards for the brand.

Several weeks after Oregon's NCAA tournament ended, the university at last sent students an email saying that a sexual assault had been reported near campus. The email came on April 10, two days after the Eugene Police Department told the university it had completed its investigation, which Lane County District Attorney Alex Gardner declined to carry any further, citing insufficient evidence. With criminal charges off the table, the university was able to handle the rape complaint as an administrative issue under the school's code of conduct, which required a disciplinary hearing. But the school's administrators once again elected to ignore protocol in favor of discretion by quietly negotiating an unusual arrangement with the athletes ahead of the disciplinary hearing: if Austin, Artis, and Dotson agreed to an administrative conference in which the outcome was decided solely by the university, with no outsiders involved, school officials could guarantee that they would not be expelled, and that there would be no mention of sexual misconduct on their transcripts, which would smooth the way for each of them to quietly transfer to another university. The school also delayed the disciplinary process until immediately after the academic quarter was over, allowing the players to finish their classes in good standing and transfer to other schools without harming the Oregon basketball program's Academic Progress Rate, which the NCAA uses to measure academic success in student-athletes. And no one, including the plaintiffs, would receive a physical copy of the final written outcome of the conference, the players were told. As more time passed, the few university officials who knew about the incident began to entertain the idea that it might remain hidden forever—a scandal that never was. They had, after all, largely avoided creating a paper trail that might become public, in part by keeping any record of the crime out of open records like the Clery crime log. But Eugene police detectives had run their own investigation, with its own paper trail, and in early May the department released a graphic twenty-four-page police report to local and national media. Shortly after seven o'clock on the evening of May 5, Julie Brown received a frantic text message from her boss, University of Oregon communications director Tobin Klinger.

"The story broke," Klinger wrote. "We need your help getting a statement from the president on his Web site. Call ASAP. We need to get it out. It's live, including the police report."

Klinger didn't need to tell Brown which story it was that had broken—this was, after all, the moment they'd prepared for since the day after the rape occurred. Now it was time for the university's public-relations staff to implement the crisis-management plan they'd been crafting, starting with a statement from Michael Gottfredson, who had taken over as university president following Lariviere's ouster.

"I am deeply troubled by the information contained in the police report released yesterday by the Eugene Police Department," Gottfredson wrote in a prepared statement. "The university has rigorous internal conduct processes that we follow when we receive a report such as this, as well as legal processes and a moral commitment to our students. We share a responsibility to provide a safe learning environment for our students, a responsibility I take very seriously."

It was, at best, a deeply disingenuous statement considering how long university officials had known about the sexual assault, how objectively lax its internal conduct and legal processes had been, and how weak its moral commitment to its students now seemed. Gottfredson personally knew about the rape accusations no later than March 19, 2014, according to court documents, which was days before Artis and Dotson played in their first NCAA tournament game of the season. But Gottfredson's statement was just one of many rolled out by the school's public-relations staff as it sought to promote Brown's "key messages" in the media. Vice President of Student Affairs Robin Holmes, who is a licensed clinical psychologist, granted an interview to the *Oregonian* to talk about the university's wealth of resources available to survivors of sexual assault—just as Brown's communications plan had outlined two months earlier.

"We have counseling center staff who have specialty in regard to sexual assault," Holmes said.

The student who accused the three basketball players of rape did, in fact, start visiting the university's Counseling and Testing Center, where students can avail themselves of affordable counseling. She met regularly with a therapist named Jennifer Morlok, unaware that university administrators would use the therapy session notes to spy on her.

At the University of Oregon's Counseling and Testing Center, a young woman's case file grew thicker, piled high with evidence of the emotional distress she'd suffered after being sexually assaulted. Her therapist, Jennifer Morlok, filled the file with notes detailing her trauma, and with details from conversations about her personal life and her family. The file was a sacred object, protected by a professional ethical code and by laws like the Federal Educational Records and Privacy Act (FERPA) and the Health Information Portability and Accountability Act (HIPAA). Like most sacred objects, a patient's counseling records are not obtained lightly; there are specific rules and rituals associated with gaining access to these kinds of records, so it was a surprise when Karen Stokes opened her email to find an oddly informal request for counseling records one day in December of 2014.

The request came from Shelly Kerr, who was part of a leadership team that Stokes supported as an executive assistant at the Counseling and Testing Center. In her email, Kerr asked Stokes to make a complete copy of the student's medical file and send it to the University of Oregon's general counsel. She asked Stokes not to stamp the copied pages, as they usually did with documents that were not originals. She also asked her not to document the fact that the file had been copied, and to discuss the matter with no one besides Kerr and two of her colleagues. Stokes was unnerved by the request, which violated a number of standard procedures and protocols, so she checked the student's file to see if it included a consent form authorizing the disclosure of medical records to the general counsel. When she found that it did not, she printed out Kerr's email and brought it to the young woman's therapist, Jennifer Morlok, who was equally confused about the request. As they talked, Stokes and Morlok soon reached a conclusion about what was going on: the university had mishandled the student's sexual-assault complaint and was anticipating a lawsuit, for which it sought to gain competitive advantage through access to the girl's confidential therapy records.

Two days later, Stokes learned that another employee had copied the file for Kerr, who personally brought it to the general counsel's office. It didn't take long for Stokes and Morlok to identify a number of potential ethical and legal breaches, and on January 25, 2015, armed with the printed email, Morlok filed complaints with the Oregon Board of Psychologist Examiners, alleging that Holmes, Kerr, and two others had committed ethics violations. She also filed complaints with the Oregon State Bar, which cleared the university's interim general counsel, Douglas Park, and associate general counsel, Samantha Hill, after finding "no evidence that the university's lawyers knew it was illegal or fraudulent" to take custody of the student's file. The U.S. Department of Education's chief privacy officer, Kathleen Styles, called this a legal loophole worthy of attention. Oregon Senator Ron Wyden and Representative Suzanne Bonamici further highlighted this loophole in a joint statement, emphasizing that it left students with fewer privacy protections than private citizens when it comes to health records.

"The last thing sexual assault victims should have to think about is whether their own words could be used against them when they seek help," they wrote.

Holmes, who encouraged sexual-assault victims to take advantage of the university's counseling services in her interview with the *Oregonian*, looked particularly untrustworthy after seeking private records from these kinds of sessions for use as opposition research to be used in the event of a lawsuit. And Shelly Kerr, who secured the records while attempting to cover her tracks, was fined $5,000 and forced to take ethics classes by the Oregon Board of Psychologist Examiners, which investigated Morlok's complaint and found that Kerr had breached the student's confidentiality. A month later, the University of Oregon reached a settlement with the student, paying her $800,000 while providing four years of free tuition, housing, and student fees.

One week after the settlement was reached, Morlok resigned in an open letter to the university's new president, Michael H. Schill, who succeeded Scott Coltrane, who had been tapped as interim president after Gottfredson resigned in the wake of the campus rape scandal, taking with him $940,000 in severance pay. Morlok was tired of the retaliation she'd faced after speaking out, she said, and discouraged by Schill's recent comments on the scandal.

"I do not believe any of our coaches, administrators, or other university personnel acted wrongfully," Schill had said. "Nor do I believe that any one of them failed to live up to the high moral standards that we value and that they embody in their work every day."

President Schill, Morlok wrote, had not spoken to her or to Kerr about their ordeal, and had failed to even consider the possibility that ethics violations had occurred, and in doing so "deflated hope by many that accountability and consequences would come to those who did wrong in leadership positions, causing harm along the way."

"I am thankful that the Oregon Board of Psychologist Examiners looks at all the evidence and does not carry blind loyalty and PR concerns as does a university," she wrote.

Early in 2011, Lisa Thornton took as job as an assistant in the public-records office at the University of Oregon. A decade and a half earlier,

Thomas Hager's News Bureau had been the office responsible for answering many requests for public records, which public universities produce constantly—emails, contracts, budgets, and virtually anything else generated by university employees are considered public-records, which are subject to the Freedom of Information Act and Oregon's generous open records laws. Gradually, more and more public-records requests went through Melinda Grier's office, earning her a reputation for keeping secret records that were meant to be public. In response to calls for greater transparency, a single public records office was created, with two full-time employees to handle all records requests, which mostly came from journalists. After just a few months on the job, Thornton was thrust into a leadership role when her boss suddenly quit, and she found herself in need of an assistant to do the job she'd been doing. The university called a local temporary work agency called Personnel Source, which sent a recent college graduate named Antonia Noori Farzan.

Farzan was hired after a brief interview and began working in October 2011. Her job was relatively straightforward: When a public records request came in, she would log it in the two internal databases used by the office of public records, noting the name of the requester, the record they were requesting, and the status of the request. Next she would send an email to the head of the department responsible for warehousing the particular record she'd need to retrieve in order to satisfy the request. Finally, she would put together an estimate of how long it would take to fulfill the request and how much it would cost in fees for the person requesting the record. On both of these points, it's useful to know something about public-records laws. The law requires that requests are fulfilled within a reasonable amount of time, and while schools may charge reasonable fees for things like copying, they may waive those fees for requests that are deemed to be in the public interest—things Farzan was surprised to learn had eluded Thornton, who once asked her what the law meant by "public interest."

Instead of serving the public interest by releasing public records according to the criteria clearly laid out in state and federal open-records laws, Thornton was largely concerned with two private fiefdoms within the university: the public relations department and the office of the general counsel.

"Lisa was particularly afraid that the public-relations department would get mad at her," Farzan said. "They have a lot of clout at the university."

Farzan witnessed this clout firsthand during her second day in the office, when members of the university public-relations staff arranged for a meeting with Thornton and her new assistant.

"She wore a fleece with the UO logo that day and told me that she had felt like she should wear some UO gear to the meeting," Farzan said. "I guess to show institutional loyalty or whatever. She seemed worried that they would ask for her to be fired if she did anything that they weren't happy with."

Institutional loyalty was precisely the point of the meeting that unfolded. In light of the ongoing NCAA investigation into Willie Lyles and his recruiting services for Oregon, the public-relations staff said it was important that any public-records request that might cast the university in a negative light be funneled through their department.

"We agreed to let them know about any request that was related to a major scandal," Farzan said. The university's public-relations department would sometimes instruct the public-records office not to release a record, or to delay its release until they said it was okay. Requests related to Nike, the NCAA, or the faculty union were among those automatically flagged for review by the public-relations department. Eventually, Thornton's office became even more stingy with public records.

"If there was a request from a professional journalist asking for anything more detailed than someone's salary or the contract for a new hire, Lisa just assumed that the topic was controversial and would flag it," Farzan said.

Controversial topics were also of special interest to Randy Geller and Douglas Park in the office of the general counsel. Thornton and Farzan cc'd Geller and Park on records requests that might prove harmful to the university's image or upsetting to important donors or corporate partners. When they didn't want some public record to be released, they had ways of making sure that it wasn't. One way of doing this was to take advantage of the fact that the school is allowed to charge requesters a fee for their records based on the cost of gathering and preparing them; by claiming the records required legal review, inflating the time it might take to conduct that review, and applying the same hourly fee they might charge a corporate client for their legal services, Geller and Park could offer to release a batch of records only if the requester was willing to pay some astronomical sum. (While reporting on the Austin, Artis, and Dotson rape scandal for *The New York Times*, I was told it would cost $9,493.95 to process my requests for emails and text messages between Oregon communications staff and administrators in the days after the rape occurred and in the immediate aftermath of the police report's release.) Thornton also liked to charge journalists as much as she could for records requests, even when they qualified for a public-interest fee waiver.

Another method favored by Geller, Park, and the assistant to the university president, Dave Hubin, was to redact entire pages whenever student privacy laws, like FERPA, gave them an opportunity to redact a student's name.

There were other things about Thornton's work that surprised Farzan.

"Her attitude toward journalists was pretty negative," Farzan said. "Right from the start she told me that she found them annoying, and there were certain reporters from the *Oregonian*, the *Register-Guard*, and the *Daily Emerald* who were making the majority of the requests, so she followed them from a private Twitter account in order to try and get a sense of what they were working on."

Thornton's policy was to charge journalists as much as she could for records requests, and to only give the "public service" waiver if a journalist could prove there was a lot of interest in what they were writing about—a crude misreading of the meaning of the term "public interest," which generally refers to the public good in the context of journalism. More than making journalists pay, Farzan said, Thornton loved giving them nothing at all.

"Lisa's policy was not to give out information if she could find any reason to withhold it," Farzan said.

This institutional obsession with secrecy trickled down from the top: Oregon administrators feared anything that might tarnish the university's brand or damage its valuable relationship with Nike, which in turn led faculty and staff to fear the school's powerful public-relations department. These fears, which led Thornton to disregard open-records laws in favor of absolute subservience to the university's public-relations arm, were not unfounded. In 2015, the University of Oregon fired two Knight Library archivists for releasing documents on Frohnmayer and Lariviere without first having them vetted for confidential information by the school's general counsel. The Society of American Archivists found the school's reaction unusually punitive considering the benign nature of the records released. The real issue, some felt, was the fact that the documents in question had been handed over to Bill Harbaugh, a University of Oregon economics professor who often criticized the school's administration on his blog.

Once a replacement was hired to take charge of special collections at the Knight Library, a new policy was implemented: student journalists, postgraduate researchers, and others requesting archival materials that were not part of an existing collection would be referred to the office of public records. It was an unusual policy, but struck most researchers as harmless, because most people had no inkling that the university's office of public records was, in fact, acting as an extension of its office of public relations.

Dave Frohnmayer was unusually active for a septuagenarian retiree fighting prostate cancer. For a few years, he remained president emeritus at the University of Oregon, and practiced law at a Eugene firm called Harrang Long Gary Rudnick. His work there sometimes veered into strange territory for someone who had spent so much of his personal life in hospitals, and so much of his professional life serving Oregon taxpayers: in April 2013, for example, he testified as a paid expert witness on behalf of major tobacco companies that were seeking to avoid the payment of hundreds of millions of dollars owed to the state of Oregon under the terms of a 1998 settlement over taxpayer funds that had been lost to tobacco-related health-care costs.

Outside of the courtroom, Frohnmayer continued to fight tirelessly against FA, which still threatened the life of his last living daughter, Amy. She was approaching thirty, which made her older than either of her big sisters had lived to be. Amy was accomplished, even for a Frohnmayer: She graduated from Stanford with a degree in psychology, then enrolled in a master's program at Oregon State University, where she studied to be a counselor. When she wasn't studying or helping her parents out with the Fanconi Anemia Research Fund, she loved hiking, white-water rafting, and scuba diving—anything that brought her outdoors. She was a natural athlete. At South Eugene High School, she'd played varsity tennis and cofounded a cross-country ski team, and she began running half marathons while she was an undergraduate at Stanford. Sometimes she logged thirty or forty miles a week, which worried her doctors, who constantly monitored her blood values. It wasn't recklessness, but an extraordinary determination to go after the experiences she truly wanted to have; watching her sisters die had shown her what it meant to miss out on those opportunities. When she was nineteen, Amy asked her doctors to let her run a full marathon, which they allowed her to do only after she agreed to take shots of EPO, a blood-boosting cancer drug that became famous after Lance Armstrong secretly used it to win the Tour de France.

"I guess I was kind of doping," Amy said. "But I made it—I did all 26.2, baby."

In 2013, Amy met Alex Winn, a pharmacist in Bend, Oregon. They began dating and by December 2014, things were serious enough that Alex went along on the Frohnmayer family's annual vacation to Hawaii. Dave and Lynn felt blessed to see their daughter so happy and healthy as she approached her thirties—a chapter of life that doctors had always said she'd never live to see.

A few months after the Frohnmayers returned from Kauai, on March 10, 2015, Dave Frohnmayer died in his sleep at the age of seventy-four. He was eulogized at length in the pages of Oregon's daily newspapers and weekly magazines, which noted both his long and storied political career and his tenure as the president who reshaped the University of Oregon more than any other—for better or for worse. In each of his obituaries, beneath his impressive list of accomplishments, was the line that would have pleased him most if he'd been able to read it:

"Dave is survived by his wife, Lynn, his sons, Mark and Jonathan, and his daughter Amy."

After her husband's death, Lynn Frohnmayer worried about the future of the Fanconi Anemia Research Fund, which continues to fund research aimed at improving and extending the lives of those living with FA. She called Phil Knight and explained how difficult it would be to raise funds without Dave's political connections and his Harvard friends.

"I asked him for $20 million," Lynn said, "and he gave me $10 million."

The following year, Knight announced the gift of $10 million to the Fanconi Anemia Research Fund, payable in annual instalments of $1 million. The gift, which was made in Dave's honor, will help identify new therapies for preventing and treating various cancers that afflict young people with FA, in the hope that more of them will live to adulthood, Lynn said.

"Phil Knight is a very honorable guy and a very caring guy," she said. "He's a very sentimental man, and a good man."

Chapter Ten

Rinse and Repeat

The University of Nike was born, in spirit, the moment Dave Frohnmayer withdrew the University of Oregon's membership in the WRC; in a more practical sense, the transformation was complete once Knight showed he could have university employees hired or fired; in an absolute sense, the takeover will not reach its apotheosis until the coming decade, with the opening of the Phil and Penny Knight Campus for Accelerating Scientific Impact.

The Knight Campus was announced ninety minutes before the sun rose over Eugene on the morning of October 18, 2016, with a series of Web sites, promotional videos, and press releases that made it seem more like a product launch than an academic undertaking: Knight pledged $500 million to fund the $1 billion Knight Campus, which will consist of three new 70,000-square-foot buildings, adjacent to the school's existing science complex, outfitted with cutting-edge laboratories, research facilities, prototyping tools, imaging facilities, and an innovation hub—an academic incubator, of sorts, that is sure to make every head in Silicon Valley bow. PayPal cofounder Peter Thiel turned heads, after all, with his fellowship program that pays a select few students to drop out of school and pursue research or business ventures. Knight, ostensibly a relic of old-school American capitalism, managed to transform what he found unprofitable about the public university.

It might not have happened if not for Richard Lariviere's vision for a more independent university, which unexpectedly came true in the middle of 2015: each of Oregon's seven public universities, long under the governance and oversight of a state board of higher education, were granted the right to have individual governing boards. Knight was approaching eighty and spending his $24-billion fortune more liberally than ever before, with gifts of $500 million to the Oregon Health & Science University and $400 million to Stanford. The time had come for Knight—with the help of Michael Schill, the fourth University of Oregon president since Frohnmayer's departure—to elevate the concept of the quasi-private public university to new heights.

The impressive speed with which they embraced such a major logistical undertaking was not what most surprised Thomas Hager, who had been in charge of the university's media relations during Frohnmayer's early years as president. As with the dramatic rebranding initiative that had been kept quiet years earlier, it was the fact that they had managed to keep it secret.

"I was struck by how the whole thing sprang full-blown, in a moment, from nothing to everything, with this packaged approach that gave no hint ahead of time that anything was coming," Hager said. "It was quite an example of PR-age."

The language of marketing and public relations seemed an appropriate vehicle for delivering news of the Knight Campus, which had been conceived, in secret, as a bridge between industry and the university. It would be "dedicated to fast-track science discoveries into innovations, products or cures," according to a press release, which said it would "reshape the higher-education landscape in Oregon by training new generations of scientists" while "forging tighter ties with industry and entrepreneurs."

Hager, along with many others on campus, struggled to understand what any of this actually meant.

"Very little was said about what kinds of things we are going to be researching, aside from bio-science and health stuff, which for me is very problematic because that means the pharmaceutical industry," he said. "There are serious ethical issues and questions over the role of the university in commercialization and product development when you're a public institution, and I haven't seen any evidence that those issues have been thought of or addressed."

Seven months later, when hundreds of Eugene residents gathered at a community center to learn more about the Knight Campus, President Schill gave no indication that he'd considered any of the ethical issues raised by members of his faculty. Instead, he offered up a buzzword-laden description of a project that seemed to border on neoliberal utopianism.

The Knight Campus, Schill said, would give researchers a way to move their laboratory discoveries more quickly into testing, so they could more quickly become "cures and solutions" for the problems facing society.

"That market signal," he said, "would turn around and benefit and inform their basic science—we call this the 'impact cycle.'

"One of the overarching goals of the Knight Campus," he added, "is to create a research-rich environment, gather together smart and innovative people, remove barriers, then that in turn would rapidly speed this impact cycle."

This raises an important question: Who will decide which barriers need to be removed from the path of the "impact cycle" at the University of Oregon's Knight Campus?

The architects and agents of the CIA's MK-Ultra program, for example, viewed basic constitutional and human rights as barriers to be eliminated. The Swiss pharmaceutical giant Novartis, in its partnership with UC Berkeley, tossed aside important ethical research practices, like the obligation to publish clinical-trial data, which it viewed as a barrier to innovation. When the Knight Campus announces its corporate partners—if it announces its corporate partners—where will the "impact cycle" lead the researchers working there? And what will they do if it leads them somewhere they had not prepared for or even imagined?

Recent history suggests that the University of Oregon will side with its corporate partners, which could be disastrous if the contracts they sign with Nike and other corporations are anything like those signed by UC Berkeley and Novartis. Under such terms, "cures and solutions," if they are unprofitable to the university's corporate partners, might be shelved; studies linking a corporation's food products to some disease or another might be buried; and clinical trials might be repeated but not published, ad nauseam, until a sponsor has the opportunity to tailor the variables in such a way that the product is shown only in the best possible light. University research, in these conditions, becomes a form of marketing rather than inquiry.

President Schill did not address precisely what barriers may be standing in the way of the University of Oregon's "impact cycle," nor how these obstacles might be removed through corporate partnerships. One of the less ominous answers is lack of funding. A state-of-the art facility might help Oregon recruit better scientists, just as its athletics facilities helped it recruit better athletes. And with the corporate backing and industry partnerships the Knight Campus promises, new tenure-track faculty might produce the kind of research needed to help the school win greater prestige and more federal grant money, both of which it could use.

Over the years, Knight's increasingly generous gifts brought athletic acclaim, brand recognition, and lucrative television and licensing deals to the University of Oregon. But they failed to bring a sense of stability to the school, and in some ways obscured the fraught reality of an institution constantly on the brink of peril. Frohnmayer and his successors relied on a crude but effective model for shoring up funds to replace declining state support for higher education: they used Knight's money to build Oregon athletics into a regional and national powerhouse, then leveraged the power of that brand to attract more out-of-state students, who pay higher tuition than Oregon residents. This worked so well that between 2004 and 2014 the percentage of Oregonians entering the school's freshman class declined from 68 percent to just under 50 percent. (It also worked well enough that, before it earned the nickname University of Nike, the school was often derisively called the University of California, Eugene.)

There was no commensurate hiring of new faculty, however, and throughout this same period, Oregon's staff remained poorly compensated relative to colleagues at peer universities. Some of these faculty were faced with ballooning class sizes, which pushed the faculty-to-student ratio beyond the point where Oregon could punch its weight, academically, against peer institutions where students had more one-on-one time with professors. To keep class size under control, administrators tended to hire adjunct professors, rather than tenure-track faculty. This saved the school money on salary and benefits, but it also won it fewer federal grants for the kind of research produced by tenured professors, and produced fewer PhD and graduate students emerging from under the tutelage of tenured faculty, whose research they often assist. In 2013, when the school at last dared to research which of its peer institutions produced fewer doctoral degrees per tenure-track faculty member, it found that the answer was none.

This strategy exacerbated the financial burden on a generation of students whose lives will be defined, in part, by the historic amount of debt they take on in order to attend college. When Measure 5 passed in 1990, students at Oregon's public universities paid for about 26 percent of the cost of their degrees, compared with 61 percent in 2015. The costs keep rising—between 2011 and 2016, out-of-state tuition at the University of Oregon jumped from $26,415 to $33,441, and that increase was preceded by a 10.2-percent increase, which itself followed just two years after a previous jump in the cost of studying at Oregon's flagship state university. These tuition increases, according to the school's vice provost for budget and planning, were aimed at shoring up the university's general fund, which subsidizes a number of programs and services that don't benefit students who are not athletes. One glaring example is the maintenance and staffing for the Jaqua Center for Student Athletes—millions of tuition dollars annually, which benefit only a select group of student-athletes. When students protested the latest tuition hikes ahead of the 2016 academic year, university administrators blamed the recent unionization of Oregon's faculty, which could be found at the bottom of its peer group of nine universities in terms of salary. And yet, annual tuition increases had been around for years before the faculty unionized, including the 10.2-percent increase that came in the academic year before Oregon professors joined the United Academics union.

These trends are set to continue for years to come, not by accident, but by design. In 2017, after five consecutive years of decreased enrollment of in-state students, the University of Oregon unveiled a $1.3 million plan to bring even more out-of-state students to Eugene. Five full-time recruiters, all based outside Oregon, were hired to bring in as many as 3,000 more out-of-state students over the course of several years.

Schill, meanwhile, has lobbied Oregon's legislature for more money to help pay for the Knight Campus. Knight's gift was the largest ever to a public university and, according to Schill, "the single most transformative event in the history of the University of Oregon since its founding." But it was also a $500-million bill that Schill is asking Oregon taxpayers to subsidize, not unlike the debt-accruing state bonds that were sold to pay for the construction of the Matthew Knight Arena. Students, meanwhile, continue to pay higher tuition with each passing year: in 2018, Oregon residents would pay double the tuition and fees they would have a decade earlier, while out-of-state students saw an increase of 60 percent.

Lack of funding aside, there are more ominous barriers University of Oregon administrators may seek to remove in the name of closing the "impact cycle" at the Knight Campus. One of them is transparency.

When it appeared that the University of Oregon had attempted to cover up rape accusations against three of the school's basketball players, lawyers for *The New York Times* filed legal motions arguing for the release of emails between certain administrators and public-relations staff. One of those lawyers was Victoria Baranetsky, who noted in legal motions that the school had demonstrated a willingness to "use privacy as both a sword and a shield" in order to prevent public scrutiny of its handling of sexual assault on campus. This argument would seem to be consistent with the methods Lisa Thornton passed down to her employees as head of the university's office of public records—methods that included allowing the school's public-relations department and its general counsel to review documents it did not want released, so that they could find reasons to claim exemptions, sometimes illegitimately. The general counsel, in particular, was happy to redact entire documents even when the law called only for certain names to be blacked out, according to Thornton's former assistant.

This pattern of behavior, combined with an important exemption from state and federal open-records laws that allows for the redaction of public records that might reveal trade secrets, suggests that much of what goes on at the future Knight Campus for Accelerating Scientific Impact may be shielded from public oversight. This is especially concerning given the potential for ethical violations at an institution hoping to raise $500 million through corporate partnerships. What kinds of promises or compromises might a school be willing to make under such circumstances? Frohnmayer's various concessions to Knight set a worrying precedent that may pale in comparison to the potential for corruption that surrounds the Knight Campus.

If there are backroom deals to be cut or promises to be made in the search for new corporate partners, they may be coming sooner rather than later: in 2017, the University of Oregon asked lawmakers to approve $100 million in state bonds to help fund the Knight Campus, and were given $50 million; a year later, they asked for another $40 million and again walked away with half of what they requested. Representative Nancy Nathanson, a key architect of the state's budget, said she was surprised the university had come back for more money so soon.

In early March 2018, when the university broke ground on the construction of the Knight Campus, just $70 million of its half-billion-dollar shortfall was covered. President Schill told the crowd that had assembled that his school would need every dollar it could get its hands on.

"We are hoping the state will provide us with more money," he said.

At the tail end of March, in 2017, head men's basketball coach Dana Altman brought the Oregon Ducks to the Final Four after a 78-year absence from college basketball's biggest stage. As with Oregon football, much of the credit went to Phil Knight, who had helped build the opulent basketball arena that then helped the school's basketball program recruit the kind of talent it needed to win. And while the school's programs have performed well, they have never managed to stay out of trouble: recruiting scandals, sexual-assault accusations, and legal troubles among student-athletes have been persistent side effects of Nike's experiment at the University of Oregon. The school's approach to these problems, much like Nike's approach to the issue of sweatshop labor, has been to strive for eliminating the appearance of trouble, rather than rooting out the trouble itself. This suggests that such problems may be a feature, rather than a bug, at the University of Nike, which would explain why the university learned no lessons from the campus rape scandal of 2014. Two years later, the school allowed Kavell Bigby-Williams to play in thirty-seven basketball games with rape allegations hanging over his head.

Bigby-Williams was a promising prospect from London, England, who transferred to Oregon from Gillette College in Wyoming, where he was named National Junior College Player of the Year before his transfer was finalized during the summer of 2016, when he joined a Ducks roster already stacked with talent. Altman's new recruit seemed like the perfect addition to help the Ducks make the jump from the NCAA's Elite Eight tournament to its first Final Four since 1939.

Bigby-Williams arrived on campus in late August and joined his new teammates on a four-game tour of Spain, then returned to Gillette to say his goodbyes to friends and former teammates before the beginning of fall term. In late September, three days after classes began, a detective at the University of Oregon's campus police department received a phone call about Bigby-Williams. Brooke Tibbetts, who worked as a campus police officer at Gillette College, was investigating a sexual assault. She told Kathy Flynn, the detective in Oregon, that Gillette's campus police received the sexual-assault complaint on the evening of September 19, when a friend of the alleged victim contacted their department. The girl was upset and acting strangely, her friend told Tibbetts, and she had a large bruise on her neck. She suspected that the girl had been drugged and raped at a party she'd attended on the evening of September 17.

When Tibbetts arrived at the girls residence, the girl told the officer that she didn't remember anything, so she couldn't say for sure that she'd been raped. But she recalled drinking whiskey and vodka, then blacking out at some point after ten o'clock on the evening of the party, and when she woke at 3:30 in the morning on September 18, she was naked and bleeding from her sore vagina. When she went to the hospital for a pregnancy test and screening for sexually transmitted diseases, she couldn't account for the painful bruises on her neck or recall the name of the man who had given them to her. But her three roommates, who were there on the night of the party, did have a name for Tibbetts: Kavell Bigby-Williams.

The girl had thrown up in a trash can around midnight, then passed out on her bed, according to her roommates. Once they noticed how strangely she was acting the next day, two of the roommates confronted Bigby-Williams, who told them he'd had consensual sex with the girl on the evening of the party. After taking photographs of the alleged victim's bruises, and collecting her sheets and clothing as evidence, Tibbetts felt confident she had enough evidence and witness testimony to move forward with an interview of Bigby-Williams. She suspected he had committed sexual assault in the first degree by having intercourse with someone who was unable to consciously consent. But by then her suspect had left for Oregon. Tibbetts repeatedly called her suspect, and sent him text messages, but he didn't respond, so she reached out to Oregon's campus police and asked Detective Flynn to conduct an interview for them. Flynn reviewed the campus police report Tibbetts sent her, as well as the photos and text messages, then tried contacting Bigby-Williams herself. The basketball player brushed the investigator off, repeatedly, until one day she heard from Gillette College's assistant basketball coach, Nick Carter, who is also an attorney in Wyoming. He called to ask her not to contact Bigby-Williams again. So, with little else to do, Detective Flynn notified the appropriate officials within the University of Oregon's administrative structure. One of the people Flynn told about the case was Darci Heroy, who had recently been hired as the Oregon's Title IX coordinator, charged with ensuring that the school acted in compliance with federal law when it came to investigating sexual harassment, sexual assault, and gender-based harassment or discrimination. The other person was Lisa Peterson, a deputy athletic director who served as Heroy's deputy Title IX coordinator.

Heroy's work on Title IX issues at the school began in April 2015, in the aftermath of the campus rape scandal that cost Michael Gottfredson his job as university president. The school's new president, Michael Schill, publicized her appointment at a time when colleges around the nation were doing all they could to signal that they had heard President Obama's stern missive urging America's universities to do more to prevent campus sexual assault and investigate its aftermath.

One of Heroy's responsibilities as Title IX coordinator was to notify the school's director of the Office of Student Conduct and Community Standards, Sandy Weintraub, whenever she learned of sexual-assault allegations against a student. Weintraub would then decide whether it would be necessary to take emergency actions, like suspending the accused student or limiting their ability to participate in activities outside of class—activities like athletics, for example. And yet, when Weintraub tallied the number of sexual-assault cases the risk-assessment team handled during the academic year beginning in 2016, the one allegedly involving Bigby-Williams was not among the twenty-one they arrived at. The Title IX investigation into the basketball player was stopped, quite literally, before it even got started. It had stopped with Heroy and Peterson.

In these early stages of an investigation into sexual misconduct on campus, establishing guilt or innocence is not the goal; instead, Weintraub and Heroy are supposed to lead an initial "risk assessment" to determine what level of protection other students on campus might require, if any, while an investigation into the allegations runs its course. It is not, therefore, up to Heroy to determine that there is no risk and that Weintraub does not need to be involved in the matter; it is, in fact, explicitly Heroy's responsibility to inform Weintraub and then, in concert, decide whether a suspension of any kind is warranted while campus police or university administrators carry out an investigation. And yet Heroy kept Weintraub out of the loop and decided, with help from a deputy Title IX director who works in the athletic department, that Bigby-Williams posed no risk to the campus community.

When news of the case was reported in the media in June 2017, the University of Oregon's massive public relations staff once again mobilized, as they had during the Artis, Dotson, and Austin scandal. Director of communications Tobin Klinger played a key role in containing both rape scandals, which the school managed by compartmentalizing information and ensuring that only public-relations professionals, like Klinger himself, spoke to the media. When circumstances demand it, an administrator or member of the athletic department might give a press conference, but under no circumstances would they answer questions from the media or the public. One reason for this was to keep university and athletic department officials from telling a lie that might end their careers if the truth came out later. Any lies Klinger might tell on behalf of someone in the school's administration or its athletic department, if revealed, could be chalked up to his own misunderstanding. And because he's a communications professional, with experience and training, Klinger excels at phrasing comments to the press for maximum deniability if they prove to be untrue or problematic later on. In the case of the Bigby-Williams incident, for example, Klinger was asked by journalists whether Coach Altman knew that his player had a sexual-assault allegation hanging over his head throughout the season. Instead of answering the question directly, Klinger merely suggested an answer by saying that it's the school's practice not to notify coaches when their student-athletes stand accused of sexual assault. It may have been a lapse in public-relations judgment that compelled Klinger to suggest Oregon's athletes are so frequently accused of sexual assault that the school needs such a policy, but it's also possible he didn't answer the question straightforwardly because a direct denial would have been a lie.

In the two days after University of Oregon officials first learned of the criminal sexual-assault investigation into Bigby-Williams, Altman's phone records show he talked five times with the school's deputy Title IX director, Lisa Peterson, who works in the school's athletic department. His phone records, which were first obtained by student reporter Kenny Jacoby, also showed that during those same two days, Altman spoke on four occasions with the player's former basketball coach at Gillette College. These calls, which began on the day that Officer Flynn informed Heroy and Peterson of the investigation, illuminated one possible reason for hiring Peterson as the school's deputy Title IX director: it was not unusual, as Klinger would later claim, for her to be speaking on the phone with Altman, who she worked with in the athletic department—even if phone records showed that the two of them ordinarily did not talk by phone.

In the end, Klinger would again claim the university's failure to investigate a basketball player accused of sexual assault was in deference to a criminal investigation, which was ironic in the Bigby-Williams case, since the referral had come to school administrators directly from sworn police officers in two different states. But it also demonstrated a certain ignorance about Title IX laws, which, Obama's task force on campus sexual assault reiterated, don't relieve a school of its obligation to investigative sexual-assault complaints in cases where a criminal investigation is also taking place.

Heroy, meanwhile, went so far as to say that it was not unusual that Weintraub was not informed about the Bigby-Williams investigation since she didn't need to hear about "absolutely every disclosure that comes in." This, too, is in violation of the school's own written procedures for a Title IX investigation. The case file, Heroy said, had been vague, without enough evidence to determine whether an assault had occurred, and so there was no formal investigation. Putting aside this bit of circular logic—he seemed innocent, so we didn't investigate, because there was no crime—and the fact that it was not Heroy's place to make these determinations unilaterally, there is a great deal of evidence suggesting the case file was not as thin as Heroy has claimed.

Jacoby, the Oregon student reporter, learned that police in Wyoming provided University of Oregon officials with a substantive police report on September 28, 2016. Inside were multiple witness statements indicating that the girl had vomited and passed out in her bed before Bigby-Williams had sex with her—sex that the basketball player claims was consensual, but which could not have been under Wyoming law unless the girl woke up clear-eyed and conscious between the hours of midnight and 3:00 a.m., then had consensual sex with Bigby-Williams and promptly forgot about it when she woke up at 3:30 that morning. The police report Oregon officials received also included text messages and more than forty photographs. Klinger nevertheless claimed there had been "insufficient" evidence to warrant an investigation—not a determination of guilt, but an investigation, under the rules of Title IX, which call for only a preponderance of evidence, not proof of guilt beyond a reasonable doubt. When the same student reporter asked President Schill whether he was aware Bigby-Williams had played an entire season for the Oregon Ducks while under investigation by law enforcement for sexual assault, Schill replied, glibly, that he could not comment on an individual student.

"What if I was asked by another reporter about you being obnoxious?" Schill said. "Would you want me to tell them that?"

———

Dana Altman's basketball team was not alone on campus with its Title IX woes in 2016. Throughout the course of the year, seven of Oregon's football players were accused of some kind of sexual misconduct or gender-based violence. One of these cases involved Tristan Wallace and Darrian Franklin, who were accused of sexually assaulting two different women at a house party that took place in late September at Eugene's Courtside Apartments. A third student-athlete was accused of a separate assault at the same house party, according to a person with knowledge of the investigation, but that individual remains anonymous because the victim chose not to move forward with her complaint.

University officials learned in early October that Wallace and Franklin were accused of vaginally penetrating two women who said they didn't want to have sex, but who were too intoxicated to resist the men's advances physically. Head coach Mark Helfrich suspended both players, but the school made no announcements, and both men remained on the Oregon Ducks roster throughout November. Finally, in December, the *Oregonian* reported on the criminal investigation that had been quietly proceeding for months, leading Craig Pintens, Oregon's senior associate athletic director for marketing and public relations, to announce that they had both been suspended indefinitely. In early January, Willie Taggart took over as head coach for Oregon's football team, and all seven players accused of Title IX violations in 2016 quietly vanished from the team's official roster.

Behind the scenes, university employees with knowledge of these cases grew increasingly frustrated with how the school handled things.

"We need to be more forthcoming when these things happen instead of waiting for the public to ask questions," one insider said. "Looking like you covered something up is worse than acknowledging there is a problem and handling it."

University employees also had serious concerns about the motives of the school's public-relations department and its general counsel.

"Decisions are being made based on how bad things might look from a public relations standpoint and how likely we are to get sued," another administrator said. "Sometimes that leads us to make the wrong decision."

At a glance, the University of Oregon's fear of litigation seems to have an outsized influence over how the school chooses to handle reports of sexual assault. The reality is even more cynical. It's all in the odds: an athlete accused of sexual assault will invariably defend themselves against the allegations at all costs, while a victim of sexual assault will often decide not to pursue justice; of the small number of rape victims who do report the crime, and who follow up on the investigation, a certain number will give up when the pressure and their trauma becomes too intense; and those few who follow a case to its conclusion will be likely to accept an out-of-court settlement, relieved to be able to move on from their ordeal. When universities bet against a victim, they rarely lose; betting against the accused, on the other hand, would cost them more financially, the math suggests, especially when one considers the great number of additional rape accusations that would be associated with the university brand and the brand of its corporate benefactor.

Only this kind of cynical calculation could explain why Klinger defended Oregon's handling of the Bigby-Williams case by claiming the Wyoming police report proved "insufficient" in determining whether a crime had been committed, when in fact there was a detailed thirty-eight-page report that Officer Tibbetts felt was evidence of sexual assault in the first degree. Wyoming police, Klinger said, had made it clear in their report that the complaint came from a third party, rather than the victim herself.

"The voice of a survivor is the key to an investigation," University of Oregon police chief Matt Carmichael said. Without it, there was no point in proceeding, he said, apparently unaware that Title IX does, in fact, demand just the opposite. But with a victim who was not pushing hard for justice, the school chose to place its usual bet. Late in the summer of 2016, Bigby-Williams transferred to LSU, where recruiters were eager to have him.

Inside the university, people involved with various aspects of dealing with the school's Title IX complaints began feeling fatigued and let down. Depressed, they began to worry about whether the same kind of reflexive, protect-the-brand mentality might infect the Knight Campus as well.

"It isn't really an athletics thing," one such person said. "It's an obsession with protecting the brand and keeping people from giving testimony in open court."

The brand, apart from its value to Nike and IMG Communications, is also an important tool for increasing enrollment at the University of Oregon, where attracting out-of-state undergraduates remains central to the school's strategy for replacing the money it has lost due to declining state funds for higher education. And this, more than anything else, may explain why American universities seem to be getting worse, not better, at dealing with campus sexual assault.

American universities that receive federal funding—all of them, basically—are required to release an annual security report that details, among other things, the number of sexual assaults reported in the campus community that year. These statistics are a source of dread for university administrators, who know that parents will be more hesitant to send their children to schools where a high number of sexual assaults have been reported. And since universities have yet to find meaningful ways of preventing campus sexual assault, some desperate administrators have decided instead to fudge the statistics by doing whatever they can to prevent formal reports of sexual harassment and assault. At the University of Oregon, one such instance occurred in 2013, when a PhD student named Erica Midttveit tried to report a professor who had clearly violated the school's policies surrounding sexual harassment and conflicts of interest. At the school's Office of Affirmative Action and Equal Opportunity, an equal-opportunity specialist named Anne Bonner advised her not to file a formal complaint against the professor.

"She told me that if I filed a formal complaint, [the professor] would know it was me and they couldn't do anything to protect me,"

Midttveit said. "They said I should just let them handle it informally, and that they'd handle it exactly the same way as if I had filed a complaint."

A year later, Midttveit was called into the office of Robin Holmes, the vice president for student life. The professor, Holmes told her, would quietly resign and move to a different institution. Midttveit, however, had no recourse for the abuse she'd suffered or the damage that had been done to her academic career. After all, she hadn't filed a formal complaint.

It was a shock for Midttveit, who saw, for the first time, how far her school would go to protect the brand it had built. Once it had been a university with an out-of-control athletic department, then it became, for a time, more like an athletic department besieged by unruly educators. Now there was harmony: it was a university united by a common mission.

Amy Frohnmayer became acquainted with death early. She spoke about it plainly; when her sisters died, she refused to use euphemisms like "passed away." Her father's death was different. It was the first time she'd had to process the death of a family member as an adult, and it was hard on her. She coped by adding extra miles to her daily run. A year after the Frohnmayer's last family vacation in Hawaii, Amy and Alex returned, and he proposed to her on the beach. She said yes.

Several months later, Amy was running along the Deschutes River Trail, in Bend, Oregon, when a sharp, sudden pain coursed through her spine. She ran through the pain, and it passed, but a few weeks later it suddenly returned. After a trip to the emergency room revealed dangerously low blood counts, she was admitted to the Knight Cancer Institute at Portland's Oregon Health and Science University (OHSU), which was made possible by a $500-million gift from the Nike billionaire. The marrow of her bones was ridden with leukemia cells. A few days after her diagnosis, she was flown to the University of Minnesota Medical Center for a cord-blood expansion, which would be followed by chemotherapy. When she wasn't too weak or too sick, Amy walked the halls of the hospital, where eleven laps added up to a mile, and on her good days she logged four miles. In June 2016, she and Alex were married in a ceremony at the hospital, dressed in scrubs. Later that month, Amy graduated from her master's program at OSU, and took part in the ceremonies using Skype. Six weeks after her procedure, it was clear that it had been a failure. She returned to the Knight Cancer Institute at OHSU.

In late September of 2016, Amy began saying goodbye to family and friends from her hospital bed. One day, while talking with her brother, she tearfully recounted the joy of completing the marathon she ran while she was an undergraduate at Stanford University. One minute she was crying and the next she was laughing, but she did both with a smile as her brother asked her to tell more stories. When Amy arrived at a difficult moment, her brother pulled her out of it by asking her to recite the final lines from a Mary Oliver poem she'd once read to him.

"In this life, you must be able to do three things," she said, paraphrasing the poem from memory. "To love what is mortal; to hold it against your bones as though your life depends on it; and three, in the end, to let it go. To let it go."

Just before dawn on October 2, she did.

What began as an attempt to save one public university has become an effective blueprint for corporatizing any number of public colleges, with proponents like David Carter, executive director of the Sports Business Institute at Southern California's Marshall School of Business.

"Phil Knight and Nike have essentially created a lab at the

University of Oregon," Carter said. "The students welcome that. As long as the programs perform well and stay out of trouble, it's rinse and repeat."

The University of Maryland, for one, has studied the Oregon blueprint exactly: in 2014, the school signed a $33-million equipment deal with Under Armour, an athletic apparel company founded by Maryland alumnus Kevin Plank. The university, which has lost 20 percent of its state funding since 2000, will also be getting renovated athletics facilities courtesy of Plank. Its football team, which joined the Big Ten conference in 2014, will help test the next generation of Under Armour products as the company sets its sights on Nike, having already overtaken Adidas as the second-largest retailer of sporting apparel in America. Maryland's athletic director, Kevin Anderson, has been happy to credit the University of Nike as his inspiration.

"I saw the beginnings of what Nike did with Oregon and that's been our conversation from day one, that we can have that kind of relationship," Anderson said. "Before Nike got involved with the University of Oregon, nobody knew where Eugene was."

And it's true: for someone in Maryland or New York, Eugene is almost certainly easier to find on a map than it was twenty years ago. But for people living there, the question of where Eugene has ended up is difficult to agree on—a land of dreams for Joey Heisman, and nightmares for Jane Doe. What they can agree on is how it got there.

Afterword

In the summer of 2018, while I was finalizing the manuscript for this book, two former Nike employees were busy preparing a sexual harassment lawsuit against the company. Kelly Cahill and Sara Johnston had each worked for years at Nike's Beaverton, Oregon headquarters, which they described as "an unclimbable pyramid" for women, who faced a culture of sexual harassment and gender bias.

Johnston, for example, was offered an annual salary of $33,000 when Nike hired her as an account service representative, and was told that the company does not negotiate starting salaries. "However, about two months after I was hired, Nike hired a man into the same role on my team, and his starting annual salary was $35,000," she said. "He was able to negotiate a higher starting salary even though I had more relevant experience and higher-level credentials. He had no idea how to do the job and I had to train him, but he was paid more than I was."

Cahill, meanwhile, was paid $20,000 less than a male colleague on her team, and was passed over for promotion despite her significant experience and expertise. When she left Nike, she said, her role was filled by a man who was paid a higher salary than she'd been earning.

"At Nike," their lawsuit alleged, "the numbers tell a story of a company where women are devalued and demeaned." They were so devalued and demeaned, in fact, that Nike's top executives had never bothered to tally, much less reckon with, the numbers that told this story. So, in early 2018, a group of women working at the company's Beaverton headquarters banded together to do it themselves. Using an informal survey, they quietly gathered evidence of the individual and collective harm women had endured at every level of Nike's corporate hierarchy: inappropriate sexual and romantic advances; lower wages than their male colleagues; and, relative to male peers within the company, fewer opportunities for advancement and promotion.

On March 5, 2018, the results of the survey landed with a thud on the desk of Nike CEO Mark Parker—a thick packet filled with documentary evidence of systemic, company-wide sexual harassment and gender discrimination. And because these surveys had been gathered in guerrilla fashion, by a group of employees not all known to Parker, the unflattering picture they painted could not be covered up; the narrative would not be set by Nike, but by *The New York Times*, which soon reported on the "exodus of male executives" that followed: Trevor Edwards, who was well positioned to succeed Parker as CEO, left the company amid accusations of inappropriate behavior. His lieutenant, Jayme Martin, also departed, along with at least ten senior managers.

Months later, in August 2018, Cahill and Johnston filed their lawsuit, which soon attracted more plaintiffs. But after dragging on for over a year, the case had slowed to a crawl, as Nike's attorneys pressed for greater secrecy concerning documents the company was asked to produce—documents Nike hopes to have marked "confidential," even if they do not contain trade secrets. Meanwhile, in a federal courtroom in Manhattan, an unrelated scandal threatened to pierce the veil of secrecy surrounding what may be the oldest of Nike's misdeeds: cheating NCAA recruiting rules.

Like so many scandals, it began with the slighting of a seemingly minor figure. Gary Franklin Sr., who spent more than a decade nurturing talent through his youth basketball club, California Supreme, took it personally when Nike opted not to renew his contract in 2018. It was a significant loss for Franklin, whose contract with Nike had for years guaranteed him at least

$70,000 annually for directing California Supreme, which was one of more than forty clubs in Nike's Elite Youth Basketball League (EYBL).

Grassroots programs like California Supreme are a direct descendant of Sonny Vaccaro's early efforts to circumvent the NCAA's rules on recruiting in college athletics. Each year, shoe companies like Nike and Adidas spend hundreds of thousands of dollars organizing spring and summer tournaments built around clubs like California Supreme, which outfit their players exclusively in gear provided by their sponsor. The players, who are aged seventeen and under, are often viewed by college recruiters as the top prospects in their respective regions.

Sonny Vaccaro told *The New York Times* that Franklin "had a reputation as one of the good guys," who avoided even a whiff of controversy. And yet, the very existence of programs like California Supreme, and the vast sums of money Nike and Adidas pay to support them, seemed to suggest that they have aims beyond distributing free sneakers to talented high school basketball players. In March 2018, after Nike opted not to renew his contract, Franklin and his friend Jeffrey Auerbach, a sports consultant, exchanged text messages regarding what the California Supreme director knew about the illicit aims of Nike's EYBL.

In one of those text messages, Auerbach discussed confronting John Slusher, Nike's executive vice president for global sports marketing, over the company's participation in "collusion, fraud and corruption," which included introducing "handlers" for the purposes of "procuring players illegally." The plan, they agreed, was to stress that Franklin was approaching Slusher out of loyalty, "with the hope Nike Corporate will do the right thing and swiftly take action, investigate and fire these rogue Nike EYBL executives, who have no place in youth and amateur basketball." Otherwise, Auerbach advised, "your plan is to go directly to the FBI within the next 5–10 days to expose everything that's transpired."

These "rogue" Nike executives were Carlton DeBose and Jamal James, and what had transpired seemed to be a lot of illegal activity:

In emails from 2016, Franklin and DeBose appeared to discuss how they could best get $10,000 to the mother of Deandre Ayton, a high school prospect who would go on to play for the Arizona Wildcats—a Nike school—before entering the 2018 NBA draft, where he was chosen first overall by the Phoenix Suns. In the end, Franklin was tasked with delivering Andrea Ayton's payment in cash, to avoid leaving a paper trail. Another $30,000 bribe, Franklin said, went to Ayton's "handler," Mel McDonald.

Seven months later, in October 2018, Franklin and Auerbach were still discussing the plan, which had come to include more concrete demands. Auerbach suggested asking Nike for "fair and reasonable reparations to the California Supreme Youth Basketball program," which he felt should be in the neighborhood of $150,000. He also suggested a stipulation that California Supreme would receive a new five-year contract with Nike. It must have seemed like an ideal moment for reminding Nike just how much Franklin knew about its recruiting practices, and how much they stood to lose by shutting him out of the scheme: earlier that month, a jury in New York had convicted two Adidas executives, and an aspiring agent, of federal charges stemming from payments they'd made to ensure that promising recruits signed with Adidas-sponsored colleges. On February 6, 2019, while those Adidas executives awaited sentencing, Auerbach at last called Nike executive John Slusher about the Franklin situation.

In a memo, Auerbach described telling Slusher that he was calling on Franklin's behalf to report the "bullying and abuse" he'd suffered under DeBose and James, and the "ongoing corruption and illicit schemes" these Nike executives had directed Franklin to engage in—"Actions similar to those in the recent DOJ-Adidas case," Auerbach wrote. The subtext, previously discussed by Auerbach and Franklin, was that the coach could be persuaded to describe Nike's illegal activities as the work of "rogue" employees, rather than a broader criminal conspiracy that was, in fact, the very essence of the EYBL.

Slusher told Auerbach that he'd turned the matter over to Nike's outside counsel at Boies, Schiller, and Flexner. Disillusioned,

Auerbach and Franklin turned to Michael Avenatti, a pugnacious attorney with a talent for litigating cases in the headlines of major newspapers. On March 18, 2019, Auerbach sent Avenatti an email detailing his correspondence with Slusher—one week later, the flamboyant attorney would find himself behind bars, accused of attempted extortion.

On the evening of March 25, Avenatti swung open the brass doors of the federal courthouse in downtown Manhattan, where dozens of reporters were waiting to greet him outside. U.S. Marshals cleared the path toward an idling SUV that would whisk the celebrity lawyer away, but Avenatti instead rushed to face the media.

"As all of you know, for the entirety of my career, I have fought against the powerful—powerful people and powerful corporations," he said. "I will never stop fighting that good fight."

His most recent fight had been with Donald Trump, who'd allegedly paid $130,000 in hush money to Avenatti's client, Stormy Daniels, to cover up an affair with the adult film star. This time, however, Avenatti's quarrel was with federal prosecutors, who had summoned him to court as a defendant, not as counsel, to face extortion charges.

The indictment against Avenatti stemmed from an ultimatum he'd laid at Nike's door: Avenatti and his client, Gary Franklin, planned to go public, in the midst of March Madness, with evidence that Nike executives had violated NCAA recruiting rules. But for a price, they would agree to handle things more quietly, Avenatti said. Nike could avoid the harsh media spotlight by paying $22.5 million for the lawyer and his client to "ride off into the sunset."

Just hours before his appearance outside of the courthouse, Avenatti had used his Twitter account to announce a press conference in which he promised to "disclose a major high school/college basketball scandal perpetrated by @Nike," which, he said, involved criminal conduct that "reaches the highest levels of Nike and involves some of the biggest names in college basketball." What he didn't know was that Nike lawyers had secretly recorded his blunt proposal, and brought the recordings to federal authorities, who later secured an indictment. Twenty-three minutes after sending the tweet, Avenatti was in FBI custody for what Geoffrey S. Berman, the U.S. District Attorney for the Southern District of New York, called an "old-fashioned shakedown."

Soon after Avenatti's arrest, I received a phone call from Kevin Draper, a reporter for *The New York Times*; the hardcover edition of this book, which had then been on sale for five months, detailed at length Nike's history of doing business in the world of college athletics, and Draper wanted to know what I thought of the accusations against Nike.

I told him first that I would not be surprised if Avenatti's allegations proved in time to be true—my reporting, after all, documented similar recruiting methods that the company had used as far back as the early 1970s. Nike's sponsorship of the distance runner Steve Prefontaine, for example, had relied on a bold lie that was designed to evade rules which disqualified professional runners from taking part in the Olympics. Instead of following that rule, Nike's co-founder and CEO, Phil Knight, gave Prefontaine a $5,000 salary and a business card that said he was Nike's National Director of Public Affairs—a subterfuge that Knight would later boast about.

Knight's success in business has depended largely on the fact that he made up his own rulebook. It should come as no surprise, then, that the company he founded continues to ignore all rulebooks which are not its own.

Before hanging up, I told Draper that there was one other way in which Nike had lived up to its past behavior: When confronted with allegations that he had slept with Stormy Daniels, and that he sought to cover up that fact, history's most shameless American president was chastened enough to deny it. Executives at Nike instead went on the attack when Avenatti offered to sell his silence.

"Avenatti's mistake," I told Draper, "was to try and shame a corporation that has spent decades demonstrating its utter shamelessness."

In November 2019, I spoke to Avenatti myself. His trial, scheduled for January 2020, would vindicate him, he said. It would also uncover more secrets that Nike might prefer to keep buried—documents associated with the case have already suggested Nike paid bribes to determine which colleges could sign young prospects like Bol Bol, Deandre Ayton, and Zion Williamson; more big names would make headlines once Avenatti had his day in court, he told me.

"What you've seen so far is just a small fraction of what's going to come out at trial," he said. "There's a mountain of evidence showing a pattern of widespread corruption that extends from Nike boardrooms to the very top NCAA programs—even the ones that like to pretend they are above that kind of behavior."

Avenatti was unrepentant when asked whether he regretted approaching Nike as bluntly as he did, and suggested the company's lawyers had sought to entrap him. A year or two earlier, this accusation might have seemed laughable. But David Boies, chairman of Boies, Schiller, and Flexner, which represented Nike in the Franklin affair, had recently experienced what *The New York Times* deemed "an unprecedented public relations disaster": Harvey Weinstein, a longtime client of the firm, was accused of numerous sexual assaults, and reporting by the *New Yorker* and the *Times* showed that Boies and his firm had for years helped the powerful producer silence his victims through the use of settlements and non-disclosure agreements—just the sort of brokered silence which the FBI deemed criminal once Avenatti suggested using it to resolve the Franklin affair.

It was not an isolated incident for the firm. In his book "Bad Blood," *Wall Street Journal* reporter John Carreyrou documented how Boies and his firm sought to intimidate whistleblowers at Theranos, a client which paid Boies half of his fees using company stock, giving him a strong financial incentive to shield the company's image in the face of mounting evidence that its founder, Elizabeth Holmes, was a fraud.

"These guys play dirty, which is why Weinstein and Theranos hired them," Avenatti said. "It's why Nike hired them, too."

Behind the company's illicit recruiting practices and its sexual harassment scandal, Avenatti believes, is a toxic "culture of corruption that reaches to the very highest levels of leadership, infecting everything the company does."

He was no longer speaking solely of his own experiences with the company. In October 2019, a new scandal emerged, and it did stretch to the highest levels of leadership at Nike: Emails contained in a decision reached by anti-doping authorities showed that Nike CEO Mark Parker had been briefed on several occasions regarding medical experiments aimed at determining how various banned substances could be used by athletes without being detected. The experiments were conducted by Alberto Salazar, who oversaw an elite Nike running program called the Oregon Project. As a result of the decision, authorities barred Salazar from track and field for four years for violating anti-doping rules.

One of Salazar's experiments, conducted at Nike's headquarters in Beaverton, involved testing the effects of a topical testosterone product called AndroGel. Two squirts of the gel, Salazar told Parker in an email, produced only a slight rise in testosterone/epitestosterone levels—nothing that would trigger concern among anti-doping authorities. Next, he wrote, they would repeat the experiment using three pumps of the performance-enhancing testosterone gel.

In an email, Parker told Salazar it "will be interesting to determine the minimal amount of topical male hormone required to create a positive test."

On October 1, when the Salazar news broke, Parker sent Nike employees an email that some found "oddly defensive."

"As for Alberto, it's clearly a difficult time for him, his family and his athletes," Parker wrote. "We will continue to support him in his appeal as a four-year suspension for someone who acted in good faith is wrong."

Three weeks later, Nike announced Parker would be stepping down from his role as CEO. In the interim, Nike once more made headlines: On October 12, the Nike-sponsored distance runner Eliud Kipchoge became the first person to finish a marathon in less than two hours. The Kenyan's miraculous time was a marvel of physiology, training, and planning: Nike outfitted Kipchoge in prototype shoes not yet available to the public, placed him behind an electric car that covered each mile in exactly four minutes and thirty-four seconds, and gave him thirty-five pacesetters, some of whom were Olympians, to share the work of shielding him from the wind. Because of these unusual advantages, Kipchoge's extraordinary achievement will not be recorded as a world record. And because of the Oregon Project scandal, some may wonder whether another asterisk will one day be affixed to Kipchoge's unbelievable marathon time of 1 hour 59 minutes and 40 seconds.

A few years ago, this level of skepticism might fairly have been called cynical—Kipchoge, after all, has never tested positive for performance-enhancing drugs. But in the wake of the Oregon Project, which sought to undermine the tests meant to catch drug cheats, it would be naïve to discount the people an athlete chooses to align themselves with. In Kipchoge's case, this means Nike and its Oregon Project, as well as the London-based professional cycling team Ineos, formerly known as Team Sky, which backed the Kenyan's marathon effort. The team and its leader, Dave Brailsford, were mired in controversy in 2017, when star rider Chris Froome tested positive for banned substances at a race in Spain, and again in 2018, when a parliamentary committee found that Team Sky had abused the anti-doping system in order to allow its athletes to use performance-enhancing drugs. More recently, Kipchoge's coach, Patrick Sang, has proved to be a liability to his reputation as a clean athlete: In April 2019, anti-doping authorities suspended Kenyan distance runner Cyrus Rutto, who is also coached by Sang.

Doping scandals create a unique kind of blowback—by undermining the legitimacy of extraordinary feats of athleticism, they lead us to doubt the kinds of achievements that draw us to sporting events in the first place. Those who want to believe in Kipchoge's achievement must convince themselves that he is a once-in-a-generation talent while also ignoring his associations with corporations, teams, and individuals who have been linked to systemic doping programs. In short, athletes who rely more than ever before on scientists and statisticians have, paradoxically, come to expect that their fans rely on faith alone.

There was a time, not so long ago, when Nike specialized in selling these kinds of dreams. Whether they still can may depend on how much damaging news emerges in open court, and the extent to which it can be pinned on rogue executives. Avenatti's tarnished reputation may help Nike limit the fallout from the Franklin affair, but widespread gender discrimination, sexual harassment, and doping programs will be tougher to blame on "rogue executives." The 2020 presidential race might make it tougher still: Democratic contenders like Elizabeth Warren and Bernie Sanders have already shown their willingness to take on corporations practicing the kind of predatory capitalism that Nike helped pioneer. Should one of them win the White House, they may be eager to take on big tech powerhouses like Facebook and Amazon; or they might instead choose to start with Nike—mired in scandal, besieged by leaks and lawsuits, and, in the wake of the Adidas case, a prime candidate for prosecution using documents the government has already obtained for the Avenatti case.

Nike would, in many ways, be a fitting appetizer for any politician who wishes to make a meal of America's tech giants: Phil Knight's company moved fast and broke things; it dealt with authoritarian regimes whenever the price was right; it put profits before country and before workers; it did everything it could to avoid paying taxes; and it subjected countless overseas laborers to untold miseries, while cultivating an atmosphere hostile to women at its U.S. headquarters.

In October 2018, during a book talk at Google's Seattle campus, I asked the crowd of employees to think back to 1998—a year in which Nike's reputation suffered so greatly that Phil Knight was forced to acknowledge publicly that his company had "become synonymous with slave wages, forced overtime, and arbitrary abuse," while quoting a columnist who said "Nike represents not only everything that's wrong with sports but everything that's wrong with the world." This, I explained, was what the world thought of American corporations in 1998, when Sergey Brin and Larry Page founded Google. And it may be why they felt it was necessary to adopt the slogan "Don't be evil." This remained a guiding principal for Google until 2018, when the slogan was retired after twenty years. The change was, perhaps, a sign that Google's ambitions have come to require greater moral flexibility. Or, just maybe, it was evidence of what really separated Phil Knight, and the company he built, from the rest of the pack: ruthless ambition, not as a last resort, but as a guiding principle, embraced from day one, while others spend years, even decades, trying to convince themselves that their corporation will be different.

Joshua Hunt
November 2019

Note on Sources

This book is based on more than a hundred interviews, supplemented by many thousands of pages of financial, legal, and archival documents. It was reported without the cooperation of some key figures, and some of the territory it covers has become clouded by mythmaking over the years, so, in the interest of accuracy, dialogue has been drawn largely from historical documents, like letters, emails, and transcripts of speeches, and from contemporaneous newspaper, magazine, and television reports.

The narrative structure of this book benefitted tremendously from consistent, excellent coverage of the University of Oregon and Nike by local and regional newspapers like the *Oregonian* and the *Register-Guard*, and weekly newspapers like *Willamette Week*. I also owe a great deal to generations of diligent young reporters at the University of Oregon's student-run newspaper, the *Daily Emerald*. My immense debt to these newspapers, and to others, will be clear to anyone who peruses the endnotes for this book.

It should also be noted that certain facts presented here will invariably be disputed by some of the parties concerned. Such facts sometimes concern trivial matters, like the fastest mile Phil Knight ran in college, which is either 4:10 or 4:13, depending on whether you believe what the billionaire told Stanford's alumni magazine in 1997 or what he told Bloomberg in 2017. Other times, the facts in dispute concern consequential moments in Nike's history, such as the parties responsible for signing Michael Jordan as Nike's pitchman. In each case, I've done my best to be dispassionate when deciding which sources to privilege, and I feel comfortable with the choices I've made.

Endnotes

Introduction

vii: **a developing story for *The New York Times*:** Joshua Hunt, "3 Oregon Basketball Players Face Rape Allegations," *The New York Times* (New York, NY), May 6, 2014.

vii: **a graphic twenty-four page police report:** Incident Case Number 14-04131, "Rape 1—Forcible," filed with the Eugene Police Department on March 13, 2014.

viii: **Uncle Phil:** Author's interviews with UO faculty, students.

ix: **University of Michigan announced a $169 million contract:** Kurt Svoboda, "Reunited: Michigan and NIKE Announce Partnership," Michigan Athletics press release, July 6, 2015.

After the details were finalized in 2016, the contract's value rose to $173.8 million.

ix: **until the University of Texas at Austin:** Matthew Watkins, "UT Signs Record-Breaking Apparel Deal with Nike," *Texas Tribune* (Austin, TX), October 30, 2015.

ix: **property-tax cuts that left state colleges to fend for themselves:** Ballot Measure 5 and Oregon's tax revolt: Chapter 5. Richard J. Ellis, *Oregon Politics and Government: Progressives versus Conservative Populists*, Edited by Richard A. Clucas, Mark Henkels, and Brent S. Steel (Lincoln: University of Nebraska Press, 2005), pages 67–69.

ix: **in 2017, for the first time, public colleges:** "State Higher Education Finance: Fiscal Year 2017," State Higher Education Executive Officers Association, pages 16–34.

Chapter One

3: **Philip Hampson Knight was seven years old:** Kerry Eggers, *The Civil War Rivalry: Oregon vs. Oregon State* (Charleston: The History Press), 2014), page 378.

Knight said he was "seven or eight," but must have been seven because Washington did not play Oregon at Multnomah Stadium at any point while he was eight.

3: **fielding teams for the first time in two or three years:** Charles Einstein, "When Football Went to War," *Sports Illustrated*, December 6, 1971.

3: **braving overcast skies:** Dick Strite, "Battling Ducks Drop Game to Washington, 7-0," *Eugene Register-Guard* (Eugene, OR), November 4, 1945.

3: **one out of every ten residents:** United States Census Bureau population data for Portland, Oregon, 1940.

3: **". . . Dad, which is the good team?'":** Kerry Eggers, *The Civil War Rivalry: Oregon vs. Oregon State* (Charleston: The History Press), 2014, page 378.

3: **perched atop the resurgent Pacific Coast Conference:** Dick Strite, "Battling Ducks Drop Game to Washington, 7-0," *Eugene Register-Guard* (Eugene, OR), November 4, 1945.

3: **"He set me straight":** Kerry Eggers, *The Civil War Rivalry: Oregon vs. Oregon State* (Charleston: The History Press, 2014), page 378.

3: **William Knight's loyalty:** University of Oregon Archives Department, university archives biographical files, 1930s–present, UA Ref 2, Box 6; UPI, "William Knight, Former Publisher, Dies at Age of 72," *Eugene Register-Guard* (Eugene, OR), February 19, 1981.

4: **fierce, union-busting lawyer:** "Duncan Says News Strike Role Doubtful," *Eugene-Register Guard* (Eugene, OR), January 22, 1960; J. B. Strasser and Laurie Becklund, *Swoosh: The Unauthorized Story of Nike and the Men Who Played There* (New York: HarperCollins, 1992), pages 8–9.

4: **Phil tried his hand:** J. B. Strasser and Laurie Becklund, *Swoosh: The Unauthorized Story of Nike and the Men Who Played There* (New York: HarperCollins, 1992), page 9.

4: **His solitary nature:** Phil Knight, *Shoe Dog: A Memoir by the Creator of Nike* (New York: Scribner, 2016), page 2.

4: **". . . I was going to Oregon":** Kerry Eggers, *The Civil War Rivalry: Oregon vs. Oregon State* (Charleston: The History Press, 2014), page 378.

4: **". . . Bowerman was the guy":** Kerry Eggers, *The Civil War Rivalry: Oregon vs. Oregon State* (Charleston: The History Press, 2014), page 378.

5: **Bill Hayward, who spent forty-four years:** University of Oregon Archives Department, sports information and media guides, 1890–2014, UA Ref 5, Boxes 26, 28, 39, and 59.

5: **coached four track world record holders:** Blaine Newnham, "Pages Out of Time," *Eugene Register-Guard* (Eugene, OR), June 22, 1980.

5: **Knight arrived at the University of Oregon:** Phil Knight, "My Fill-In Father," *The New York Times* (New York, NY), June 17, 2016.

5: **". . . weird, dope-fueled ideas":** Chip Brown, "Ken Kesey Kisses No Ass," *Esquire*, September 1992.

5: **earned him the nickname Buck:** Phil Knight, *Shoe Dog: A Memoir by the Creator of Nike* (New York: Scribner, 2016), pages 13, 20.

5: **brought the childhood nickname to college with him:** J. B. Strasser and Laurie Becklund, *Swoosh: The Unauthorized Story of Nike and the Men Who Played There* (New York: HarperCollins, 1992), page 10.

5: **"I hadn't broken a rule, let alone a law":** Phil Knight, *Shoe Dog: A Memoir by the Creator of Nike* (New York: Scribner, 2016), page 2.

5: **which had become the family business:** UPI, "William Knight, Former Publisher, Dies at Age of 72," *Eugene Register-Guard* (Eugene, OR), February 19, 1981.

5: **imagined becoming a novelist or a statesman:** Phil Knight, *Shoe Dog: A Memoir by the Creator of Nike* (New York: Scribner, 2016), page 3.

5: **TrackTown, U.S.A.:** University of Oregon Archives Department, University Archives sports information and media guides, 18902-2014, UA Ref 5, Boxes 26, 28, 38, 39, 41, 45, 59, 57, and 66.

6: **He felt that the sport was for "sissies":** Geoff Hollister, *Out of Nowhere: The Inside Story of How Nike Marketed the Culture of Running* (Maidenhead: Meyer and Meyer Sport, 2008), page 17.

6: **Spencer Butte:** Geoff Hollister, *Out of Nowhere: The Inside Story of How Nike Marketed the Culture of Running* (Maidenhead: Meyer and Meyer Sport, 2008), page 17.

6: **group photographs:** University of Oregon Archives Department, University Archives sports information and media guides, 18902-2014, UA Ref 5, Boxes 26 and 28.

6: **"the white mole":** J. B. Strasser and Laurie Becklund, *Swoosh: The Unauthorized Story of Nike and the Men Who Played There* (New York: HarperCollins, 1992), page 7.

6: **"a good squad man":** J. B. Strasser and Laurie Becklund, *Swoosh: The Unauthorized Story of Nike and the Men Who Played There* (New York: HarperCollins, 1992), page 10.

6: **running the mile in just four minutes and thirteen seconds:** David Rubenstein, *The David Rubenstein Show* (June 28, 2017; Bloomberg TV), television broadcast.

7: **"That was one of the great games of the rivalry":** Kerry Eggers, *The Civil War Rivalry: Oregon vs. Oregon State* (Charleston: The History Press, 2014), pages 378–379.

7: **the last drops of Confederate and Union blood:** Richard Gardiner, "The Last Battlefield of the Civil War and Its Preservation," *Journal of America's Military Past*, vol. 38, spring/summer 2013, pages 5–22.

7: **gathered around a sawdust field:** Author unknown, *Daily Eugene Guard* (Eugene, OR), November 5, 1894.

7: **"an absence of slugging on either side":** Author unknown, *Corvallis Gazette* (Corvallis, OR), November 3, 1894.

7: **when Rutgers beat Princeton:** William H. S. Demarest, *A History of Rutgers College, 1766–1924* (New Brunswick: Rutgers College, 1924), pages 425–430.

7: **"demand a high grade of classwork . . .":** Kerry Eggers, *The Civil War Rivalry: Oregon vs. Oregon State* (Charleston: The History Press, 2014), page 22.

8: **An "athlete's code of honor . . .":** Henry Beach Needham, "The College Athlete: How Commercialism is Making Him a Professional," *McClure's Magazine*, June 1905, page 115.

8: **In February 1898, Brown University hosted a conference:** Henry Beach Needham, "The College Athlete: How Commercialism is Making Him a Professional," *McClure's Magazine*, June 1905, page 115.

8: **"It is obvious":** Henry Beach Needham, "The College Athlete: How Commercialism is Making Him a Professional," *McClure's Magazine*, June 1905, page 115.

8: **" men of weight and muscle":** Henry Beach Needham, "The College Athlete: How Commercialism is Making Him a Professional," *McClure's Magazine*, June 1905, page 118.

8: **resorted to hiring ringers:** Robert McCaughey, *Stand, Columbia: A History of Columbia University in the City of New York, 1754-2004* (New York: Columbia University Press, 2003), page 279.

8: **"the virus of the game":** John Watterson, "Reputation Reclaimed," *College Football Historical Society*, vol. 17, no. 1, November 2003.

8: **the sport had grown to be immensely popular:** Kerry Eggers, *The Civil War Rivalry: Oregon vs. Oregon State* (Charleston: The History Press, 2014), page 23.

9: **there were 18 deaths and 159 serious injuries recorded:** Joseph C. Maroon, Christina Mathyssek, and Jeffrey Bost, "Cerebral Concussion: A Historical Perspective," *Progress in Neurological Surgery, vol. 28, Concussion*, edited by A. Niranjan and L. D. Lunsford, page 2.

9: **President Theodore Roosevelt:** Author unknown, "Teddy Roosevelt Jr. Hurt on Football Field," the *Salt Lake Herald* (Salt Lake City, UT), October 15, 1905; Author unknown, "Nineteen Killed on Gridiron," the *San Francisco Call* (San Francisco, CA), November 27, 1905; Author unknown, "For Reform of Football," *New York Tribune* (New York, NY), December 13, 1905; Author unknown, "How to Play Football Under New Rules," *New York Tribune* (New York, NY), September 23, 1906.

9: **Football schools increasingly sought to distinguishs:** Henry Beach Needham, "The College Athlete: How Commercialism is Making Him a Professional," *McClure's Magazine*, June 1905.

9: **The turnaround was so swift and absolute:** University of Oregon Archives Department, sports information and media guides, 1890s–2014, UA Ref 5, boxes 9 and 37.

10: **Oregon's profound cultural and economic divisions:** Chapter 1, Richard A. Clucas and Mark Henkels, *Oregon Politics and Government: Progressives versus Conservative Populists*, Edited by Richard A. Clucas, Mark Henkels, and Brent S. Steel (Lincoln: University of Nebraska Press, 2005), pages 1–16.

10: **much more than pride on the line:** Kerry Eggers, *The Civil War Rivalry: Oregon vs. Oregon State* (Charleston: The History Press, 2014), page 260.

10: **"This is what I've wanted ever since . . .":** Kerry Eggers, *The Civil War Rivalry: Oregon vs. Oregon State* (Charleston: The History Press, 2014), page 311.

11: **A good amount of that attention fell on Danny O'Neil:** Kerry Eggers, *The Civil War Rivalry: Oregon vs. Oregon State* (Charleston: The History Press, 2014), page 312.

11: **"The value of my life was directly related . . .":** Phil Milani, *Blast from the Past: Danny O'Neil Keeping the Faith* (July 2011; Eugene, OR: KVAL, an affiliate of Central Broadcasting Service), television broadcast.

11: **On game day:** *University of Oregon at Oregon State University*, (November 19, 1994; Corvallis, OR: American Broadcasting Company), television broadcast.

12: **". . . and it's for real":** University of Oregon Archives Department, University Archives sports information and media guides, 18902-2014, UA Ref 5, Box 8.

12: **Stanford and Michigan contested the first Rose Bowl:** "All Is Ready for Contest: Gridiron Warriors in Fine Fettle, Michigan and Stanford Rest Before the Fray," *Los Angeles Herald* (Los Angeles, CA), January 1, 1902.

12: **America's first nationally broadcast college football game:** Edward Gruver, *Nitschke* (Lanham: Taylor Trade Publishing, 2002), page 48.

12: **when Oregon faced Ohio State in the 1958 Rose Bowl:** *The Rose Bowl Game: Oregon vs. Ohio State*, (January 1, 1958; Pasadena, CA: National Broadcasting Company), television broadcast.

12: **By 1983, NBC was paying $7 million:** Gerald R. Gems, Linda J. Borish, and Gertrud Pfister, *Sports in American History: From*

Colonization to Globalization (Champaign: Human Kinetics, 2008), page 322.

12: **guaranteed each team more than $6 million:** Andrew Zimbalist, "Unpaid Professionals," *The Business of Sports* (Sudbury: Jones and Bartlett, 2004), edited by Scott R. Rosner and Kenneth L. Shropshire, page 505.

13: **Oregon's unexpected return to Pasadena:** *Rose Bowl: Oregon vs. Penn State*, (January 2, 1995; Pasadena, CA: American Broadcasting Company), television broadcast.

13: **with no grander plan:** Author's interviews with Dave Frohnmayer.

13: **Beverly and Robert Lewis:** Office of the Vice President for Research and Innovation, "Robert and Beverly Lewis: A History of Giving at the University of Oregon," *University of Oregon* (Eugene, OR), February 25, 2013: http://research.uoregon.edu/news/around-campus/robert-and-beverly-lewis-history-giving-university-oregon

13: **raising the funds he would need:** Author's interviews with Dave Frohnmayer.

13: **Ballot Measure 5:** Chapter 13. Mark Henkels, *Oregon Politics and Government: Progressives versus Conservative Populists*, Edited by Richard A. Clucas, Mark Henkels, and Brent S. Steel (Lincoln: University of Nebraska Press, 2005), pages 213–215.

13: **a whopping 10.5 percent:** David Sarasohn, "State Colleges: Onward and Downward," the *Oregonian* (Portland, OR), February 12, 1995.

13: **Frohnmayer knew that the University of Oregon:** University of Oregon Archives Department, Dave Frohnmayer, major speeches, box 1, "State of the University Address," 150 Columbia, University of Oregon, 3:00 p.m. on October 5, 1994.

13: **Tom and Carol Williams:** Melody Ward Leslie, "The Williams Effect," *Oregon Quarterly*, winter 2016, pages 16–18.

13: **Jim Rippey:** University of Oregon Archives Department, Dave Frohnmayer, major speeches, box 1, "State of the University Address," University of Oregon, September 27, 1995.

14: **forced the university to raise its tuition:** University of Oregon Archives Department, Dave Frohnmayer, major speeches, box 1, "The Promise of Public Higher Education," Portland City Club, December 8, 1995.

14: **"one of the great men of our times":** Telephone message left for Dave Frohnmayer by Bill Bowerman at 12:30 p.m. on April 24, 1994, transcribed by Frohnmayer's assistant.

14: **The NCAA had just instituted new limits:** William C. Rhoden, "NCAA Cuts Practice, Scholarships and Seasons," *The New York Times* (New York, NY), January 10, 1991.

14: **an obstacle no NCAA rule could affect:** Author's interviews; Austin Murphy, "Waiting for the Hate," *Sports Illustrated*, November 4, 2013.

14: **The University of Oregon's most prominent alumnus:** Kenny Moore, *Bowerman and the Men of Oregon* (New York: Rodale, 2006), page 156.

15: **"Never underestimate yourself":** Kenny Moore, *Bowerman and the Men of Oregon* (New York: Rodale, 2006), page 86.

15: **Herbert Hoover founded Stanford Graduate School of Business:** John Pearce Mitchell, *Stanford University: 1916–1941* (Stanford: Stanford University Press, 1958), pages 79–80.

15: **responsible for half the world's manufacturing:** "World Economic Survey 1956," *United Nations Department of Economic and Social Affairs*, New York, 1957.

15: **"a little on the wimpy side . . .":** J. B. Strasser and Laurie Becklund, *Swoosh: The Unauthorized Story of Nike and the Men Who Played There* (New York: HarperCollins, 1992), page 12.

15: **". . . it was unclear whether he did have goals":** J. B. Strasser and Laurie Becklund, *Swoosh: The Unauthorized Story of Nike and the Men Who Played There* (New York: HarperCollins, 1992), page 11.

15: **a small business class taught by Frank Shallenberger:** Kenny Moore, *Bowerman and the Men of Oregon* (New York: Rodale, 2006), page 156.

15: **"Adidas was taking advantage":** Kenny Moore, *Bowerman and the Men of Oregon* (New York: Rodale, 2006), page 157.

16: **He was reminded of something:** Jackie Krentzman, "The Force Behind the Nike Empire," *Stanford Magazine*, January/February 1997.

16: **a plane bound for Japan on Thanksgiving Day:** J. B. Strasser and Laurie Becklund, *Swoosh: The Unauthorized Story of Nike* *and the Men Who Played There* (New York: HarperCollins, 1992), page 15.

16: **He visited the track at the University of Tokyo:** Kenny Moore, *Bowerman and the Men of Oregon* (New York: Rodale, 2006), pages 157–158.

17: **"Faked out Tiger Shoe Co.":** J. B. Strasser and Laurie Becklund, *Swoosh: The Unauthorized Story of Nike and the Men Who Played There* (New York: HarperCollins, 1992), page 17.

17: **He penned a letter to his father:** Phil Knight, *Shoe Dog: A Memoir by the Creator of Nike* (New York: Scribner, 2016), page 31.

17: **Kihachiro Onitsuka:** Author unknown, "An Era's Leader: Kihachiro Onitsuka, President of Asics," *Nikkei Business* (Tokyo, Japan), August 19, 1985; J. B. Strasser and Laurie Becklund, *Swoosh: The Unauthorized Story of Nike and the Men Who Played There* (New York: HarperCollins, 1992), pages 18–21.

18: **Knight received his first shipment of samples:** J. B. Strasser and Laurie Becklund, *Swoosh: The Unauthorized Story of Nike and the Men Who Played There* (New York: HarperCollins, 1992), pages 30–31.

18: **Onitsuka's sole U.S. distributor since 1959:** J. B. Strasser and Laurie Becklund, *Swoosh: The Unauthorized Story of Nike and the Men Who Played There* (New York: HarperCollins, 1992), page 36.

18: **"Here is a sample . . .":** J. B. Strasser and Laurie Becklund, *Swoosh: The Unauthorized Story of Nike and the Men Who Played There* (New York: HarperCollins, 1992), pages 31–33.

19: **". . . one of my former half-milers . . . ":** Geoff Hollister, *Out of Nowhere: The Inside Story of How Nike Marketed the Culture of Running* (Maidenhead: Meyer and Meyer Sport, 2008), page 42.

19: **Bowerman pulled aside Geoff Hollister:** Geoff Hollister, *Out of Nowhere: The Inside Story of How Nike Marketed the Culture of Running* (Maidenhead: Meyer and Meyer Sport, 2008), pages 16–21.

19: **Hollister turned down a generous scholarship to attend Oregon State:** J. B. Strasser and Laurie Becklund, *Swoosh: The Unauthorized Story of Nike and the Men Who Played There* (New York: HarperCollins, 1992), page 65.

19: **Bowerman continued to give valuable feedback:** Kenny Moore, *Bowerman and the Men of Oregon* (New York: Rodale, 2006), pages 181–184.

19: **Bowerman's endorsement was crucial:** J. B. Strasser and Laurie Becklund, *Swoosh: The Unauthorized Story of Nike and the Men Who Played There* (New York: HarperCollins, 1992), page 34.

19: **Bowerman also helped Knight:** Geoff Hollister, *Out of Nowhere: The Inside Story of How Nike Marketed the Culture of Running* (Maidenhead: Meyer and Meyer Sport, 2008), pages 42–43.

19: **Hollister's first meeting with Knight:** Geoff Hollister, *Out of Nowhere: The Inside Story of How Nike Marketed the Culture of Running* (Maidenhead: Meyer and Meyer Sport, 2008), page 42.

19: **at a Dairy Queen restaurant:** Author's visits.

20: **"Buck forgot his wallet":** Geoff Hollister, *Out of Nowhere: The Inside Story of How Nike Marketed the Culture of Running* (Maidenhead: Meyer and Meyer Sport, 2008), page 42.

20: **dedicated sales representatives like Jeff Johnson:** Kenny Moore, *Bowerman and the Men of Oregon* (New York: Rodale, 2006), pages 260-262.

20: **The Hollister family home:** Geoff Hollister, *Out of Nowhere: The Inside Story of How Nike Marketed the Culture of Running* (Maidenhead: Meyer and Meyer Sport, 2008), page 42.

20: **Hollister took it upon himself:** Geoff Hollister, *Out of Nowhere: The Inside Story of How Nike Marketed the Culture of Running* (Maidenhead: Meyer and Meyer Sport, 2008), page 55.

20: **"You'd think I was bleeding Buck dry . . .":** Geoff Hollister, *Out of Nowhere: The Inside Story of How Nike Marketed the Culture of Running* (Maidenhead: Meyer and Meyer Sport, 2008), page 55.

21: **the company soon opened retail outlets:** J. B. Strasser and Laurie Becklund, *Swoosh: The Unauthorized Story of Nike and the Men Who Played There* (New York: HarperCollins, 1992), pages 58, 61.

21: **doubts about the size of Knight's operation:** District of Oregon Court, *Blue Ribbon Sports vs. Onitsuka Co., 1973*.

21: **"Get it as high as you can without lying":** J. B. Strasser and Laurie Becklund, *Swoosh: The Unauthorized Story of Nike and the Men Who Played There* (New York: HarperCollins, 1992), page 82.

21: **Knight was cultivating a spy:** J. B. Strasser and Laurie Becklund, *Swoosh: The Unauthorized Story of Nike and the Men Who Played There* (New York: HarperCollins, 1992), pages 80–81.

21: **". . . the illogical Japanese mind . . .":** J. B. Strasser and Laurie Becklund, *Swoosh: The Unauthorized Story of Nike and the Men Who Played There* (New York: HarperCollins, 1992), page 80.

21: **". . . schools for industrial spies . . .":** J. B. Strasser and Laurie Becklund, *Swoosh: The Unauthorized Story of Nike and the Men Who Played There* (New York: HarperCollins, 1992), page 81.

22: **"While it is somewhat remote . . .":** J. B. Strasser and Laurie Becklund, *Swoosh: The Unauthorized Story of Nike and the Men Who Played There* (New York: HarperCollins, 1992), page 81.

22: **growing pains on both sides of the Pacific:** District of Oregon Court, *Blue Ribbon Sports vs. Onitsuka Co., 1973;* J. B. Strasser and Laurie Becklund, *Swoosh: The Unauthorized Story of Nike and the Men Who Played There* (New York: HarperCollins, 1992), pages 88–90.

22: **Nissho Iwai:** J. B. Strasser and Laurie Becklund, *Swoosh: The Unauthorized Story of Nike and the Men Who Played There* (New York: HarperCollins, 1992), page 92.

22: **the birth of a shadow brand called Nike:** J. B. Strasser and Laurie Becklund, *Swoosh: The Unauthorized Story of Nike and the Men Who Played There* (New York: HarperCollins, 1992), page 116.

22: **a new swoosh logo:** J. B. Strasser and Laurie Becklund, *Swoosh: The Unauthorized Story of Nike and the Men Who Played There* (New York: HarperCollins, 1992), pages 111–112.

22: **Knight had the logo tattooed:** Kenneth Labich, "Nike vs. Reebok," *Fortune*, September 18, 1995.

23: **Johnson had a dream about the Greek goddess:** Kenny Moore, *Bowerman and the Men of Oregon* (New York: Rodale, 2006), page 269.

23: **Dimension 6:** J. B. Strasser and Laurie Becklund, *Swoosh: The Unauthorized Story of Nike and the Men Who Played There* (New York: HarperCollins, 1992), pages 114–116.

23: **". . . a parallel development to our Tiger line":** Kenny Moore, *Bowerman and the Men of Oregon* (New York: Rodale, 2006), page 270.

23: **What distinguished them among competitors like Adidas and Puma:** J. B. Strasser and Laurie Becklund, *Swoosh: The Unauthorized Story of Nike and the Men Who Played There* (New York: HarperCollins, 1992), page 129.

24: **acts of corporate espionage:** District of Oregon Court, *Blue Ribbon Sports vs. Onitsuka Co., 1974, deposition of Philip H. Knight.*

24: **One step ahead of Japanese backers:** Phil Knight, *Shoe Dog: A Memoir by the Creator of Nike* (New York: Scribner, 2016), pages 165–166; J. B. Strasser and Laurie Becklund, *Swoosh: The Unauthorized Story of Nike and the Men Who Played There* (New York: HarperCollins, 1992), page 116.

24: **Knight could more easily hide the New England factory:** J. B. Strasser and Laurie Becklund, *Swoosh: The Unauthorized Story of Nike and the Men Who Played There* (New York: HarperCollins, 1992), page 156.

24: **Steve Prefontaine discovered his love of running:** Bill McChesney, *Stories of Steve Prefontaine: The "Legend" of Tracktown, U.S.A.*, 1981. University of Oregon Archives of Northwest Folklore, 1981_027.

24: **Marshfield High School:** Author's visit to Coos Bay, Oregon.

24: **his father worked as a carpenter:** University of Oregon Archives Department, university archives biographical files, 1930s–present, UA Ref 2, Box 8.

24: **"Coos Bay is a sports-minded town":** Pat Putnam, "The Freshman and the Great Guru," *Sports Illustrated*, June 15, 1970.

25: **didn't really impress coach Walt McClure:** Kenny Moore, *Bowerman and the Men of Oregon* (New York: Rodale, 2006), page 235.

25: **". . . I didn't want to lose":** Pat Putnam, "The Freshman and the Great Guru," *Sports Illustrated*, June 15, 1970.

25: **he put Prefontaine on a special thirty-week training program:** Michael Musca, "Steve Prefontaine's High School Career," *Runner's World*, October 1, 2006.

25: **Instead, he sent two of his best distance runners:** Kenny Moore, *Bowerman and the Men of Oregon* (New York: Rodale, 2006), page 235.

25: **"If you want to come to Oregon":** Kenny Moore, *Bowerman and the Men of Oregon* (New York: Rodale, 2006), page 236.

26: **he appeared on the cover of the June 1970 issue:** Pat Putnam, "The Freshman and the Great Guru," *Sports Illustrated*, June 15, 1970.

26: **by the time he was nineteen:** University of Oregon Archives Department, Bill Bowerman Papers, 1932–1999, UA 003, Box 17, Folder 8.

26: **Bowerman was obsessed with every aspect of running:** University of Oregon Archives, Bill Bowerman Papers, 1932–1999, UA 003, Box 71, folder 14; box 72, folders 5 and 16.

26: **Wearing a pair of Bowerman's waffles:** Geoff Hollister, *Out of Nowhere: The Inside Story of How Nike Marketed the Culture of Running* (Maidenhead: Meyer and Meyer Sport, 2008), page 72.

27: **usually wore Onitsuka Tigers:** J. B. Strasser and Laurie Becklund, *Swoosh: The Unauthorized Story of Nike and the Men Who Played There* (New York: HarperCollins, 1992), pages 133–134.

27: **"you have to have spikes on your feet":** Geoff Hollister, *Out of Nowhere: The Inside Story of How Nike Marketed the Culture of Running* (Maidenhead: Meyer and Meyer Sport, 2008), page 72.

27: **By the time the Olympic trials came to Eugene:** University of Oregon Archives Department, sports information and media guides, 1890–2014, UA Ref 5, Boxes 26, 27, 28, 56, and 59.

27: **". . . I've never seen anything like when Pre ran in Eugene":** Gerald Scott, "The Legend Lives On," *Los Angeles Times* (Los Angeles, CA), May 6, 1985.

27: **His running style:** University of Oregon Archives Department, film collection, 1919–2009, UA 026_027, Box 3.

27: **sometimes called Pre a "rube":** Kenny Moore, *Bowerman and the Men of Oregon* (New York: Rodale, 2006), page 240.

27: **for Pre, any other way of running was "chickenshit":** Kenny Moore, *Bowerman and the Men of Oregon* (New York: Rodale, 2006), pages 238 and 247.

27: **On the final day of the 1972 Olympic trials:** University of Oregon Archives Department, sports information and media guides, 1890s–2014, UA Ref 5, Boxes 25 and 27.

28: **Pre was in peak physical condition:** Kenny Moore, *Bowerman and the Men of Oregon* (New York: Rodale, 2006), pages 280–304.

28: **"The Arabs are in our building":** Kenny Moore, *Bowerman and the Men of Oregon* (New York: Rodale, 2006), page 290.

28: **"If they loaded us all into a plane . . .":** Kenny Moore, *Bowerman and the Men of Oregon* (New York: Rodale, 2006), page 296.

29 **"Fourth Street":** Geoff Hollister, *Out of Nowhere: The Inside Story of How Nike Marketed the Culture of Running* (Maidenhead: Meyer and Meyer Sport, 2008), page 83.

29: **The company signed its first endorsement deal:** Phil Knight, *Shoe Dog: A Memoir by the Creator of Nike* (New York: Scribner, 2016), pages 214–215.

29: **"They were in my shoes":** Phil Knight, *Shoe Dog: A Memoir by the Creator of Nike* (New York: Scribner, 2016), page 216.

29: **The timing was ideal for Pre:** Kenny Moore, *Bowerman and the Men of Oregon* (New York: Rodale, 2006), page 305–307.

30: **"I build these shoes to last one race":** Geoff Hollister, *Out of Nowhere: The Inside Story of How Nike Marketed the Culture of Running* (Maidenhead: Meyer and Meyer Sport, 2008), pages 86–87.

30: **Pre ran some of the best races of his life:** Geoff Hollister, *Out of Nowhere: The Inside Story of How Nike Marketed the Culture of Running* (Maidenhead: Meyer and Meyer Sport, 2008), page 88.

30: **Knight decided to give him a job:** Phil Knight, *Shoe Dog: A Memoir by the Creator of Nike* (New York: Scribner, 2016), pages 221–223.

31: **Just after midnight, he swerved into a cliff:** Gerald Scott, "The Legend Lives On," *Los Angeles Times* (Los Angeles, CA), May 6, 1985.

31: **"five cool guys":** Joyce D. Duncan, *Sport in American Culture: From Ali to X-Games* (Santa Barbara: ABC-CLIO, 2004), page 337.

31: **It opened with a shot of a basketball rolling:** "Jordan Flight," Chiat/Day advertising.

32: **banning his prototype red-and-black Air Jordan shoes:** Russell T. Granik, NBA executive vice president, "re: . . . wearing of certain red and black NIKE basketball shoes . . .", typed letter to Nike's Rob Strasser, February 25, 1985.

32: **It took Knight ten years:** Geoff Hollister, *Out of Nowhere: The Inside Story of How Nike Marketed the Culture of Running* (Maidenhead: Meyer and Meyer Sport, 2008), page 90.

32: **his company's annual revenues were nearly $700 million:** Nike annual reports.

32: **the disaster that was waiting at the tail:** J. B. Strasser and Laurie Becklund, *Swoosh: The Unauthorized Story of Nike and the Men Who Played There* (New York: HarperCollins, 1992), page 437.

32: **in 1981, Nike helped upend the manufacturing world:** Philip M. Rosenzweig, "International Sourcing in Athletic Footwear: NIKE and Reebok," *Harvard Business School* case study, July 14, 1994; Debora L. Spar and Jennifer Burns, "Hitting the Wall: Nike and International Labor Practices," *Harvard Business School* case study, September 6, 2002.

32: **Nike's annual advertising budget:** Donald R. Katz, *Just Do It: The Nike Spirit in the Corporate World* (Holbrook: Adams, 1994), page 7.

32: **"What Phil and Nike have done":** Donald R. Katz, *Just Do It: The Nike Spirit in the Corporate World* (Holbrook: Adams, 1994), page 8.

33: **Nike was raking in $2.2 billion:** Nike annual reports.

33: **by 1993, that figure climbed to almost $4 billion:** Donald R. Katz, *Just Do It: The Nike Spirit in the Corporate World* (Holbrook: Adams, 1994), page 9.

33: **Profits soared nearly 1000 percent:** Donald R. Katz, *Just Do It: The Nike Spirit in the Corporate World* (Holbrook: Adams, 1994), page 9.

33: **when one out of every three pairs of shoes sold in America:** Donald R. Katz, *Just Do It: The Nike Spirit in the Corporate World* (Holbrook: Adams, 1994), page 8.

33: **all but vanquished:** Seth Stevenson, "How to Beat Nike," *The New York Times* (New York, NY), January 5, 2003.

33: **Nike sold two hundred pairs of shoes each minute:** Donald R. Katz, *Just Do It: The Nike Spirit in the Corporate World* (Holbrook: Adams, 1994), pages 9–10.

33: **It began with an unexpected phone call:** Donald R. Katz, *Just Do It: The Nike Spirit in the Corporate World* (Holbrook: Adams, 1994), page 8.

33: **Gathered on the second floor:** Donald R. Katz, *Just Do It: The Nike Spirit in the Corporate World* (Holbrook: Adams, 1994), pages 3–4.

33: **Air Jordan merchandise accounted for just 5 percent:** Nike annual reports.

33: **schoolchildren in China:** Donald R. Katz, *Just Do It: The Nike Spirit in the Corporate World* (Holbrook: Adams, 1994), page 10.

33: **"anyone with a body":** University of Oregon Archives Department, Bill Bowerman Papers, 1932–1999, UA 003.

33: **Still, Knight knew that there were billions:** Donald R. Katz, *Just Do It: The Nike Spirit in the Corporate World* (Holbrook: Adams, 1994), page 14.

34: **When Ballot Measure 5 passed in 1990:** Chapter 5. Richard J. Ellis, *Oregon Politics and Government: Progressives versus Conservative Populists*, Edited by Richard A. Clucas, Mark Henkels, and Brent S. Steel (Lincoln: University of Nebraska Press, 2005), pages 67–69.

34: **Oregonians who had once thought of themselves as citizens:** Chapter 13. Mark Henkels, *Oregon Politics and Government: Progressives versus Conservative Populists*, Edited by Richard A. Clucas, Mark Henkels, and Brent S. Steel (Lincoln: University of Nebraska Press, 2005), pages 212–215.

34: **conservative anti-tax activists like Don McIntire:** Jeff Mapes, "Don McIntire, Activist Who Led Property Tax Revolt, Dies at 74," the *Oregonian* (Portland, OR), October 12, 2012.

35: **which was called the Oregon system by political reformers:** Chapter 5. Richard J. Ellis, *Oregon Politics and Government: Progressives versus Conservative Populists*, Edited by Richard A. Clucas, Mark Henkels, and Brent S. Steel (Lincoln: University of Nebraska Press, 2005), pages 63–67.

36: **It was often just a matter of finding the right title:** Bill Sizemore's testimony before the Oregon Senate Committee on Rules and Elections, February 9, 1999.

36: **as important for state and local economies:** R. Haveman and T. Smeeding, "The Role of Higher Education in Social Mobility." *The Future of Children*, vol. 16, no. 2, fall 2006, pages 125–150.

36: **When Myles Brand became the University of Oregon's president:** David Sarasohn, *Failing Grade: Oregon's Higher-Education System Goes Begging* (Portland: New Oregon Publishers, 2010), page 19.

36: **Bill Sizemore championed more than a dozen ballot initiatives:** Chapter 5. Richard J. Ellis, *Oregon Politics and Government: Progressives versus Conservative Populists*, Edited by Richard A. Clucas, Mark Henkels, and Brent S. Steel (Lincoln: University of Nebraska Press, 2005), pages 69–74.

37: **Lon Mabon and the Oregon Citizens Alliance:** Chapter 6. Russ Dondero and William Lunch, *Oregon Politics and Government: Progressives versus Conservative Populists*, Edited by Richard A. Clucas, Mark Henkels, and Brent S. Steel (Lincoln: University of Nebraska Press, 2005), page 94.

38: **Knight bought his own suite:** Kerry Eggers, *The Civil War Rivalry: Oregon vs. Oregon State* (Charleston: The History Press, 2014), page 379.

38: **caught himself thinking about how much he'd like:** Kerry Eggers, *The Civil War Rivalry: Oregon vs. Oregon State* (Charleston: The History Press, 2014), page 379.

38: **the potential for Nike to cut deals to outift NFL teams:** Mark Asher, "NCAA Schools Search for Shoe Deals That Fit," *Washington Post* (Washington, D.C.), November 19, 1995.

38: **Knight presented his first major gift:** Author's interviews.

38: **the football team's new head coach, Mike Bellotti:** Chad Peppars, "Interview Project," audio recording, University of Oregon Archives of Northwest Folklore, 2008_197, folder 1.

39: **Rich Brooks, who had led the Ducks**: Kerry Eggers, *The Civil War Rivalry: Oregon vs. Oregon State* (Charleston: The History Press, 2014), pages 254–289.

39: **"What would it take to get to the next level?":** Kerry Eggers, *The Civil War Rivalry: Oregon vs. Oregon State* (Charleston: The History Press, 2014), page 380.

Chapter Two

40: **Throughout 1987, a team of eighteen volunteers:** University of Oregon Archives Department, Dave Frohnmayer, major speeches, box 1, "A Race Against Time: A Narrative of the Frohnmayer Family's Search for a Bone Marrow Donor," January 1991; "Fanconi

Anemia Symposium Keynote Address," October 2008; author's interviews with Dave and Lynn Frohnmayer.

41: **"I was raised to believe . . .":** Montgomery Brower, "A Desperate Quest into a Family's Past," *People*, January 11, 1988.

42: **In 1989, they registered the Fanconi Anemia Research Fund:** University of Oregon Archives Department, Major Speeches of Dave Frohnmayer, box 1, "The Fanconi Anemia Research Fund Story: Building Something from Nothing," October 5, 2008; Author's interviews with Dave and Lynn Frohnmayer.

42: **"We knew the next step was to go to Canada":** Montgomery Brower, "A Desperate Quest into a Family's Past," *People*, January 11, 1988.

43: **"every fresh truth and every new idea . . .":** Alexis de Tocqueville, *Democracy in America* (New York: Penguin Classics, 2003), introduction.

43: **The story of Otto Frohnmayer and his descendants:** University of Oregon Archives Department, Dave Frohnmayer, major speeches, box 1, "A Personal Journey," October 4, 1996.

43: **Otto's son, David Braden Frohnmayer:** University of Oregon Libraries, Special Collections and University Archives, biographical files, ca. 1930s–present, UA Ref 2, Box 4.

43: **before his career unexpectedly veered into politics:** Hardy Myers, "Dave Frohnmayer and the Oregon Legislature," *Oregon Law Review*, vol. 94, 2016, pages 541–560.

43: **a California Republican named Robert Finch:** "Speeches of Robert H. Finch," Richard M. Nixon Presidential Library and Museum, FG 23, Boxes 56–58.

44: **Frohnmayer was twenty-nine and living in Washington, D.C.:** Garrett Epps, *Peyote vs. the State: Religious Freedom on Trial* (Norman: University of Oklahoma Press, 2009), pages 22–24; author's interviews with Dave and Lynn Frohnmayer.

44: **The other case emerged from a strange series of events:** Marion Goldman, "Dave Frohnmayer and the Apocalypse That Evaporated," *Oregon Law Review*, vol. 94, 2016, pages 633–658.

44: **Bill Bowerman's oldest son, Jon**: Kenny Moore, *Bowerman and the Men of Oregon* (New York: Rodale, 2006), pages 369–379.

46: **". . . that'd be the worst thing . . .":** Kenny Moore, *Bowerman and the Men of Oregon* (New York: Rodale, 2006), page 375.

46: **an Oregon legislator asked Frohnmayer:** University of Oregon Archives Department, Dave Frohnmayer, major speeches, Box 1, "Rajneesh," Southtowne Rotary, Eugene, Oregon, August 31, 2006.

47: **". . . we've got to keep the peace . . .":** Marion Goldman, "Dave Frohnmayer and the Apocalypse That Evaporated," *Oregon Law Review*, vol. 94, 2016, page 655.

48: **". . . come to a family reunion a little too late":** Montgomery Brower, "A Desperate Quest into a Family's Past," *People*, January 11, 1988.

48: **"I thought I won the lottery":** Robert James Reese, "Running for Her Life, *Runner's World*, April 22, 2017.

49: **"a lot of people have bad things happen to them":** Montgomery Brower, "A Desperate Quest into a Family's Past," *People*, January 11, 1988.

49: **"It was a horrible thing to do . . .":** Ellen Licking, "Gene Therapy: One Family's Story," *BusinessWeek*, July 12, 1999.

49: **"I have never ever seen a person with this disease":** Ellen Licking, "Gene Therapy: One Family's Story," *BusinessWeek*, July 12, 1999.

50: **"I already knew the real reason . . .":** Robert James Reese, "Running for Her Life, *Runner's World*, April 22, 2017.

50: **a popular incumbent named Neil Goldschmidt:** Tom Wicker, "Mr. Mayor at 31," *The New York Times* (New York, NY), May 25, 1972.

50: **his decision to run for governor:** Nigel Jaquiss, "The 30-Year Secret," *Willamette Week*, May 11, 2004.

51: **Adding to his worries:** Author's interview with Neil Goldschmidt, 2016.

51: **"I gotta believe the best family will win":** Nigel Jaquiss, "The 30-Year Secret," *Willamette Week*, May 11, 2004.

51: **become as skilled at raising money:** Garret Epps, *Peyote vs. the State: Religious Freedom on Trial* (Norman: University of Oklahoma Press, 2009), page 221.

51: **"Dave Frohnmayer is a man of integrity . . .":** Public Papers of the Presidents of the United States of America, George H. W. Bush, "Remarks at a Fundraising Breakfast for Gubernatorial Candidate David Frohnmayer in Portland, Oregon," May 21, 1990.

53: **"She was trapped inside":** Garret Epps, *Peyote vs. the State: Religious Freedom on Trial* (Norman: University of Oklahoma Press, 2009), page 225.

53: **"Mom, I'm just so glad . . .":** Ellen Licking, "Gene Therapy: One Family's Story," *BusinessWeek*, July 12, 1999.

53: **"It's not a time for comfort":** Garret Epps, *Peyote vs. the State: Religious Freedom on Trial* (Norman: University of Oklahoma Press, 2009), page 228.

54: **"University of Oregon's accidental president":** Diane Dietz, "Iconic Public Servant Dies," *Eugene Register-Guard* (Eugene, OR), March 11, 2015.

54: **"Our research universities . . .":** University of Oregon Archives Department, Dave Frohnmayer's Major Speeches, "State of the University Address," 150 Columbia, University of Oregon, 3:00 p.m. on October 5, 1994.

54: **making Oregon the only state:** David Sarasohn, "State Colleges: Onward and Downward," *Oregonian* (Portland, OR), February 12, 1995.

54: **"We must raise more outside money":** University of Oregon Archives Department, Dave Frohnmayer's Major Speeches, "State of the University Address," 150 Columbia, University of Oregon, 3:00 p.m. on October 5, 1994.

55: **Knight committed to giving the school:** Mike Fish, "Just Do It," *ESPN*, January 13, 2006.

55: **a full-length artificial field with ceilings:** Author's visits to the University of Oregon campus.

56: **"In higher education you have more hoops . . .":** Mike Fish, "Just Do It," *ESPN*, January 13, 2006.

56: **It avoided paying international tariffs:** Jeff Steck, "Sneaking Through U.S. Customs with Converse All-Star Invention," *Gazette Cetera*, August 26, 2010.

56: **Knight circumvented many of the:** Author's interviews.

56: **using names like "Penny and I, LLC":** LLC registrations for Phil and Penny Knight.

56: **an endless source of frustration:** Greg Bolt and David Steves, "Legislators Demand Transparency from UO Arena Project," *Eugene Register-Guard* (Eugene, OR), May 25, 2010; Author's interviews with Eugene labor representatives.

57: **the Nike CEO had committed to giving:** Anonymous Author, "Matching Gifts Endow Knight Chairs," *News & Views: Faculty and Staff Newsletter of the University of Oregon*, June 11, 1998; author's interviews.

57: **In 1986, the University of Oklahoma spent:** Richard W. Stevenson, "Supplying the Athletes: A High-Stakes Business," *The New York Times* (New York, NY), June 10, 1986.

58: **Nike's college basketball dealmaker:** J. B. Strasser and Laurie Becklund, "Vaccaro: The Dean of Shoes," *Los Angeles Times* (Los Angeles, CA), February 15, 1992.

58: **"That's how my basketball life started":** Jon Weinbach and Dan Marks, *Sole Man*, documentary film, 2015.

58: **"He wasn't hesitant to tell you":** Jon Weinbach and Dan Marks, *Sole Man*, documentary film, 2015.

59: **"I looked him in the eye . . .":** Jon Weinbach and Dan Marks, *Sole Man*, documentary film, 2015.

60: **In 1978, college basketball coaches:** Bill Brubaker, "In Shoe Companies' Competition, the Coaches are the Key Players," *Washington Post* (Washington, D.C.), March 11, 1991.

60: **"I was charmed by Sonny":** Curry Kirkpatrick, "The Old Soft Shoe with Some Fancy Footwork, Super Sneaker Salesman Sonny Vaccaro Has Become a Power in College Basketball," *Sports Illustrated*, November 16, 1988.

60: **an enterprise called College Colors:** Richard W. Stevenson, "Supplying the Athletes: A High-Stakes Business," *The New York Times* (New York, NY), June 10, 1986.

61: **"You gotta give the kid everything you got":** Jon Weinbach and Dan Marks, *Sole Man*, documentary film, 2015.

61: **helped arrange a meeting at Tony Roma's restaurant:** Roland Lazenby, *Michael Jordan: The Life* (New York: Little, Brown and Company, 2014).

61: **Nike's Air Jordan brand generated:** Nike annual reports.

62: **bringing America's most promising:** Jon Weinbach and Dan Marks, *Sole Man*, documentary film, 2015.

62: **"We're wondering if the property . . .":** Richard W. Stevenson, "Supplying the Athletes: A High-Stakes Business," *The New York Times* (New York, NY), June 10, 1986.

63: **"The athletes are considered":** Richard W. Stevenson, "Supplying the Athletes: A High-Stakes Business," *The New York Times* (New York, NY), June 10, 1986.

63: **"We were the first corporate entity . . .":** Joe Nocera and Ben Strauss, "A Reformed 'Sneaker Pimp' Takes on the NCAA," *The New York Times* (New York, NY), February 12, 2016.

63: **"Basically that's probably true":** Jon Weinbach and Dan Marks, *Sole Man*, documentary film, 2015.

64: **the NBA and the NFL were each:** Mark Asher, "NCAA Schools Search for Shoe Deals That Fit," *Washington Post* (Washington, D.C.), November 19, 1995.

64: **Nike signed a slew of all-school apparel deals**: Joe Drape, "College Football Coaches Receive Both Big Salaries and Big Questions," *The New York Times* (New York, NY), January 1, 2004.

65: **One prototype tested by the Ducks:** Rick Bakas, "How the Oregon Ducks Brand Was Created," *Bakas Media* blog post, December 16, 2014; author's interviews.

65: **"getting our apparel products on the playing field . . .":** Nike investor conference call, 1996.

65: **"became a total brand":** Nike annual report, 1996.

65: **Nike's tailwind was suddenly slowed:** Nike annual report, 1996.

65: **it had already lost five:** Robert J. Dolan, "Nike, Inc. in the 1990s: Strategy and Management Changes, 1993–1994," *Harvard Business School*, case study, March 15, 1995.

66: **Autzen Stadium in Eugene:** University of Oregon Archives Department, Architecture of the University of Oregon, "Autzen Stadium."

66: **contributing $40,000 toward President Dave Frohnmayer's:** Oregon State Board of Higher Education.

66: **by becoming the Fanconi Anemia Research Fund's:** Author's interviews with Dave and Lynn Frohnmayer; 990 forms filed with the Internal Revenues Service by the Fanconi Anemia Research Fund.

66: **In February 1995, Kirsten traveled:** Ellen Licking, "Gene Therapy: One Family's Story," *BusinessWeek*, July 12, 1999.

Chapter Three

68: **Jonah Peretti made his first piece:** Email exchange between Jonah Peretti and Nike, first published by shey.net, later republished by the *Guardian* (London, UK), February 19, 2001.

69: **Nike's manufacturing operations:** Philip M. Rosenzweig, "International Sourcing in Athletic Footwear: Nike and Reebok," *Harvard Business School*, case study, July 14, 1994.

70: **seeking out the poorest nations:** Ann Harrison and Jason Scorse, "Improving the Conditions of Workers? Minimum Wage Legislation and Anti-Sweatshop Activism," *California Management Review*, vol. 48, no. 2, winter 2006.

70: **Just outside of Jakarta, Indonesia:** Jeff Ballinger, "The New Free-Trade Heel," *Harper's*, August 1992.

71: **It was highly unusual for a corporation:** Donna Everatt and Kathleen Slaughter, "Nike Inc.: Developing an Effective Public Relations Strategy," *Richard Ivey School of Business*, 1999.

71: **"They have protested, disingenuously . . .":** Mark Clifford, "Keep the Heat on Sweatshops," *BusinessWeek*, December 23, 1996.

72: **The shoes that Nguyen Thi Thu Phuong:** Debora L. Spar and Jennifer Burns, "Hitting the Wall: Nike and International Labor Practices," *Harvard Business School* case study, September 6, 2002.

72: **"We don't make shoes":** Richard P. McIntyre, *Are Worker Rights Human Rights?* (Ann Arbor: University of Michigan Press, 2008), page 1.

73: **he turned to a firm called GoodWorks:** Dana Canedy, "Nike's Asian Factories Pass Young's Muster," *The New York Times* (New York, NY), June 25, 1997.

73: **"It is my sincere belief that Nike":** Full-page Nike advertisement, *The New York Times* (New York, NY), June 25, 1997.

74: **The widely criticized Andrew Young report:** Bob Herbert, "Mr. Young Gets It Wrong," *The New York Times* (New York, NY), June 27, 1997.

74: **a series of formal audits:** Steven Greenhouse, "Nike Shoe Plant in Vietnam Is Called Unsafe for Workers," *The New York Times* (New York, NY), November 8, 1997.

75: **a moment in which student activism:** Liza Featherstone, "The Student Movement Comes of Age," *Nation*, September 28, 2000.

76: **students at the University of North Carolina:** Archie B. Carroll, Jim Brown, and Ann K. Buchholtz, *Business & Society: Ethics, Sustainability & Stakeholder Management* (Boston: Cengage Learning, 2015), page 674.

76: **"I don't want to be a billboard . . .":** William McNall, "Nike Fighting Uphill Battle Over Bad Image," *Los Angeles Times* (Los Angeles, CA), October 11, 1998.

76: **"Away in a Sweatshop":** "Santa and Sweatshops," *Wall Street Journal* (New York, NY), December 22, 2000.

76: **the common battleground shared by activists:** Aaron Bernstein, Michael Shari, and Elisabeth Malkin, "A World of Sweatshops," *BusinessWeek*, November 6, 2000.

76: **"It really is quite sick":** Nancy Cleeland, "Students Give Sweatshop Fight the College Try," *Los Angeles Times* (Los Angeles, CA), April 22, 1999.

77: **"Nike has chosen to strike out . . .":** Author unknown, "Statement Regarding Nike Negotiations," University of Michigan press release, April 27, 2000.

77: **Sarah Jacobson made her way:** Author's interview.

78: **"standard protest issue":** Author's interview with Jim Earl.

78: **"The idea of academics . . .":** Author's interview with Jim Earl.

79: **"We want you to sign . . .":** Author's interviews with Sarah Jacobson and Dave Frohnmayer.

79: **". . . fumbling a teachable moment":** Phil Knight, email, April 24, 2000.

80: **Frohnmayer was recovering from a full cardiac arrest:** University of Oregon Archives Department, Dave Frohnmayer's Major Speeches, "MBA Graduation Ceremony Remarks," June 21, 2009.

80: **"personally and soul-searchingly":** University of Oregon Archives Department, "Dave Frohnmayer, Letters from a Controversy," 10.091.A, Box 3, file 47.

81: **Some letters, like the one:** University of Oregon Archives Department, "Emails received prior to 4/24/00 announcement by Phil Knight," 10.091.A, Box 1, file 48.

82: **Alcoholics Anonymous (AA) had just:** Nan Robertson, "The Changing World of Alcoholics Anonymous," *The New York Times* (New York, NY), February 21, 1988.

82 **because of men like Arthur Golden:** Arthur Golden, obituary, April 2016; author's interview with Arthur Golden.

82: **"Arthur was a wonderful, kind, honest man":** Author's interview with Lynn Frohnmayer.

84: **so shocked by Knight's cruelty:** Letter from Arthur M. Golden, January 2001; author's interviews with Arthur Golden and the recipient of his letter.

84: **"Arthur would not have lied":** Author's interview with Lynn Frohnmayer.

Chapter Four

85: **". . . my regret is enormous":** University of Oregon Archives Department, "Dave Frohnmayer, Letters from a Controversy," 10.091.A, Box 3, file 47.

88: **"Nike will do the right thing":** Bob Baum, "Jordan's Critics Say It Must Be the Shoes," *Associated Press*, June 6, 1996.

88: **Knight joined President Clinton:** President Bill Clinton, *Fair Labor Practices* (C-Span; August 2, 1996), television broadcast.

89: **Silas Trim Bissell:** Associated Press, "Silas Trim Bissell, 60, Longtime Antiwar Fugitive," *The New York Times* (New York, NY), June 25, 2002.

91: **"I had a lot of experience . . .":** Lynn S. Paine, "A Conversation with Jill Ker Conway," *Harvard Business Review*, July–August 2014.

91: **"My worry was that . . .":** Lynn S. Paine, "A Conversation with Jill Ker Conway," *Harvard Business Review*, July–August 2014.

92: **"What I did at the meeting. . .":** Lynn S. Paine, "A Conversation with Jill Ker Conway," *Harvard Business Review*, July–August 2014.

92: **Knight agreed, and asked Ker Conway:** "Note from Frohnmayer on Conway," University of Oregon Archives Department, Jill Conway, Nike Board of Directors, 10.091.A, Box 3, file 47.

92: **He had his secretary fax:** University of Oregon Archives Department, "Jill Conway, Nike Board of Directors," 10.091.A, Box 3, file 47.

Chapter Five

95: **a professor named Jonathan Baldwin Turner:** Jonathan Baldwin Turner Papers, 1836–1895, Abraham Lincoln Presidential Library & Museum, 1910–1912, Boxes 1 and 2.

97: **years for the Morrill Act:** Derek Bok, *Higher Education in America* (Princeton: Princeton University Press, 2015), pages 11, 17, 18, 29, 30, 31, 34, 45, 48, 65, 81, 361, and 380.

97: **By 1867, twenty-two states had accepted:** Donald R. Brown, "Jonathan Baldwin Turner and the Land-Grant Idea," *Journal of the Illinois State Historical Society*, vol. 55, no. 4, winter, 1962, pages 370–384.

97: **". . . especially to sons of toil":** Christopher P. Loss, "Why the Morrill Land-Grant Colleges Act Still Matters," *Chronicle of Higher Education*, July 16, 2012.

98: **National Defense Act of 1958:** Barbara Barksdale Clowse, *Brainpower for the Cold War: The Sputnik Crisis and the National Defense Education Act of 1958* (Santa Barbara: Greenwood Press, 1958).

98: **Higher Education Act of 1965:** Derek Bok, *Higher Education in America* (Princeton: Princeton University Press, 2015), page 213.

99: **funding America's public universities:** Hanna Holborn Gray, *Searching for Utopia: Universities and Their Histories* (Berkeley: University of California Press, 2011).

99: **"as a guinea pig in an experiment . . .":** Associated Press, "U.S. Guilty in Man's Death During Secret Drug Testing," *Los Angeles Times* (Los Angeles, CA), May 5, 1987.

99: **One many-tendrilled program called MK-Ultra:** Alfred W. McCoy, *A Question of Torture: CIA Interrogation, From the Cold War to the War on Terror* (New York: Henry Holt and Company, 2006), pages 21–60.

100: **MK-Ultra and related programs:** Alfred W. McCoy, *A Question of Torture: CIA Interrogation, From the Cold War to the War on Terror* (New York: Henry Holt and Company, 2006), page 29.

100: **"researcher were most reluctant . . .":** Alfred W. McCoy, *A Question of Torture: CIA Interrogation, From the Cold War to the War on Terror* (New York: Henry Holt and Company, 2006), page 28.

102: **"breaking down a prisoner":** Alfred W. McCoy, *A Question of Torture: CIA Interrogation, From the Cold War to the War on Terror* (New York: Henry Holt and Company, 2006), page 33.

102: **anthropology professor Hugo Nutini:** Bill Toland, "Obituary: Hugo G. Nutini/Well-Travelled Student, Teacher, Mexico Expert," *Pittsburgh Post-Gazette* (Pittsburgh, PA), April 25, 2013.

102: **program called project Camelot:** Ellen Herman, "Project Camelot and the Career of Cold War Psychology," *Universities and Empire: Money and Politics in the Social Sciences During the Cold War*, Edited by Christopher Simpson (New York: The New Press, 1998), pages 97–133.

103: **Princeton University's Listening Center:** Lawrence C. Soley, *Radio Warfare* New York: Praeger, 1989), page 59.

104: **"I think the military should be free . . .":** Ellen Herman, *The Romance of American Psychology: Political Culture in the Age of Experts* (Berkeley: University of California Press, 1995), page 165.

104: **An important shift came in 1967:** National Science Foundation, *Federal Funds for Research, Development, and Other Scientific Activities: Fiscal Year 1967*, vol. 15, page 102.

104: **research through Project THEMIS:** Elinor Langer, "Themis: DOD Plan to Spread the Wealth Raises Questions in Academe," *Science*, vol. 156, no. 3771, April 7, 1967, pages 48–50.

105: **Universities expanded and enrollments increased:** Lawrence Soley, "The New Corporate Yen for Scholarship," *Universities and Empire: Money and Politics in the Social Sciences During the Cold War*, Edited by Christopher Simpson (New York: The New Press, 1998), page 230.

105: **the year when subsidies and grants:** National Science Foundation, "Table B-2: Federal Obligations for Science and Engineering Going to Colleges and Universities by Type of Activity and Agency: Fiscal Years 1963–1993."

105: **"Doubt is our product":** Author unknown, Brown & Williamson corporate memorandum, 1969.

105: **The tobacco industry's methodology:** Lisa Bero, "Tobacco Industry Manipulation of Research," *Public Health Reports*, vol. 120, March–April 2005, pages 200–208.

106: **law firms like Covington & Burling:** Charles Ferguson, *Inside Job: The Financiers Who Pulled off the Heist of the Century*, (London: Oneworld Publications, 2012), page 303.

106: **the Council for Tobacco Research:** Lisa Bero, "Tobacco Industry Manipulation of Research," *Late Lessons from Early Warnings: Science, Precaution, Innovation*, European Environment Agency report, 2013.

107: **the University of Wisconsin made an agreement:** Millard Johnson, "Majoring in Technology Transfer," *Corporate Report Wisconsin*, September 1994.

107: **Harvard Medical School received:** Edward B. Fiske, "Monsanto Research Pact Aims to Cut Academic Controversy," *The New York Times* (New York, NY), June 4, 1982.

107: **Hammerhill Paper Company not only funded:** Ronald Alsop, "Capitalism 101: "Programs to Teach Free Enterprise Sprout on College Campuses," *Wall Street Journal* (New York, NY), May 10, 1978.

108: **Republican congressman New Gingrich:** Peter Applebome, "In Gingrich's College Course, Critics Find a Wealth of Ethical Concerns," *The New York Times* (New York, NY), February 20, 1995.

108: **The 1996 Minnesota–Coke deal:** F.J. Gallagher, "U Gets Ready for Coke Deal," *Minnesota Daily* (Minneapolis, MN), January 10, 1996.

109: **". . . first school district in the nation . . .":** Steven Manning, "Students for Sale," *Nation*, September 27, 1999.

110: **"Research shows that vendor purchases . . .":** Kenneth J. Saltman, *Collateral Damage: Corporatizing Public Schools—A Threat to Democracy* (Lanham: Rowman & Littlefield, 2000), page 59.

110: **in 1997, children aged four to twelve:** *American Demographic*, 1998.

110: **"Our philosophy he said":** Steven Manning, "Students for Sale," *Nation*, September 27, 1999.

110: **"Let's just say everyone drinks one product a day":** Constance L. Hays, "Today's Lesson: Soda Rights; Consultant Helps Schools Sell Themselves to Vendors," *The New York Times* (New York, NY), May 21, 1999.

111: **"From now until she's graduated":** Constance L. Hays, "Today's Lesson: Soda Rights; Consultant Helps Schools Sell Themselves to Vendors," *The New York Times* (New York, NY), May 21, 1999.

111: **"The thought of generating that kind of revenue . . .":** Constance L. Hays, "Today's Lesson: Soda Rights; Consultant Helps Schools Sell Themselves to Vendors," *The New York Times* (New York, NY), May 21, 1999.

112: **"I think it would be a real negative":** Marc Kaufman, "Pop Culture," *Washington Post* (Washington, D.C.), March 23, 1999.

112: **". . . all that Pepsi has done . . .":** Marc Kaufman, "Pop Culture," *Washington Post* (Washington, D.C.), March 23, 1999.

113: **"It really would have been acceptable . . .":** Associated Press, "A Pepsi Fan Is Punished in Coke's Backyard," *The New York Times* (New York, NY), March 26, 1998.

113: **"The lobbyists kicked my ass":** Steven Manning, "The Littlest Coke Addicts," *Nation*, June 25, 2001.

113: **in 1965, the federal government:** Jennifer Washburn, "Science's Worst Enemy: Corporate Funding," *Discover*, October 11, 2007.

114: **Research comparing different cholesterol medications:** Will Dunham, "U.S. Study Sees Bias in Company-Funded Statin Trials," *Reuters*, June 5, 2007.

115: **"Usually they're lying on their way to the bank":** Jennifer Washburn, "Science's Worst Enemy: Corporate Funding," *Discover*, October 11, 2007.

115: **One startling example of this:** Paul Jacobs, "Stanford Medical School Staff Violate Paid Speech Policy," *San Jose Mercury News* (San Jose, CA), July 9, 2006.

115: **presidential administration of George W. Bush:** Juliet Eilperin, "Chemical Industry Funds Aid EPA Study," *The Washington Post* (Washington, D.C.), October 26, 2004.

115: **it was America's livestock producers:** Jennifer Washburn, "Science's Worst Enemy: Corporate Funding," *Discover*, October 11, 2007.

115: **Pharmaceutical representatives visit the campus:** Molly McCluskey, "Public Universities Get an Education in Private Industry," *Atlantic*, April 3, 2017.

116: **at Purdue University, it's food and chemical companies:** Purdue University "Industrial Associates Program," Department of Food Science brochure.

116: **"help your company avoid. . .":** Anahad O'Conner, "Coca-Cola Funds Scientists Who Shift Blame for Obesity Away from Bad Diets," *The New York Times* (New York, NY), August 9, 2015.

117: **a claim so outrageous that the candy company:** Candice Choi, "Snickers Maker Criticizes Industry-Funded Paper on Sugar," *Associated Press*, December 21, 2016.

117: **Iowa State University's athletics department:** Author unknown, "Dow AgroSciences, Iowa State University Enter into Research Agreement Using EXZACT™ Precision Technology in Algae," *Business Wire*, April 16, 2010; Sara Miller, "Iowa State University Announces New Monsanto Chair in Soybean Breeding," *Monsanto Public Affairs*, May 26, 2011.

117: **the University of Michigan receives financial consideration:** Press Release, "Industry Partners Invest in Second Phase of Mcity Funding," October 31, 2017.

117: **the University of Washington has Amazon Catalyst:** Jay Greene, "Amazon Launches New Program to Fund University Research," *Seattle Times* (Seattle, WA), November 5, 2015.

117: **"It's getting more difficult . . .":** Jennifer Washburn, "Science's Worst Enemy: Corporate Funding," *Discover*, October 11, 2007.

118: **drug called Sofosbuvir:** Harmeet Kaur Bhatia, Harmanjit Singh, Nipunjot Grewal, and Navreet Kaur Natt, "Sofosbuvir: A Novel Treatment Option for Chronic Hepatitis C Infection," *Journal of Pharmacology and Pharmacotherapeutics*, vol. 5, number 4, October–December 2014, pages 278–284.

118: **Under the trade name Sovaldi:** Andrew Pollack, "Sales of Sovaldi, New Gilead Hepatitis C Drug, Soar to $10.3 Billion," *The New York Times* (New York, NY), February 3, 2015.

118: **in states like Louisiana:** Sarah Jane Tribble, "Louisiana Proposes Tapping a Century-Old Patent Law to Cut Hepatitis C Drug Prices," *Washington Post* (Washington, D.C.), May 2, 2017.

118: **Which costs Americans $1,000 per pill:** Ketaki Gokhale and Makiko Kitamura, "$10 Copy of Gilead Blockbuster Sovaldi Appears in Bangladesh," *Bloomberg News*, March 9, 2015; author's interviews and visits to counterfeit markets in India.

119: **a British pharmaceutical corporation called Boots UK:** Ralph T. King Jr., "How a Drug Firm Paid for a University Study, Then Undermined It," *Wall Street Journal* (New York, NY), April 25, 1996.

119: **In 2006, a Cleveland cardiologist named Steve Nissen:** Steven E. Nissen and Kathy Wolski, "Effect of Rosiglitazone on the Risk of Myocardial Infarction and Death from Cardiovascular Causes," *The New England Journal of Medicine*, June 14, 2007.

120: **including Valentin Fuster:** Author unknown, "World-Renowned Cardiologists Announce the Launch of the GlaxoSmithKline Research and Education Foundation, Pledging Their Commitment to Inspiring Leadership in New Scientists," GlaxoSmithKline press release, November 10, 2001.

120: **a historic and highly unusual partnership:** Eli Kintisch, "BP Bets Big on UC Berkeley for Novel Biofuels Center," *Science*, vol. 315, issue 5,813, February 9, 2007.

121: **UC Berkeley's first chancellor, Clark Kerr:** Clark Kerr, *The Uses of the University* (Cambridge: Harvard University Press, 1963).

121: **"The university ought to remain a neutral agency . . .":** Jennifer Washburn, *University, Inc.: The Corporate Corruption of Higher Education* (New York: Basic Books, 2005), page 2.

121: **prompted by UC Berkeley's 1998 partnership:** Jesus Mena and Robert Sanders, "Swiss Pharmaceutical Company Novartis Commits $25 million to Support Biotechnology Research at UC Berkeley," press release, November 23, 1998.

121: **UC Berkeley professor Ignacio Chapela:** Kristen Philipkoski, "Professor, Biotech Butt Heads," *Wired*, December 13, 2003.

122: **"I'm not opposed to . . .":** Jennifer Washburn, *University, Inc.: The Corporate Corruption of Higher Education* (New York: Basic Books, 2005), page 4.

122: **Senator Steve Peace:** Jennifer Washburn, *University, Inc.: The Corporate Corruption of Higher Education* (New York: Basic Books, 2005), page 10.

122: **an independent review conducted by a team:** Rex Dalton, "Biotech Funding Deal Judged to be "a mistake" for Berkeley," *Nature*, August 5, 2004.

123: **"All renewables are going to have to weather the storm":** Erik Neumann, "Not So Fast: At UC Berkeley, Biofuel Research Takes Hit as BP Oil Company Backs Away," *California Alumni Magazine*, February 4, 2015.

Chapter Six

124: **Arthur Golden told just a few people:** Author's interviews with Arthur Golden and people he told.

124: **breathed new life into the stadium expansion:** University of Oregon Archives Department, "Autzen Expansion: September 1999–December 2001," 11.151.A, Box 3, file 3.

125: **the expansion would cost $89 million:** University of Oregon Archives Department, "UO Building Costs 97–06," 11.151.A, Box 3, file 3.

125: **$1.3 million worth:** Bob Clark, "Oregon Heads in New Direction with FieldTurf," *Eugene Register-Guard* (Eugene, OR), February 22, 2002; Greg Bolt, "UO Students Can Stake Out New Turf in Fall," *Eugene Register-Guard* (Eugene, OR), May 12, 2002; Bob Clark, "FieldTurf Takes Hold at Autzen, Elsewhere," *Eugene Register-Guard* (Eugene, OR), August 29, 2002.

125: **Knight would pay nearly twice that:** Author's interviews.

125: **the remaining $29 million was funded:** University of Oregon Archives Department, "UO Building Costs 97–06," 11.151.A, Box 3, file 3.

125: **Its faculty was earning less:** Figures provided by Nathan Tublitz, then president of the faculty senate at the university.

125: **"Coughing up $90 million . . .":** Jere Longman, "College Football: At Oregon, Pigskin and Sheepskin Collide," *The New York Times* (New York, NY), October 20, 2001; author's interviews with Jim Earl.

125: **the faculty was at loggerheads:** Dan Wyant, "UO Stadium Named for $250,000 Donor," *Eugene Register-Guard* (Eugene, OR), June 15, 1966.

126: **"football programsa time bomb":** Jere Longman, "College Football: At Oregon, Pigskin and Sheepskin Collide," *The New York Times* (New York, NY), October 20, 2001; author's interviews with Nathan Tublitz.

126: **A massive 80-by-100-foot billboard:** "Billboard Quarterback," *The New York Times* (New York, NY), August 8, 2001.

127: **"It frustrated me":** Jere Longman, "College Football: At Oregon, Pigskin and Sheepskin Collide," *The New York Times* (New York, NY), October 20, 2001.

127: **Tublitz was cautiously optimistic:** Author's interview.

127: **"We don't want to become a pseudo-professional team":** Jere Longman, "College Football: At Oregon, Pigskin and Sheepskin Collide," *The New York Times* (New York, NY), October 20, 2001.

127: **an "unusual grant" of $2 million:** Author's interviews with Dave and Lynn Frohnmayer, Arthur Golden; 990 forms filed with the Internal Revenues Service by the Fanconi Anemia Research Fund.

128: **a new brand identity for the Ducks:** Rick Bakas, "How the Oregon Ducks Brand Was Created," Bakas Media blog post, December 16, 2014; author's email exchanges with Rick Bakas.

128: **"to raise Oregon's status . . .":** Rick Bakas, "How the Oregon Ducks Brand Was Created," Bakas Media blog post, December 16, 2014.

129: **"I took the shape of the track . . .":** Rick Bakas, "How the Oregon Ducks Brand Was Created," Bakas Media blog post, December 16, 2014.

129: **director of communications Thomas Hager:** Author's interview with Thomas Hager.

130: **Nike's Gulfstream V corporate jet:** Author's visits to area airports; flight registries and logs.

130: **"while Nike suits became":** Author's interviews with a number of UO faculty.

130: **the school's founders dared to challenge:** Lucia W. Moore, Nina W. McCornack, and Gladys W. McCready, *The Story of Eugene* (Eugene: Lane County Historical Society, 1995), pages 131–195.

133: **starting quarterback Joey Harrington:** University of Oregon Archives Department, "Sports Information and Media Guides," UA REF 5, boxes 32, 33, and 34.

133: **"Hoping to hear from you . . .":** Joey Harrington, "Born to Be a Duck," *Eugene Register-Guard* (Eugene, OR), August 2, 2009;

133: **"For the better part of six months . . .":** Joey Harrington, "Perceptions of Perfection," *TEDxPortland*, May 17, 2016.

134: **cheerleaders who were encouraged:** Author's interviews with past athletes, cheerleaders, and university staff.

135: **Two hundred state police officers:** Fact-finding mission reports authored by Worker Rights Consortium volunteers; Steven Greenhouse, "Rights Group Scores Success with Nike," *The New York Times* (New York, NY), January 27, 2001; author's interviews.

136: **"Are you frightened yet?":** Lane Van Ham, "Workers Struggle at Nike Factory—Kukdong in Puebla, Mexico," *Labor Standard*, February 3, 2001.

138: **"People are drawn in by the horror stories":** Daniel E. Bender and Richard A. Greenwald, *Sweatshop USA: The American Sweatshop in Historical and Global Perspective* (New York: Routledge, 2003), page 260.

139: **"neither the time nor the place . . .":** Liza Featherstone, *Students Against Sweatshops* (New York: Verso, 2002), page 103.

139: **more than 400 college campuses:** Liza Featherstone, *Students Against Sweatshops* (New York: Verso, 2002), page 103.

140: **"We were a bunch of shoe geeks . . .":** Ravina Shamdasani, "Soul-Searching by 'Shoe Geeks,' Led to Social Responsibility," *South China Morning Post* (Hong Kong), May 17, 2001.

141: **Oregon allowed the Stanford marching band:** Ted Brock, "Oregon Fans Yell Foul, Stanford Banned," *Los Angeles Times* (Los Angeles, CA), November 1, 1990.

141: **Marc Kasky had learned:** *Kasky v. Nike, Inc.* (2002), Superior Court of the City and County of San Francisco, No. 994446, David A. Garcia, Judge.

142: **"Nike makes a very good product":** Steve Rubenstein, "Marc Kasky: S.F. Man Changes from Customer to Nike Adversary," *SF Gate* (San Francisco, CA), May 3, 2002.

142: **Nike then appealed to the U.S. Supreme Court:** Linda Greenhouse, "Nike Free Speech Case is Unexpectedly Returned to California," *The New York Times* (New York, NY), June 27, 2003.

143: **The settlement which left intact:** Adam Liptak, "Nike Move Ends Case Over Firms' Free Speech," *The New York Times* (New York, NY), September 13, 2003.

143: **"as invisible and unwatchable . . .":** E.J. Schultz, "See the Anti-Smoking TV Ads Big Tobacco is Forced to Run," *Ad Age*, November 22, 2017.

143: **the formation of Sitemex:** Associated Press, "Labor: Workers at Mexican Nike Factory Plan to Unionize," *Kitsap Sun* (Bremerton, WA), September 28, 2001.

144: **"I was the kid that helped . . .":** Joey Harrington, "Perceptions of Perfection," *TEDxPortland*, May 17, 2016.

144: **"For any kid in the country . . .":** Associated Press, "On Eve of Big Game, Ahmad Rashad Recalls His Days as a Duck," *ESPN*, November 10, 2006.

Chapter Seven

146: **On an otherwise ordinary Saturday:** Josh Moyer, Dan Murphy, and Mitch Sherman, "Joy and Pain: The Miracle at Michigan," *ESPN*, September 24, 2014.

147: **". . . never before in my life . . .":** Josh Moyer, Dan Murphy, and Mitch Sherman, "Joy and Pain: The Miracle at Michigan," *ESPN*, September 24, 2014.

147: **"So many things had to . . .":** Josh Moyer, Dan Murphy, and Mitch Sherman, "Joy and Pain: The Miracle at Michigan," *ESPN*, September 24, 2014.

147: **When his $1-million contract with Washington:** Associated Press, "Neuheisel Goes Back to Boulder After Bitter Departure," *The New York Times* (New York, NY), September 17, 2000.

148: **It was driven, in part:** University of Oregon Archives Department, Bowl Championship Series correspondence, 13.083.A, Box 3, files 7 and 8; revenue and expenses elements, file 11.

148: **Before long, college football:** James K. Gentry and Raquel Meyer Alexander, "From the Sideline to the Bottom Line," *The New York Times* (New York, NY), December 31, 2011.

148: **when Neuheisel's first University of Washington contract:** Associated Press, "Just Don't Do it, Neuheisel: Ethics Board Nixes Nike Deal," *Kitsap Sun* (Bremerton, WA), May 5, 2001.

149: **"We do not know . . .":** Ken Armstrong and Nick Perry, *Scoreboard, Baby: A Story of College Football, Crime, and Complicity* (Lincoln: Bison Books, 2010), page 136.

150: **Neuheisel was enjoying a leisurely game:** Nick Perry and Ken Armstrong, "Convicted of Assault and Accused of Rape, Star Player Received Raft of Second Chances," *Seattle Times* (Seattle, WA), January 27, 2008.

153: **"I thought he should have been charged":** Nick Perry and Ken Armstrong, "Convicted of Assault and Accused of Rape, Star Player Received Raft of Second Chances," *Seattle Times* (Seattle, WA), January 27, 2008.

156: **"Things like this just blow me away":** Austin Murphy, "Make Way for the Ducks Wild Uniforms, Space-Age Lockers and a Stunning Win Over Michigan," *Sports Illustrated*, September 29, 2003.

156: **"Just because we have a nice locker . . .":** Austin Murphy, "Make Way for the Ducks Wild Uniforms, Space-Age Lockers and a Stunning Win Over Michigan," *Sports Illustrated*, September 29, 2003.

157: **"We'll market you in ways no one ever imagined":** Austin Murphy, "Make Way for the Ducks Wild Uniforms, Space-Age Lockers and a Stunning Win Over Michigan," *Sports Illustrated*, September 29, 2003.

157: **"dispel some prevalent misinformation . . .":** University of Oregon Archives Department, 13.083.A, Box 10, files 5 and 6.

157: **"Locally, the symbolism . . .":** University of Oregon Archives Department, 13.083.A, Box 10, files 5 and 6.

158: **"It's difficult to understand . . .":** University of Oregon Archives Department, 13.083.A, Box 10, files 5 and 6.

158: **"Hopefully Clemens said":** Austin Murphy, "Make Way for the Ducks Wild Uniforms, Space-Age Lockers and a Stunning Win Over Michigan," *Sports Illustrated*, September 29, 2003.

159: **"There are 28 bowls":** Richard Sandomir, "College Bowl Scene is Flush with Corporate Dollars," *The New York Times* (New York, NY), December 28, 2004.

159: **like Knight T. Boone Pickens:** T. Boone Pickens, *Boone* (Boston: Houghton Mifflin, 1987).

160: **"I don't like that feeling":** Oliver Staley, "T. Boone Pickens: OSU's Big, Big Man on Campus," *Bloomberg*, April 15, 2011.

161: **"They pandered to whatever Boone wanted:"** Oliver Staley, "T. Boone Pickens: OSU's Big, Big Man on Campus," *Bloomberg*, April 15, 2011.

162: **The BCS system was created:** University of Oregon Archives Department, 13.083.A, Box 3, files 14, 15, 16, and 17; Box 4, files 1, 2, 3, 4, and 5; 10.091.A, Box 1, file 3; Box 3, file 3; Box 4, file 3; Box 1, 2, 3, 4, 5, 6, 7, 8, 9, 10, 11, and 12, file 54.

163: **"Our preference, Cowen said":** Chris Dufresne, "Have-Nots Are Uniting Against BCS," *Los Angeles Times* (Los Angeles, CA), July 23, 2003.

163: **"face up to the reality":** Harvey Perlman, email to Dave Frohnmayer, February 16, 2004.

163: **When Phil Knight stepped down:** Associated Press, "Nike Co-Founder Knight Steps Down as Chief Executive," *The New York Times* (New York, NY), November 18, 2004.

163: **Knight was ready to help build:** Frohnmayer's new basketball arena: Anonymous author, "Frohnmayer Oks New Arena," *Inside Oregon: Newsletter of the University of Oregon*, August 6, 2003.

164: **Frohnmayer sent Knight a fax:** Handwritten note alongside a photocopied newspaper editorial, with a UO cover page, faxed to

Phil Knight (FAX: 503-644-6655) on November 22, 2004; Author's interviews.

164: **offensive coordinator named Chip Kelly:** University of Oregon Archives Department, sports information and media guides, 2007–2011.

164: **"When we started this offense":** Michael Sokolove, "Speed-Freak Football," *The New York Times* (New York, NY), December 2, 2010.

165: **". . . we were dictating":** Michael Sokolove, "Speed-Freak Football," *The New York Times* (New York, NY), December 2, 2010.

164: **"I could do the best job . . .":** Kerry Eggers, *The Civil War Rivalry: Oregon vs. Oregon State* (Charleston: The History Press), 2014), page 391.

164: **"hitting the sled until . . .":** Michael Sokolove, "Speed-Freak Football," *The New York Times* (New York, NY), December 2, 2010.

166: **". . . I call it a no-breathing offense":** Michael Sokolove, "Speed-Freak Football," *The New York Times* (New York, NY), December 2, 2010.

166: **"It's still football":** Michael Sokolove, "Speed-Freak Football," *The New York Times* (New York, NY), December 2, 2010.

167: **"to bombard our kids":** Michael Sokolove, "Speed-Freak Football," *The New York Times* (New York, NY), December 2, 2010.

168: **"It's time for the athletic department . . .":** Billy Witz, "Off-Field Turmoil Causes Soul Searching at Oregon," *The New York Times* (New York, NY), April 30, 2010.

169: **"He can't keep up":** Michael Sokolove, "Speed-Freak Football," *The New York Times* (New York, NY), December 2, 2010.

169: **In early 2005, the property Knight wanted:** University of Oregon Archives Department, Arena File #1–#8, 10.091.A, Box 3, files 1, 2, 3, and 4; Greg Bolt and David Steves, "Legislators Demand Transparency from UO On Arena Project," *Eugene Register-Guard* (Eugene, OR) May 25, 2010.

Chapter Eight

170: **"Will you wear our shoes?":** Bud Withers, "New Cougars AD Bill Moos, WSU Stories Intertwined," *Seattle Times* (Seattle, WA), May 8, 2010.

171: **". . . rather step in it . . .":** John Canzano, *Bald-Faced Truth Podcast.*

171: **"I created the monster . . .":** Jim Moore, "How a Monster Ate Former UO Athletic Director Moos," *Seattle Post-Intelligencer* (Seattle, WA), October 18, 2007.

171: **Matthew Knight Arena:** University of Oregon Archives Department, Arena File #1–#8, 10.091.A, Box 3, files 1, 2, 3, and 4.

172: **He began by cleaning house:** Jeff Manning, "Melinda Grier, Attorney at Center of Mike Bellotti Scandal, on the Way Out," *Oregonian* (Portland, OR), April 22, 2010.

173: **"enforcing the culture of secrecy . . .":** Stevie Duin, "Melinda Grier's Brief Tenure as UO's 'General Counsel Emeritus,'" *Oregonian* (Portland, OR), August 27, 2012.

173: **the John E. Jaqua Academic Center:** University of Oregon Archives Department, 11.151.A, box 3, file 2; author's visit to Jaqua Center and interviews with student athletes.

175: **"We receive no funding . . .":** Rachel Bachman, "Oregon Athletic Department Uses State Money for Academic Needs Despite Claims of Self-Sufficiency," *Oregonian* (Portland, OR), October 7, 2010.

175: **the $68-million Football Performance Center:** Greg Bishop, "Oregon Embraces 'University of Nike' Image," *The New York Times* (New York, NY), August 2, 2013; author's visits and interviews.

175: **"We are the University of Nike":** Greg Bishop, "Oregon Embraces 'University of Nike' Image," *The New York Times* (New York, NY), August 2, 2013.

176: **"It's the densest wood . . .":** Greg Bishop, "Oregon Embraces 'University of Nike' Image," *The New York Times* (New York, NY), August 2, 2013.

176: **packing his suitcase for a flight:** Bill Graves, "The Rise and Fall of Richard Lariviere, University of Oregon President, Fired Monday," *Oregonian* (Portland, OR), December 3, 2011; author's interviews.

177: **"I owe everything . . .":** Bill Graves, "University of Oregon President Richard Lariviere Finds Academic Goals Overshadowed by Sports Controversies," *Oregonian* (Portland, OR), April 20, 2010.

177: **"But it's entertainment . . .":** Henry Stern and Mark Zusman, *Willamette Week* (Portland, OR), May 18, 2010.

179: **"At that point, I realized . . .":** Laura Gunderson, "Matt Donegan, Who Turned Love of the Outdoors into Millions, Emerges as Oregon Leader," *Oregonian* (Portland, OR), May 25, 2013.

179: **"signature accessory The Hat":** Tamar Lewin, "University of Oregon President Is Ousted," *The New York Times* (New York, NY), November 28, 2011.

180: **"You are not qualified . . .":** Lynn Zinser, "After UConn Picks Coach, Donor Asks for His Money Back," *The New York Times* (New York, NY), January 25, 2011.

181: **"Do you think our university is getting better?":** William C. Rhoden, "UConn Probably Has No Second Thoughts in Booster Feuds, *The New York Times* (New York, NY), January 29, 2011.

182: **". . . the resources have helped them":** Greg Bishop, "Television Revenue Fuels a Construction Boom in the Pac-12," *The New York Times* (New York, NY), November 29, 2013.

183: **"We had to play catch-up":** Greg Bishop, "Television Revenue Fuels a Construction Boom in the Pac-12," *The New York Times* (New York, NY), November 29, 2013.

183: **few college football prospects:** Chris Foster, "Lache Seastrunk of UCLA Bowl Foe Baylor Has Regained Stride," *Los Angeles Times* (Los Angeles, CA), December 23, 2012.

183: **talent scout named Willie Lyles:** Gary Klein, "Lane Kiffin Claims No Knowledge of Alleged Violation," *Los Angeles Times* (Los Angeles, CA), September 27, 2011.

184: **"Willie said he was a trainer":** Joe Schad and Mark Schlabach, "Sources: Man Who Helps Ducks Probed," *ESPN*, March 5, 2011.

184: **LaMichael James rushed for 1,731 yards:** University of Oregon Archives Department, sports memorabilia and media guides, 2011.

185: **Nike desginer Tinker Hatfield:** Donald R. Katz, *Just Do It: The Nike Spirit in the Corporate World* (Holbrook: Adams, 1994), page 5.

185: **"What is a more visible way . . .":** Michael Kruse, "How Does Oregon Football Keep Winning?" *Grantland*, September 7, 2011.

188: **"I really don't know":** Ken Goe, "Ducks Depart Southern California, Rose Bowl Victory in Hand," *Oregonian* (Portland, OR), January 3, 2012.

188: **"We don't run a gimmick deal":** George Schroeder, "Oregon 2011 Team Preview," *Sports Illustrated*, August 10, 2011.

189: **"I don't know how it works":** Interview with Marcus Mariota, December 31, 2012.

189: **". . . Tim Tebow type of quarterback":** Chip Kelly, "Coach of the Year Clinics Football Manual," 2011.

191: **"We're fast becoming people's second-favorite team":** Darren Rovell, "The Incredible Rise of Oregon as a Merchandising Powerhouse," *ESPN*, January 9, 2015.

Chapter Nine

193: **Shortly after eleven on the morning of Saturday:** Beverly Beyette, "Campus Crime Crusade: Howard and Connie Clery Lost Their Daughter to a Crazed Thief—Now They're Angry and Fighting Back," *Los Angeles Times* (Los Angeles, CA), August 10, 1989.

194: **It was the happiest year of her life":** Ken Gross and Andrea Fine, "After Their Daughter is Murdered at College, Her Grieving Parents Mount a Crusade for Campus Safety," *People*, February 19, 1990.

195: **Sundays were an ideal time:** Author's interviews with current and former UO police officers.

197: **"UO Sexual Violence Prevention Communications Plan March 2014":** Julie Brown email to Rita Radostitz.

198: **"No one wants to talk to you":** Incident Case Number 14-04131, "Rape 1—Forcible," Eugene Police Department, March 13, 2014, police report.

199: **Altman's fifteen-page contract:** University of Oregon, fifteen-page contract for Dana Altman.

201: **"The story broke Klinger broke":** Text message from Tobin Klinger to Julie Brown.

202: **"We have counseling center staff . . .":** Andrew Greif, "Q&A: Oregon VP Robin Holmes Speaks on Rape Accusations and Oregon's Response," *Oregonian* (Portland, OR), May 8, 2014.

202: **At the University of Oregon's Counseling and Testing Center:** *Stokes and Morlok v. University of Oregon*, et al. (2016), U.S. District Court for the District of Oregon.

204: **"I am thankful that . . .":** Jennifer Morlok, open letter to Michael Schill.

205: **Early in 2011, Lisa Thornton:** Author's interviews with Antonia Noori Farzan.

209: **His work there sometimes veered:** Nigel Jaquiss, "Reputation For Rent," *Willamette Week* (Portland, OR), September 24, 2013.

209: **"I guess I was kind of doping":** Mark Frohnmayer, "Amy Frohnmayer Winn," September 2016, home video.

210: **Dave Frohnmayer died in his sleep:** Jeff Mapes, "Dave Frohnmayer, Former UO President and Oregon Attorney General, Dies at 74," *Oregonian* (Portland, OR), March 10, 2015.

210: **Knight announced the gift of $10 million:** Andrew Theen, "Phil and Penny Knight Will Give $10 Million to Fanconi Anemia Research Fund Started by Frohnmayer Family," *Oregonian* (Portland, OR), April 5, 2016.

Chapter Ten

211: **Phil and Penny Knight Campus:** Tobin Klinger, "Knight Campus news release," October 18, 2016.

211: **Thiel turned heads:** Lora Kolodny, "Why a Nonprofit Backs Dropping Out of School: PayPal Founder's Foundation Encourages Learning by Doing," *Wall Street Journal* (New York, NY), December 18, 2013.

211: **Knight pledged $500 million:** Mike Rogoway, "Phil and Penny Knight's Charitable Contributions Top $2 Billion," *Oregonian* (Portland, OR), October 17, 2016.

212: **"I was struck by how . . .":** Author's interview with Thomas Hager.

213: **President Schill gave no indication:** "Science Talk Draws a Large Crowd to Hear About Knight Campus," *Around the O*, May 15,

2017, Web site with embedded YouTube video: https://around.uoregon.edu/content/science-talk-draws-large-crowd-hear-about-knight-campus.

218: **"We are hoping the state will provide . . .":** Dylan Darling, "University Breaks Ground on Knight Science Campus," *Eugene Register-Guard* (Eugene, OR), March 3, 2018.

218: **allowed Kavell Bigby-Williams:** Author's interviews, police documents, and public records.

220: **"One of the people Flynn told about the case was Darci Heroy . . .":** Kenni Jacoby, "Why Oregon's Title IX Investigation of Kavell Bigby-William's Alleged Rape Stalled Before it Began," *Sports Illustrated*, October 25, 2017.

220: **"And yet, when Weintraub tallied the number of sexual-assault cases . . .":** Kenni Jacoby, "Why Oregon's Title IX Investigation of Kavell Bigby-William's Alleged Rape Stalled Before it Began," *Sports Illustrated*, October 25, 2017.

221: **"And yet Heroy kept Weintraub out of the loop . . .":** Kenni Jacoby, "Why Oregon's Title IX Investigation of Kavell Bigby-William's Alleged Rape Stalled Before it Began," *Sports Illustrated*, October 25, 2017.

222: **"Heroy, meanwhile, went so far as to say that it was unusual . . .":** Kenni Jacoby, "Why Oregon's Title IX Investigation of Kavell Bigby-William's Alleged Rape Stalled Before it Began," *Sports Illustrated*, October 25, 2017.

222: **His phone records which were:** Kenny Jacoby, "Phone Records Contradict Oregon's Stance on How Much Dana Altman Knew of Player's Rape Case," *Sports Illustrated*, December 7, 2017.

223: **"What if I was asked by another reporter . . .":** Suhauna Hussain, "U. of Oregon Athlete Played a Season While Under Investigation for Sexual Assault," *Chronicle of Higher Education*, June 22, 2017.

224: **Dana Altman's basketball team was not alone:** Author's interviews with an anonymous source inside the university administration.

225: **"The voice of a survivor is the key to an investigation . . .":** Kenni Jacoby, "Why Oregon's Title IX Investigation of Kavell Bigby-William's Alleged Rape Stalled Before it Began," *Sports Illustrated*, October 25, 2017.

226: **PhD student named Erica Midttveit:** Author's interviews with Erica Midttveit.

226: **"In this life . . .":** Mark Frohnmayer, "Amy Frohnmayer Winn," September 2016, home video.

229: **"Phil Knight and Nike . . .":** Eddie Pells, "Nike's Knight is Oregon's Chief Duck," *Associated Press*, March 30, 2017.

229: **The University of Maryland, for one :** Marc Tracy, "Under Armour Seeks to Do for Maryland What Nike Did for Oregon," *The New York Times* (New York, NY), August 25, 2015.

Afterword

231: **"Kelly Cahill and Sarah Johnston had each worked…":** Kelly Cahill and Sara Johnston v. Nike, Inc., Case No. 3:18-cv-01477; Class and Collective Action Allegation Complaint, page 2.

231: **"However, about two months after I was hired…":** Kelly Cahill and Sara Johnston v. Nike, Inc., Case No. 3:18-cv-01477; Class and Collective Action Allegation Complaint, Exhibit A, page 1.

231: **"Cahill, meanwhile, was paid $20,000 less…":** Kelly Cahill and Sara Johnston v. Nike, Inc., Case No. 3:18-cv-01477; Class and Collective Action Allegation Complaint, Exhibit B, page 1.

231: **"At Nike,' their lawsuit alleged…":** Kelly Cahill and Sara Johnston v. Nike, Inc., Case No. 3:18-cv-01477; Class and Collective Action Allegation Complaint, page 2.

232: **"…exodus of male executives…":** "At Nike, Revolt Led by Women Leads to Exodus of Male Executives," Julie Creswell, Kevin Draper, Rachel Abrams, *The New York Times*, April 28, 2018.

232: **"Months later, in August 2018…":** Kelly Cahill and Sara Johnston v. Nike, Inc., Case No. 3:18-cv-01477; Document 77.

232: **"Meanwhile, in a federal courtroom in Manhattan…":** United States of America v. Michael Avenatti, Case 1:19-cr-00373-PGG, indictment, page 1.

232: **"Like so many scandals…":** Author's interview with Michael Avenatti, November 1, 2019.

232: **"It was a significant loss for Franklin…":** United States of America v. Michael Avenatti, Case 1:19-cr-00373-PGG, Document 30, Exhibits B & C.

233: **"Sonny Vaccaro told *The New York Times*…":** "Avenatti's Client: The Basketball Club Coach Caught Up in a Federal Case," Scott Cacciola, Marc Tracy, *The New York Times*, March 29, 2019.

233: **"In one of those text messages…":** United States of America v. Michael Avenatti, Case 1:19-cr-00373-PGG, Document 30, Exhibits F, G, I, and K.

233: **"These rogue Nike executives…":** United States of America v. Michael Avenatti, Case 1:19-cr-00373-PGG, Document 30, Exhibits E and P.

234: **"Seven months later…":** United States of America v. Michael Avenatti, Case 1:19-cr-00373-PGG, Document 30, Exhibits F, G, I, and K.

234: **"Earlier that month, a jury in New York…":** "All Three Defendants Found Guilty of Wire Fraud in College Basketball Corruption Trial," Will Hobson, Kevin Armstrong, *Washington Post,* October 24, 2018

234: **"In a memo…":** United States of America v. Michael Avenatti, Case 1:19-cr-00373-PGG, Document 30, Exhibit J.

235: **"On the evening of March 25…":** "Avenatti Charged with Trying to Extort Millions from Nike," Brian Melley, Larry Neumeister, Associated Press, March 26, 2019.

235: **"As all of you know…":** "Avenatti Charged with Trying to Extort Millions from Nike," Brian Melley, Larry Neumeister, Associated Press, March 26, 2019.

235: **"The indictment against Avenatti…":** Author's interview with Michael Avenatti, November 1, 2019.

237: **"What you've seen so far…":** Author's interview with Michael Avenatti, November 1, 2019.

237: **"…an unprecedented public relations disaster.":** "David Boies Pleads Not Guilty," James B. Stewart, *The New York Times*, September 21, 2018.

238: **"These guys play dirty…":** Author's interview with Michael Avenatti, November 1, 2019.

238: **"Emails contained in a decision…":** United States Anti-Doping Agency v. Alberto Salazar, Final Award, American Arbitration Association Commercial Arbitration Tribunal, Case No. 01-17-0004-0880.

238: **"An email that some found oddly defensive…":** Mark Parker, email to Nike staff, October 1, 2019; author's interviews with Nike employees.

238: **"Three weeks later…":** "Nike's Chief Executive, Mark Parker, is Stepping Down," Julie Creswell, Matthew Futternam, *The New York Times*, October 22, 2019.

239: **"…Nike once more made headlines.":** "Eliud Kipchoge Breaks Two-Hour Marathan Barrier," Andrew Keh, *The New York Times*, October 12, 2019.

239: **"…London-based professional cycling team Ineos…":** "Sir Dave Brailsford and Team Ineos Help Eliud Kipchoge Run First Ever Sub-2 Hour Marathon," Simon MacMichael, Road.CC, October 12, 2019.

239: **"….mired in controversy in 2017…":** "Chris Froome Fights to Save Career After Failed Drugs Test Result," Sean Ingle, Martha Kelner, *The Guardian*, December 13, 2017.

239: **"…and again in 2018…":** "Remarkable Drugs Report Shatters Team Sky's Illusion of Integrity," Martha Kelner, *The Guardian*, March 5, 2018.

239: **"In April 2019…":** "Kenyan Runner Cyrus Rutto Suspended in Doping Case," Associated Press, April 11, 2019.

Acknowledgments

This book only exists because of a single girl who decided to tell Eugene police about the worst night of her life. I'm grateful for her courage. I'm also grateful to Jason Stallman, the sports editor at *The New York Times*, for publishing my first stories about campus rape at the University of Oregon. And I'm indebted to David McCraw, Victoria D. Baranetsky, and the entire legal team at *The New York Times*, who dedicated considerable time and effort toward challenging the university's efforts to withhold public records from public scrutiny.

What little I know about the craft of book writing was learned in Samuel Freedman's remarkable seminar at the Columbia University Graduate School of Journalism. I owe whatever success I may have as an author to Sam's mentorship and to the wonderful group of people who went through his seminar with me: Asaf Shalev, Candice Thompson, Ben Taub, Geetika Rudra, Ian Port, Julia Bosson, Kristin Ciccone Gole, Tim Patterson, Janell Ross, Theresa Bradley, Dasha Lisitsina, Catherine Mullaly, Damien Lamar McDuffie, Joy Resmovits, Mohamad Yaghi, Emily Palmer, Eli Hager, Valerie Edwards, Jacqueline Mansky, and Irena Choi Stern.

I was fortunate to have many other mentors during my time at Columbia Journalism School, including John Bennet and Dale Maharidge, who made me a better writer; Laura Muha and Deborah

Amos, who made me a better reporter; Sheila Coronel, Jim Mintz, Steve Coll, and Duff Wilson, who each helped make me a better investigator; and Nicholas Lemann, who made me a better thinker.

It takes so many people to make a nonfiction book, but in the interest of brevity, I'll stick with thanking the people who helped most directly with the making of this one: Mark Krotov, for giving the book a home at Melville House; Ryan Harrington, for his patient, thoughtful editing of the manuscript once it arrived there; Noah Ballard, my agent, for always believing in the project; Jonathan Hawthorne, my brilliant researcher, for his diligent work in the archives at the University of Oregon; and every single person who shared their story, their documents, or their time.

Index

INDEX

INDEX